THE HOLY SPIRIT

Books by Alasdair I. C. Heron
Published by The Westminster Press

The Holy Spirit
A Century of Protestant Theology

The Holy Spirit

Alasdair I. C. Heron

THE WESTMINSTER PRESS
Philadelphia

Published by The Westminster Press ®
Philadelphia, Pennsylvania

PRINTED IN THE UNITED STATES OF AMERICA
9 8 7 6 5 4 3 2 1

Library of Congress Cataloging in Publication Data

Heron, Alasdair.
  The Holy Spirit.

  Bibliography : p.
  Includes index.
  1. Hòly Spirit—History of doctrines. I. Title.
BT119.H47 1983   231'.3   82-24705
ISBN 0-664-24439-4 (pbk.)

CONTENTS

INTRODUCTION

Of all the themes of Christian theology, that of the Holy Spirit may well seem the most elusive and difficult. How can one speak at all adequately of the power that alone enables any authentic discernment and speaking of God? How convey within the pages of what must in the end of the day seem simply an academic text-book the real and vital energy of God himself? How avoid reducing the Spirit of Jesus Christ crucified and risen to a mere item in a catalogue of the history of ideas? The short answer is that one cannot by any means guarantee any of these things, and certainly not when, as here, one must approach the subject from the most oblique angle imaginable. For the following chapters focus only indirectly on the reality of the Holy Spirit. Their primary topic is the witness to and interpretation of the Spirit in the Bible, in the history of Christian theology, in central issues in modern exploration. This is not said defensively, for it is always only through such prisms that Christian reflection traces the refracted beams of the light by which it lives. But it is as well to make it clear from the start that the true subject lies behind and beyond what can here be said, and can only be pointed towards by it.

The broad pattern of the book is to give, in fairly brief compass, the biblical, historical and contemporary dimensions, and the author's task is essentially one of reportage with occasional comment. This is not an essay in systematic or dogmatic theology, but an initial survey of those aspects of the matter about which a modicum of basic information is needed before more ambitious constructive attempts can either be undertaken or subjected to an informed evaluation. Of necessity it is highly selective in the issues it raises and the examples it cites—especially in the second and third parts, where I am all too painfully aware of how much more could (and ideally should) have been said, had only space permitted—but I hope it may prove of some help as an introduction to the field, and as an encouragement to further study.

Some explanation ought to be given of a feature which some readers will perhaps find jarring: throughout, in defiance of normal convention, the Spirit is referred to as 'it' rather than 'he'. The initial (and not entirely superficial) reason is the difficulty of deciding when in a study of this sort to change from the impersonal to the personal pronoun, or indeed which personal pronoun should be used. *Ruach* in Hebrew is feminine; *pneuma* in Greek is neuter; *spiritus* in Latin is masculine. To make matters worse, English does not normally use the neuter form for personal subjects. There is no similar difficulty in German, as Mark Twain once illustrated with his literal translation of an everyday conversation: 'Where is the *girl*?' '*It* is in the *kitchen*?' Where is *she*?' 'The *kitchen* is downstairs.' One might simply cut the Gordian knot and refer to God's Spirit throughout as 'he' or even, in deference to the criticism of sexism, as 'she'. There are, however, solid exegetical and theological reasons for seeking to avoid making the impression that the Spirit is 'a third he' (or 'she') alongside the Father and the Son. This is not to deny that the Spirit is, in the proper sense of the term, the 'third person of the Trinity', nor is it to 'depersonalise' the Spirit, but it is to underline the Spirit's distinctive identity, character and status as the Spirit *of God*, the Spirit *of Christ*. These problems are briefly taken up in the last chapter, but I should perhaps say at the outset that I am far from wishing to assert that 'it' is the only proper pronoun to use. Its employment can draw attention to a point that I feel to be of some importance, but is exposed to objections as valid as may be advanced against 'he'. Here we run against the boundaries of language, and it is in the end more important to be aware of *that* than to insist dogmatically that this or that expression must be made binding.

In preparing and, as it seemed, endlessly rewriting these

pages, I have repeatedly been acutely aware of a debt to many others—to my own teachers, to my past and present students in Tübingen, Dublin and Edinburgh, to the many colleagues, whether known personally or only through their writings, from whom I have learned both in agreement and in occasional disagreement. I think back with special appreciation to the meetings at Klingenthal in 1978 and 1979 of the World Council of Churches working party on the *filioque*, and at Maynooth in 1980 of the British/Irish Theological Society. Several of those to whom I owe most are mentioned in footnotes throughout the book, but I would place on record here particular thanks to Roland Walls for his teaching on the Holy Spirit in my B.D. student days, to George Anderson for his incisive yet encouraging comments on my earlier attempts to analyse the Old Testament material, to Thomas Torrance and Ulrich Wickert for their support and guidance of my initial researches into the pneumatology of the Greek fathers. My wife Helen has added to so many other good works this also, that she has typed out the manuscript and thereby saved me much time, strain, and Tipp-Ex. Truly her price is above rubies, while our junior theological consultants are best described as priceless:

For Helen
Jeanette
Patricia

Edinburgh
January 1981

Alasdair Heron

ABBREVIATIONS

DS   Denzinger/Schönmetzer, *Enchiridion Symbolorum* ...,
ed. xxxiv. Herder, 1967

JBL   *Journal of Biblical Literature*

JSSt   *Journal of Semitic Studies*

JTS   *Journal of Theological Studies*

NTS   *New Testament Studies*

SJTh   *Scottish Journal of Theology*

TDNT   Kittel/Friedrich, *Theological Dictionary of the New
Testament*, translated and edited by G. W. Bromiley.
Eerdmans, 1963ff.

TU   *Texte und Untersuchungen*

PART ONE

THE SPIRIT IN SCRIPTURE

CHAPTER ONE

THE RUACH OF YAHWEH

The Old Testament references to the Spirit of God do not easily form a simple pattern. The Spirit is spoken of in the Book of Judges, for example, in a very different way from the Psalms. Nor indeed is the Spirit at all as central in the Old Testament as in the New. The very term, 'Holy Spirit', appears in only two places (Ps. 51.11; Isa. 63.10-11); and even when all the other ways of speaking are taken into account, they offer a less definite picture than can be traced in the New Testament.

Nevertheless, the Old Testament is the place to begin. Here are the Scriptures which formed the belief and understanding of Jesus and his earliest followers, and which in turn were interpreted afresh in the light of Jesus' own life, death and resurrection. Here is the indispensable entrance to the world of ideas, memories and hopes which lies behind the New Testament itself. As modern Christian theology has increasingly come to recognise, the Old Testament becomes far more richly illuminating when it is not simply dismissed as an unimportant preface to the New, and when the temptation is resisted to read into it what is really only properly to be found in the New. It has its own light to throw on our theme.

What, then, does the Old Testament mean by 'spirit'? What does 'spirit' have to do with God? What is 'the Spirit of God'? That can best be seen by looking to see how it uses one particular world: *ruach*. We cannot here mention every instance and every nuance of meaning, but we can pick out and highlight the main points.[1]

1. The Meanings of Ruach

The root meaning of *ruach* probably had to do with the

movement of air, but from this beginning it acquired a whole variety of other senses, including 'wind', 'breath' and 'life'. It then came to be applied to the human 'spirit' or 'self', and also to what we would describe as 'mood' or 'temper'. Some examples of these uses can lead us into its meaning in connexion with God.

Ruach as 'wind' commonly refers to the strong wind of the storm, the raging blast from the desert, like the one that divided the Red Sea at the Exodus (Exod. 14.21). This driving wind is not identical with the *ruach* of God himself, but its elemental power made it a powerful image of divine strength. 'Therefore thus says the Lord God: I will make a stormy wind break out in my wrath; and there shall be a deluge of rain in my anger, and great hailstones in wrath to destroy it. And I will break down the wall that you have daubed with whitewash ... and you shall know that I am the Lord.' (Ezek. 13.13-14; also e.g. Hos. 8.7; 13.15) Here is one obvious association that talk of God's own *ruach* must have had in the minds of the people of the Old Testament. It was the surging energy of the Lord of hosts, the terrible force of his invincible judgment. *Ruach* conveyed a sense of the devastating impact of God on men and on their world. The same contrast of divine power with human resources is tersely expressed in Isa. 31.3: 'The Egyptians are men, and not God; and their horses are flesh, and not *ruach*.'[2]

At this level, *ruach* is largely an impersonal concept: it has to do with natural or supernatural strength, force, power, and energy. But it could also carry another meaning as applied to influences and moods of a personal kind, or to 'spirits' conceived of as quasi-personal entities. Instances of the last of these meanings are fairly rare in the Old Testament. It does not have the same interest in good or evil 'spirits' as some strands of later Jewish thought and indeed of the New Testament were to display. Nor is it always easy to draw the line between a 'spirit' as a mood or attitude and a 'spirit' as a more independent agent. When, for example, Num. 5.14 mentions 'a spirit of jealousy' that 'comes upon' a man when he suspects his wife of unfaithfulness, it would seem most natural, at least to modern readers, to take this simply as describing his psychological state, not the activity of a roaming 'spirit'. The ancient Hebrew, however, like many African villagers today, would not make such a sharp or straightforward distinction as we are familiar with between what is 'in the mind' and what comes 'from outside'. The human self as he visualised it was more permeable than we normally assume, more open to external influences which could themselves be spoken of in more or less personal terms. It was part of the same view of things that a 'spirit' could be described as passing from one person to another. So God promises Moses that he will 'take some of the *ruach* which is upon you and put it upon them' (Num. 11.17: the recipients are the seventy elders), while Elisha asks for a 'double share' of the *ruach* of Elijah (II Kings 2.9).

This way of thinking appears to be characteristic especially of the older strata of the Old Testament. God 'sent an evil *ruach* between Abimelech and the men of Shechem; and the men of Shechem dealt treacherously with Abimelech ...' (Judges 9.23); 'an evil *ruach* from the Lord tormented' Saul (I Sam. 16.14 etc.); and God allowed a 'lying *ruach*' to deceive the prophets advising Ahab (I Kings 22.22ff = II Chron. 18.21ff). In the case of Saul, the arrival of the evil *ruach* follows the departure of 'the *ruach* of the Lord': the two are spoken of in similar terms, and are presumably thought of in much the same way. It is significant that all these 'evil spirits' come *from* God. There are no 'free-lance' demons in the Old Testament, though hints of such an idea, stemming from more primitive times, may perhaps be detected here and there—as in the reference to Azazel in the ritual for the Day of Atonement (Lev. 16.8-10). Even Zech. 13.2, where God promises to 'cut off the names of the idols from the land,' and to 'remove from the land the prophets and the unclean spirit,' refers to alien religious cults rather than to the kind of 'evil spirits' mentioned in the New Testament. The Old Testament in fact offers very little by way of demonology, but it can and does use *ruach* to speak of a good or evil influence coming from God and exerting an impact on the lives of individuals or groups. Here

we are in the area of *personal* activity—not that the *ruach* is
necessarily thought of as 'a person' in our modern sense; but it
functions at the level of persons to mould their attitudes and
behaviour. Closely connected with this is the sense that is still
preserved in English when we say that someone is 'in poor
spirits', 'high-spirited', or behaving 'in an angry spirit'. *Ruach*
very commonly has this sense, as when Pharaoh's *ruach* is
'troubled' by his dream (Gen. 41.8).

Yet a further use, which becomes especially prominent in
the later strands of the Old Testament, makes *ruach* mean more
or less 'person' or 'self'. This was a natural further
development from the idea of the 'breath of life', coupled with
the 'psychological' application just mentioned. As 'breath',
ruach might be expected to stand for what in English once used
to be called the 'animal soul', in Latin *anima*, and in Greek
psyche. In most of the Old Testament, however, this role is
played by the different term *nephesh*. This names the power of
life, which, although the root meaning of *nephesh* also has to do
with *breathing*, tended in the Old Testament, and particularly
in the older writings, to be associated with the *blood*. Every
living creature, human or animal, possesses *nephesh*, the
'blood-soul'. (Hence came the prohibition of drinking the
blood of slaughtered animals: it was to be poured out as an
offering to God—Lev. 17.10-14.) *Ruach* can also be ascribed on
occasion to animals; but it is more characteristically applied to
humans. Here it tends to mean not simply 'the power of life',
but rather the 'mind' or 'self'. *Nephesh* can also on occasion
bear this sense, so that we should not draw too absolute
distinctions between them. Nor ought we to over-systematise
Hebrew psychology, as if the Old Testament presented a
single neat pattern which divided man into body, blood-soul
(*nephesh*) and spirit (*ruach*). What seems to have happened is
that as time went on the older concentration on the *nephesh*, the
blood-soul, was replaced by an increasing focus on the *ruach* of
man as the centre of his personal self.[3] It is in this sense that
ruach is usually translated as (human) 'spirit', as, for example,
in Ps. 31.5, 'Into thy hand I commit my spirit,' or 32.2,
'Blessed is the man ... in whose spirit there is no deceit.' What

is meant here is not the idea of 'an immortal spirit' or 'soul'. It is the distinctively personal character of human beings, able to think, feel, be aware, act and bear responsibility. So, when Malachi warns the people, 'take heed to your *ruach* and do not be faithless,' (Mal. 2.16), *ruach* is best translated simply as 'yourselves', as the RSV renders it. Similarly, when Num. 16.22 speaks of 'the God of the spirits of all flesh,' it does not mean 'the God of immortal souls', but 'the God of all that lives.'

Just as the thought of *ruach* as elemental force or as personal influence contributes to the understanding of the *ruach* of God, so too does this more fully personal conception; for it is the conviction of the Old Testament that man's *ruach* is not something that he possesses simply by himself. It is a gift from God, and depends continually on God. So Ps. 51.10 prays, 'Create in me a clean heart, O God, and put a new and right *ruach* within me. Cast me not away from thy presence, and take not thy holy *ruach* from me.' It is a moot point whether the second use of *ruach* here should be translated as 'Spirit' or 'spirit', as God's own *ruach* or the *ruach* of man which he renews. The two senses are so intimately bound up together that to insist on the one rather than the other is to drive into the text a distinction which was not in that fashion in the author's mind. It is not that he made no difference between God and man—*that* contrast is fundamental to the whole Old Testament—but he saw man as existing by his very nature in relation to God. *Ruach* (and 'holy *ruach*') refer both to God acting upon man, and to the result of that action in man himself. So *ruach* even as applied to man has an implicit reference to God as man's creator and sustainer; thus it becomes a linking term which refers both to God and to human life in its dependence upon God.

These illustrations indicate the range of meanings that *ruach* could have, and so introduce us to its significance when applied to God. We have just touched on one vital clue: *ruach* is used to speak of God as present and active in the world and in particular among human beings. It is in fact only one of a whole series of terms employed by the Old Testament in this way. It can also talk of God's 'arm', 'hand', or 'finger'; of his 'face' (usually translated as his 'presence'); of his 'name' or his 'glory' especially as dwelling in the temple in Jerusalem; of his 'word' or his 'angel' ('messenger') declaring his will and purpose. All of these images are more or less pictorial and anthropomorphic: they use analogies drawn from human experience to describe God in action. The *ruach* of Yahweh is not detachable, as it were, from Yahweh himself: it is his living impact here and now.

The use of this kind of language and imagery is an essential element in the way the Old Testament speaks of God. He can 'send' his *ruach*, his angel or his word; he can make his name dwell in the temple; he can withdraw his glory from it, as in Ezekiel's vision (Ezek. chs 8-11). In all of these, it is God himself who is present. They are, so to speak, extensions of his own being, means of his touching upon the affairs of Israel.[4] At the same time, if they are not detachable from him, he is not simply reduced to them. The account of the dedication of the temple by Solomon (II Chron. chs 5-7) brings that out very clearly. On the one hand, the temple is filled with God's glory; it is the place where his name dwells and where he is present in the ark of the convenant; but in his prayer Solomon repeatedly affirms that God's dwelling-place is in heaven, and that the heaven of heavens cannot contain him, 'much less this house which I have built.' (II Chron. 6.18) This does not, however, mean that God's presence in the temple is artificial, unreal, or even only indirect: it is precisely because he transcends earth and heaven that he can be directly and immediately *present* in that place, though not *contained* in it or limited by it. *Ruach*, like these other linking terms, speaks of God reaching out from his remoteness without ceasing to be himself. But this note of 'reaching out' must not be lost: *ruach* as applied to God in the Old Testament does not as a rule describe God's 'inner personality' by analogy with the human *ruach*. Rather, as man's *ruach* is constituted by its relation to God who gives it, the *ruach* of God is God's activity in relation to the world and to men.

This use of *ruach* and other words in the Old Testament is

sometimes described in modern writing by saying that God's *transcendence*, his utter otherness, is balanced and complemented by his *immanence*, his universal presence 'in' everything. This pair of categories can, however, be somewhat misleading if uncritically applied to the Old Testament (or indeed the New). On the whole, it is not some *general* (and abstractly conceived) 'immanence' of God that they set over against his 'transcendence', but his *specific* and *particular* 'making of himself present' *at points of his own choosing*. The element of particularity cannot be ironed out without drastic distortion of the biblical evidence. At the same time, the sheer diversity of the material in the Old Testament, and the developments that can be traced in it, demand two qualifications.

First, it is likely that some of the more primitive strands in the Old Testament reflect notions of a super-natural *ruach* which was originally thought of as a distinct 'power', and only gradually drawn in, subordinated to Yahweh, and consequently also refined. The cases of the 'evil spirits from God' noted above may reflect this process, as also some examples to be mentioned below of particularly violent, ecstatic manifestations of *ruach*. As we shall shortly see, at one key stage in the Old Testament development the whole idea of the *ruach* of God seems to have been driven into the background, and this too probably witnesses to the problems of integrating such older concepts with the main line of Old Testament theology. The main line remains nonetheless clear enough.

Conversely, there are also signs in the later Old Testament period of the emergence of a more universal, less particular understanding of the *ruach* as divine presence. The classic example is Ps. 139:

> Whither shall I go from thy *ruach*?
>   Or whither shall I flee from thy presence?
> If I ascend to heaven, thou art there!
>   If I make my bed in Sheol, thou art there!
> If I take the wings of the morning

and dwell in the uttermost parts of the sea,
    even there thy hand shall lead me,
        and thy right hand shall hold me. (vv. 7–10)

The movement of thought so finely expressed here was to be carried further in Hellenistic Judaism, and is to some degree in tension with the more central Old Testament focus on the historical particularity of God's presence and action.

2. *God's* Ruach *in Action*

It remains now to look more closely at four main contexts in which the *ruach* of God is spoken of in the Old Testament: creation; outstanding gifts; prophecy; future hope. These do not add up to a single system of doctrine, but they can illustrate the range and forms of activity associated with the *ruach* of Yahweh.

(i) *Creation and the Maintenance of Life*

This theme is not in fact very extensively treated in the Old Testament. Insofar as a connection is indicated, it generally comes by the association of *ruach* and another word, *neshamah* (also meaning 'breath'), with the giving and preserving of life. So Job 33.4 has, 'The *ruach* of God has made me, and the *neshamah* of the Almighty gives me life,' while the corollary follows at 34.14-15: 'If he should take back his *ruach* to himself, and gather to himself his *neshamah*, all flesh would perish together, and man would return to dust.' The same twofold thought is in Ps. 104.27-31, which sings of all living things:

These all look to thee,
    to give them their food in due season...
When thou hidest thy face, they are dismayed;
    When thou takest away their *ruach* they die and return to
        their dust.
When thou sendest forth thy *ruach* they are created;
    and thou renewest the face of the ground.

Similar uses of *ruach* and/or *neshamah* as life 'breathed in' by God or returning to him are found, for instance, in Gen. 2.7;

Ezek. 37.9; Eccl. 12.7. In all these cases, *ruach* and *neshamah* seem to refer primarily to *created life* as the gift of God rather than to a distinct creative activity of God's *ruach*, though *ruach* does have the double reference to God and to created beings that we have already noted.

More explicit references to the *ruach* of God as acting in creation are both rare and imprecise. It is hard to know what weight to place on the description of the '*ruach*' as 'hovering' (like a bird) or alternatively as 'sweeping' (like a wind) over the face of the waters in Gen. 1.2. Nor does Job 26.12-13 carry us at all further:

> By his power he stilled the sea;
>   by his understanding he smote Rahab.
> By his *ruach* the heavens were made fair;
>   his hand pierced the fleeing serpent.

Ruach is simply used here as one of a series of images—along with 'power', 'understanding', and 'hand'—to depict God's activity in creation, expressed in terms of the ancient myth of a cosmic battle which also appears in Isa. 51.9. Finally, the text which at first sight seems most specific turns out to offer less than we might imagine. Ps. 33.6 proclaims, 'By the word of the Lord the heavens were made, and all their host by the *ruach* of his mouth.' This, like Gen. 1, rests on the theologically more advanced conception of creation by mere divine *fiat*. *Ruach* is coupled with *dabhar*, 'word', and now means 'the breath of speech' rather than 'the breath of life'. The dominant model is, however, that of *word*. No *distinct* role is ascribed to the *ruach*, and the reference to it is in effect a way of stressing that creation occurs at God's *command*.

These rather vague, scattered references may seem to offer very little support for the later Christian doctrine of the Holy Spirit as Creator. Indeed, as we shall see later, the early church was to have some difficulty on the point—a difficulty compounded by the fact that the New Testament offers even less of a direct connection of the Spirit with creation. The problem should, however, be kept in proper perspective. The topic of creation appears relatively infrequently in the entire

Old Testament, and the explicit doctrine of *creatio ex nihilo*, 'creation out of nothing', only emerges later (II Macc. 7.28). Similarly, the figure, so to speak, of the *ruach* of Yahweh is much less sharply focused in the Old Testament than is the Holy Spirit in the New. The question the early church had to face was whether it was more profoundly consistent with the Old Testament witness to recognise the Holy Spirit as active in creation, or to conceive of a Holy Spirit that was not involved in it. It was sound theological judgment that led it in the first of these directions, and to trace even in these imprecise Old Testament hints the appropriate guidelines. If God's *ruach* is God himself in action, and if his activity includes creation, the doctrine of the Spirit as Creator must follow unless the Spirit is to be detached from God himself in a fashion running directly counter to the thrust of the Old Testament teaching. Clearly, however, this conclusion could not be reached on the basis of the Old Testament alone: it was rather a matter of detecting the bearing of its message in the fresh horizon of Christian reflection upon the implications of the New.[5]

(ii) Outstanding Gifts

After Joseph had interpreted Pharaoh's dream, Pharaoh asked, 'Can we find such a man as this, in whom is the *ruach* of God?' and added, 'Since God has shown you all this, there is none so discreet and wise as you are.' (Gen. 41.38-39) Under similar circumstances (and no doubt by conscious literary imitation) Nebuchadnezzar is made to speak of Daniel as 'one in whom is the *ruach* of the holy god(s)' (Dan. 4.8). Nor is it only apparently supernatural powers of divination or discernment that are so described. God fills those who are to make Aaron's priestly garments with a '*ruach* of wisdom' (Exod. 28.3), and Bezaleel 'with the *ruach* of God, with ability, with intelligence, with knowledge, and with all craftsmanship.' (Exod. 35.31) Joshua likewise is one 'in whom is the *ruach*' (Num. 27.18), and 'full of the *ruach* of wisdom' (Deut. 34.9). In passages such as these, and the prophecy of the *ruach*-endowed king in Isa. 11 which we quote below, it is not mere innate human capacity that is being described.

Rather, as the talk of 'filling' with *ruach* indicates, these talents and abilities are understood to be imparted by special divine gift. The line between 'natural' and 'supernatural' is not drawn in quite the way that we today might incline to draw it.

To these should be added the fairly limited number of cases where extraordinary feats of strength or leadership are ascribed to the irruption of the *ruach* of God upon an individual. Judges in particular supplies striking examples. It is because of such a surge of divine *ruach* that Samson can tear apart the lion (14.6), slay thirty men at Ashkelon (14.19), snap the ropes of new cord (15.14), and thereafter slaughter a thousand men with the jawbone of an ass (15.15). 'Berserk frenzy' would seem to be the most appropriate description of this exalted state. In the same sort of way, though we are not supplied with such dramatic details, the *ruach* is said to come upon Othniel (3.10), Gideon (6.34), Jephthah (11.29), and also upon Saul (I Sam. 11.6) before they take the field against the enemies of Israel. This is something very different from unusual gifts, skills, or wisdom. It is a violent and temporary possession of a person by a force rushing upon him from without, manifested in an ecstatic form comparable with that associated with some kinds of prophecy. The case of Saul in fact supplies a remarkable connection between the military and prophetic forms.

(iii) *Prophecy*.[6]

In two passages in I Samuel—chs 10 and 19—the proverb, 'Is Saul also among the prophets?' is explained. Each describes an occasion when Saul 'prophesied' under the influence of the divine *ruach*. On the first, he attached himself to a group of singing prophets, and 'became another man' (10.6); on the second, he was diverted from attacking David, who had taken refuge with Samuel, and danced in naked frenzy before Samuel all day and all night (19.24). Strange indeed though this behaviour may seem to us, it well conveys the understanding of 'prophecy' at that period of Israel's history. It was a state of wild, ecstatic possession which was ascribed to the influence of God's *ruach*: 'prophet' meant much the same as

the Islamic 'dervish'. This is probably not quite what we
normally have in mind when we repeat the words of the Nicene
Creed and say of the Holy Spirit that he 'spoke by the
prophets'; but it is the association between *ruach* and prophecy
that was apparently uppermost in that age.

The affirmation of the Creed begins to look even stranger,
however, when we turn to the classical pre-Exilic prophets of
Israel—to men like Amos, Hosea, Micah, Isaiah of Jerusalem,
and indeed Jeremiah as well. They do not seem to have
claimed to be possessed or guided by the *ruach* of Yahweh at
all. The one apparent exception is Micah 3.8: 'But as for me, I
am filled with power, with the *ruach* of the Lord, and with
justice and might, to declare to Jacob his transgression and to
Israel his sin'; but the text here is doubtful. (So too, for that
matter, is Isa. 48.16, 'And now the Lord God has sent me and
his *ruach*'—which is in any case not to be ascribed to the
original Isaiah of Jerusalem, belonging as it does to the much
later sections of the book of Isaiah.)

The reason for this reticence is almost certainly that the
classical prophets in the period before the destruction of
Jerusalem were conscious of having a different role from that
of the traditional ecstatics. So while Hosea can speak of 'the
prophets' as having a divine mission (6.5; 9.8; 12.10, 13), he
also seems to pass a negative verdict on their execution of it
(4.4-5; 9.7; cf. Isa. 3.2). Amos makes the contrast very clear: 'I
am no prophet nor a prophet's son ... the Lord took me from
following the flock, and the Lord said to me, "Go, prophesy to
my people Israel."' (7.14-15) This new kind of prophet came
because the Lord had spoken, not because his vocation was ecstatic
behaviour believed to be divinely inspired; and the message
itself, the *dabhar* ('word') of the Lord, rather than any
accompanying signs of supernatural possession, carried its
own authority. 'The lion has roared; who will not fear? The
Lord God has spoken; who can but prophesy?' (Amos 3.8) It is
hard to suppress the suspicion that the kind of activity
associated with *ruach* had come to appear utterly disreputable,
and unworthy of genuine communication from God.

Later, however, the climate was to change once more. In the

period of the Exile, Ezekiel regularly ascribed his visions and prophecies to the inspiration of the *ruach* of God, with particular emphasis on its direct, even physical impact upon himself (2.1-2; see also 3.12ff; 8.3; 11.1ff; 37.1). A little later, in the Isaianic school, we find what was to become the most resonant of all prophetic appeals to the *ruach*:

> The *ruach* of the Lord God is upon me,
>   because the Lord has anointed me
> to bring good tidings to the afflicted;
>   he has sent me to bind up the brokenhearted,
> to proclaim liberty to the captives,
>   and the opening of the prison to those who are bound;
> to proclaim the year of the Lord's favour,
>   and the day of vengeance of our God;
> to comfort all who mourn ... (Isa. 61.1ff)

It now came to be taken for granted that *all* true prophecy had been inspired by that same *ruach*. So Zech. 7.12 looked back over the whole history of Israel and summed it up: 'They made their hearts like adamant lest they should hear the law and the words which the Lord of hosts had sent by his *ruach* through the former prophets. Therefore great wrath came from the Lord of hosts.' This ascription of classical prophecy to the *ruach* of God was established when the great prophets already belonged to the past. Indeed, it became the general conviction in subsequent generations that the age of prophecy itself was now over, and the gift of the prophetic *ruach* a matter of history. The coupling of the *ruach* of God with prophecy was simultaneously bound up with the consolidation of a body of 'inspired prophetic literature' from earlier days, days that were looked back upon as having been guided by the *ruach* in a fashion no longer known in the present. That did not, however, mean that the Old Testament had no sense of a counterbalancing *future* hope as well; which leads to our last theme.

(iv) *The Future Hope*

(a) *The Davidic King*   The classic promise of a future ruler endowed with God's *ruach* is in Isa. 11:

> There shall come forth a shoot from the stump of Jesse,
>   and a branch shall grow out of his roots.
> And the *ruach* of Yahweh shall rest upon him,
>   the *ruach* of wisdom and understanding,
>   the *ruach* of counsel and might,
>   the *ruach* of knowledge and the fear of Yahweh.
> And his delight shall be in the fear of Yahweh.
>
> He shall not judge by what his eyes see,
>   or decide by what his ears hear;
> but with righteousness he shall judge the poor,
>   and decide with equity for the meek of the earth;
> and he shall smite the earth with the rod of his mouth,
>   and with the breath of his lips he shall slay the wicked.
> Righteousness shall be the girdle of his waist,
>   and faithfulness the girdle of his loins ...
>
> In that day the root of Jesse shall stand as an ensign to the peoples; him shall the nations seek, and his dwelling shall be glorious. (vv. 1–5, 10)

Nothing fresh by comparison with other passages we have mentioned is said here about the *ruach* as such. This oracle's distinctiveness lies rather in the clear promise that it will fill the hoped-for heir of David. It is most probable that this, like the equally familiar prophecy of Isa. 9.2-7, originally referred to a child just born to or expected by the royal house of Judah; and it is even possible that the very preservation of these passages is due to the conviction of some in the Isaianic school that they had been fulfilled in Josiah, the last outstanding (and theologically approved) king of Judah.[7] But beyond all such hopes and disappointments, these intimations were destined to shape the longing for the Messiah, the Anointed One, who would be supremely endowed with the *ruach* of God. The same is true of the promise formulated in the period of the Exile by 'Second Isaiah':

Behold my servant, whom I uphold,
   my chosen, in whom my soul delights;
I have put my *ruach* upon him,
   he will bring forth justice to the nations.
He will not cry or lift up his voice,
   or make it heard in the street;
A bruised reed he will not break,
   and a dimly burning wick he will not quench;
   he will faithfully bring forth justice.
He will not fail nor be discouraged
   till he has established justice in the earth;
   and the coastlands wait for his law.

(Isa. 42. 1–4)

It is uncertain here whether the 'servant' is an individual or Israel itself—or indeed who the individual might be. But as with Isa. 11, the real significance of this passage lies in its subsequent influence: it too formed the picture of the coming Messiah. As in later generations the sense intensified that the *ruach* had departed from Israel, so too did the anticipation of the figure on whom it would rest in all its fullness.

(b) The people of Israel This future hope was not only focused in the person of the coming ruler. Even the promises gathering around him were promises *for the whole people*. So we also find in the Old Testament a wider conception of the presence of the *ruach* of God in Israel, and a longing for its comprehensive restoration. Their most poignant expression is given in Isa. 63, which looks back in the dark days following the return from the Exile, and speaks with heartfelt longing of the 'holy *ruach*' as the power of God's own presence with his chosen people:

I will recount the steadfast love of Yahweh,
   the praises of Yahweh,
according to all that Yahweh has granted us,
   and the great goodness to the house of Israel
which he has granted them according to his mercy,

according to the abundance of his steadfast love.
For he said, Surely they are my people,
   sons who will not deal falsely;
   and he became their Saviour.
In all their affliction he was afflicted,
   and the angel of his presence saved them;
in his love and in his pity he redeemed them;
   he lifted them up and carried them all the days of old.
But they rebelled and grieved his holy *ruach*;
   therefore he turned to be their enemy,
   and himself fought against them...
Where is he who put in the midst of them
   his holy *ruach*,
who caused his glorious arm
   to go at the right hand of Moses,
who divided the waters before them
   to make for himself an everlasting name,
   who led them through the depths?
Like a horse in the desert,
   they did not stumble.
Like cattle that go down into the valley,
   the *ruach* of Yahweh gave them rest...
Look down from heaven and see,
   from thy holy and glorious habitation.
Where are thy zeal and thy might?
   The yearning of thy heart and thy compassion are
   withheld from me.
For thou art our Father,
   though Abraham does not know us
   and Israel does not acknowledge us;
Thou, Yahweh, art our Father,
   our Redeemer from of old is thy name...
Return for the sake of thy servants,
   the tribes of thy heritage...
We have become like those over whom thou hast never
   ruled,
   like those who are not called by thy name.

                     (vv. 7–19)

These verses, which contain two of the only three instances of 'holy *ruach*' in the entire Old Testament, make it very clear that this *ruach* is nothing other than God's own active presence. Indeed one reason for quoting it at such length is that it so clearly illustrates what was said above about the use of *ruach*, 'angel', 'arm' and the like to describe that nearness of God. That apart, it also shows how profoundly the entire previous history of Israel was coming to be seen as marked by God's faviour, Israel's rebellion, and the consequent withdrawal of his presence. Out of this bitter diagnosis, the hope of Israel's restoration to friendship with God was naturally expressed in terms of a new outpouring of his *ruach* upon them. Long before, Moses' wish had been recorded: 'Would that all the people of Yahweh were prophets, that Yahweh would put his *ruach* upon them!' (Num. 11.29) That pious hope later became a more definite conviction, most dramatically formulated in Joel 2.28-29:

> And it shall come to pass afterward,
>   that I will pour out my *ruach* upon all flesh;
> your sons and your daughters shall prophesy,
>   your old men shall dream dreams,
>   and your young men shall see visions.
> Even upon the menservants and maidservants
>   in those days I will pour out my *ruach*.

Such an outpouring of *ruach* need not simply be thought of in terms of ecstatic, prophetic and visionary experiences. More commonly it was bound up with a wider hope for the renewal of the ravaged land, of the nation, and of its relation to God. Three excerpts from the books of Isaiah and Ezekiel bring this out:

> For the palace will be forsaken,
>   the populous city deserted...
> until the *ruach* is poured upon us from on high,
>   and the wilderness becomes a fruitful field,
>   and the fruitful field is deemed a forest.
> Then justice will dwell in the wilderness,

and righteousness abide in the fruitful field . . .
My people will abide in a peaceful habitation,
    in secure dwellings and in quiet resting places.
                                        (Isa. 32.14-18)

For I will pour water on the thirsty land
    and streams on the dry ground;
I will pour my *ruach* on your descendants,
    and my blessing on your offspring.
They shall spring up like grass amid waters,
    like willows by flowing streams.
This one will say, I am Yahweh's,
    another will call himself by the name of Jacob . . .
                                        (Isa. 44.3-5)

For I will take you from the nations, and gather you from all
the countries, and bring you to your own land. I will
sprinkle clean water upon you, and you shall be clean . . . A
new heart I will give you, and a new *ruach* I will put within
you; and I will take out of your flesh the heart of stone, and
give you a heart of flesh. And I will put my *ruach* within you,
and cause you to walk in my statutes . . . You shall dwell in
the land which I gave to your fathers; and you shall be my
people, and I will be your God. (Ezek. 36.24-38; cf. also
37.12-14)

It is very much a *corporate* hope that is offered here; the *ruach*
of God's presence is the power of the restored life of Israel, not
merely the inspiration of individuals. In this connection it is
worth noticing that in the last two of these passages the image
of *water* rather than of air, wind, or life, is drawn upon. Water
is also a symbol of the support of life; but beyond that, it also
speaks of washing and refreshing, and so is well fitted to
convey the sense of renewal and repairing, the overcoming of
past defilement—in a word, the reconciliation with God which
is Israel's hope, and the promise of its future life.

(c) The individual   Very similar language to that just quoted

could also be used to speak of the individual's relation to God, and of the overcoming and forgiving of his personal sins. The classic example is the other passage in the Old Testament referring to 'holy *ruach*'—Ps. 51:

> Have mercy on me, O God, according to thy steadfast love;
>> according to thy abundant mercy blot out my transgressions.
> Wash me thoroughly from my iniquity,
>> and cleanse me from my sin...
> Behold thou desirest truth in the inward being;
>> therefore teach me wisdom in my secret heart.
> Purge me with hyssop, and I shall be clean;
>> wash me, and I shall be whiter than snow....
> Create in me a clean heart, O God,
>> and put a new and right *ruach* within me.
> Cast me not away from thy presence
>> and take not thy holy *ruach* from me.
> Restore to me the joy of thy salvation,
>> and uphold me with a willing *ruach*.
>
>> (vv. 1–2, 6–7, 10–12)

While the forms of expression here are very similar to those in the prophets, the perspective (as in many of the Psalms) is different. It is not the withdrawal of the *ruach* from Israel, or its restoration, that is here in view, but the rupture and repair of the individual's relation to God. The two perspectives are of course complementary, but they are not identical, and they could fall apart. This can be seen in two quite different ways of speaking about the *ruach* of God which can be traced in later rabbinic Judaism, and which could scarcely be integrated with each other.[8] According to one, the *ruach* had definitely departed from Israel when the glory of Yahweh arose and left the temple (Ezek. chs 8–11). It was now absent, and would return only with the messianic age; and in the present time the only source of divine inspiration was the *bath qol*, the 'daughter (or echo) of the voice'—which, furthermore, was not very highly valued. According to the other, the *ruach* of God continued to rest upon 'the righteous', and was seen virtually as a reward for their righteousness. The horizon in the first case was shaped by Israel's history; in the second by the individual's personal goodness or sinfulness. But the roots of both run back to the Old Testament; and this, like the other tensions and contrasts to be traced there, continued to have outworkings in later ages.

CHAPTER TWO

RUACH AND PNEUMA
BETWEEN THE TESTAMENTS

In the Jewish literature from the period between the Old and
New Testaments, several lines of thought about the Spirit of
God, or indeed about 'spirit' and 'spirits' in general, can be
traced. For our purposes, a broad distinction can be made
between Palestinian Judaism and the more Hellenistic
atmosphere of the Diaspora, especially in Alexandria.

1. Palestinian Judaism and the Dead Sea Scrolls

In Palestinian Judaism the relatively slight Old Testament
connection of the Spirit of God with creation seems to have
faded even further into the background. The predominant
association of the Spirit was with prophecy, and this became
entrenched in the increasingly systematic formalisation of
Jewish thought by the rabbis.[1] The Old Testament
anticipations of a future giving of the Spirit are, however, also
taken up in some of the writings looking forward to the
Messiah. One example is to be found in the Psalms of
Solomon, which probably date from the first century BC, and
reflect the outlook and piety of the Pharisaic school. The 17th
describes the 'Anointed of the Lord' (v.32), the 'Son of David'
(v.21), who will purify Jerusalem and defeat the foreigners
(v.30), and 'smite the land with the word of his mouth' (v.35).
Of him it is said,

> And he shall not fail in his days before his God,
>   for God has made him strong in holy spirit,
>   and wise in counsel of wisdom with strength and
>   righteousness.
> The blessing of the Lord is with him in strength,
>   and he shall not weaken.

His hope is in the Lord,
and who shall be able to resist him? (vv.37-39)

Nothing new is said here about the 'holy spirit': the language simply echoes what we have seen in the Old Testament, with the same ambiguity as in Ps. 51—is this 'Spirit' or 'spirit'? But the passage does show how the Messiah could be associated with it.[2]

Much more striking is a messianic hymn preserved in the Testaments of the Twelve Patriarchs.[3] These writings were probably composed in the century before Christ, but they betray signs of subsequent Christian editing. This makes it hard to know what value to place upon the sections which most strongly resemble themes in the New Testament: they may open up for us part of the background to the New Testament itself, but equally they may simply reflect the hand of Christian redactors. With that proviso, however, this hymn is still so remarkable as to be worth quoting: it should be compared especially with the Gospel accounts of Jesus' baptism in the Jordan.

The heavens shall be opened,
And from the temple of glory shall come upon him
    sanctification,
With the Father's voice as from Abraham to Isaac.
And the glory of the Most High shall be uttered over him,
And the spirit of understanding and sanctification
    shall rest upon him in the water.
For he shall give the majesty of the Lord to his sons
    in truth for evermore ...

And he shall open the gates of paradise,
And shall remove the threatening sword against Adam.
And he shall give to the saints to eat of the tree of life,
And the spirit of holiness shall be on them.
And Beliar shall be bound by him,
And he shall give power to his children to tread upon evil
    spirits.
And the Lord shall rejoice in his children,

And be well pleased in his beloved ones for ever.

(Test. Lev. 18.6-8, 10-12)

This 'new priest' (v.2), whose 'star shall rise in the heavens as of a king' (v.3), will himself be endowed with the spirit that God will give, and also give it to 'the saints', his 'children'. This is a remarkable anticipation (or echo) of what the New Testament has to say about Jesus. So too is the reference to the overcoming of 'evil spirits' and of 'Beliar' (= 'Belial', one of the names given to Satan).[4] These hint at the extensive outgrowth of demonology in the time between the Testaments, a development which was further coloured by anticipation of the final apocalyptic conflict between good and evil—a conflict that was a very common theme in Palestinian Jewish literature, and appears in various parts of the New Testament, most dramatically in the Book of Revelation.

The struggle between good and evil takes on a distinctive shape in some of the Dead Sea Scrolls,[5] which since their discovery a generation ago have cast much new light on Palestinian Judaism around the time of Christ. Admittedly, some of the exaggerated claims that were made in the first flush of excitement—for instance, that the message of Jesus, or of John the Baptist, could now be entirely explained by the Scrolls—have turned out on more sober reflection to be quite unsound.[6] If John was ever one of the Qumran sect, he had certainly ceased to be an orthodox subscriber by the time he came preaching his baptism of repentance in the Judaean wilderness, while Jesus' teaching was a world apart from the rigid puritanism of the Scrolls. Both in resemblance and in contrast, however, they do illuminate the New Testament in various aspects.

Many of the uses of the word 'spirit' in the Scrolls are similar to those we have already noted. It can be used of the human 'spirit', of supernatural 'spirits', and also of the 'Holy Spirit' or 'Spirit of Holiness'. The inspiration of the Scriptures is ascribed to the Holy Spirit, and in the *Hymns* (1QH) the dependence of man's spirit upon God's is expressed in very similar style to Ps. 51.[7] The really distinctive feature is the teaching on the 'two spirits', which are very fully described in the third and fourth pages of the *Community Rule* (1QS iii-iv). The passage deserves to be quoted at some length, but for the sake of clarity we shall break it up, with some rearranging, into the main points.

Fundamental to the whole view is the primeval antithesis between 'the spirit of truth' and the 'spirit of falsehood', or, as they are also called, the Prince or Angel of Light and the Angel of Darkness or of Malevolence. (In another of the Scrolls, the *War Rule*, the latter is identified with Satan, the former apparently with Michael—1QM xiii, xvii.) These govern the nature and behaviour of human beings, and are locked in unremitting conflict:

> (God) has created man to govern the world, and has appointed for him two spirits in which to walk until the time of his visitation: the spirits of truth and falsehood. Those born of truth spring from a fountain of light, but those born of falsehood spring from a fountain of darkness. All the children of righteousness are ruled by the Prince of Light and walk in the ways of light; but all the children of falsehood are ruled by the Angel of Darkness and walk in the ways of darkness.
>
> The nature of all the children of men is ruled by these (two spirits), and during their life all the hosts of men have a portion in their divisions and walk in (both) their ways. And the whole reward for their deeds shall be, for everlasting ages, according to whether each man's portion in their two divisions is great or small. For God has set the spirits in equal measure until the final age, and has set everlasting hatred between their divisions. Truth abhors the works of falsehood, and falsehood hates all the ways of truth. And their struggle is fierce for they do not walk together.

This sense of a cosmic conflict between the forces of good and evil may owe something to the impact of Iranian religion upon Judaism in the centuries preceding the New Testament era. Zoroastrianism was strongly dualistic, and explained the existence of evil and suffering by interpreting the universe as a battle-ground between two eternally opposed powers of light and darkness. Even if there is direct or indirect Iranian influence in the Scrolls, however, it has been sharply qualified by the Jewish conviction of the ultimate sovereignty of God, for the dualism of the two spirits is not ultimate. Both have been appointed *by God*, who has set them in equal balance against each other *until the final age*; it is also made quite clear that 'it is he who created the spirits of light and darkness and founded every action upon them and established every deed (upon) their (ways).' There is in fact a certain resemblance here to the doctrine which developed about this time in Judaism of the 'good and evil inclinations' which compete against each other in man, and which are both firmly subordinated to God himself.[8] The contest between them is nonetheless quite real and absolutely serious for the destiny of each individual.

God himself, further, is by no means ultimately neutral in the struggle. Those who belong to the spirit of truth can have confidence in ultimate victory:

But the God of Israel and his Angel of Truth will succour all the sons of light. For ... he loves the one everlastingly and delights in its works for ever; but the counsel of the other he loathes and for ever hates its ways.

But in the mysteries of his understanding and in his glorious wisdom, God has ordained an end for falsehood, and at the time of his visitation he will destroy it for ever. Then truth, which has wallowed in the ways of wickedness during the dominion of falsehood until the appointed time of judgment, shall arise in the world for ever. God will then purify every deed of man with his truth; he will refine for himself the human frame by rooting out all spirit of falsehood from the bounds of his flesh. He will cleanse him of all wicked deeds with the spirit of holiness; like purifying waters he will shed upon him the spirit of truth (to cleanse him) of all abomination and falsehood. And he shall be plunged into the spirit of purification that he may instruct the upright in the knowledge of the Most High and teach the wisdom of the sons of heaven to the perfect of way. For God has chosen them for an everlasting covenant, and all the glory of Adam shall be theirs. There shall be no more lies and all the works of falsehood shall be put to shame.

The strongly predestinarian note here deserves notice. There seems to be something of the idea that the sons of light belong by their very nature to the spirit of truth, and are therefore foreordained to ultimate salvation, but that in this present life they are besmirched by a certain admixture of the spirit of falsehood, which will at the last be expunged. Those on the other hand whose 'portion in the division' of the spirit of falsehood is greater are predestined to destruction.

Finally, as the spirits are not simply supernatural, cosmic beings, but powers at work in human life, their influence can be described in quite practical religious and ethical terms. So the 'ways of the spirit of truth', and the eventual reward of those who share in it, are portrayed:

> ... a spirit of humility, patience, abundant charity, unending goodness, understanding and intelligence; (a spirit of) mighty wisdom which trusts in all the deeds of God and leans on his great loving-kindness; a spirit of discernment in every purpose of zeal for just laws, of holy intent with steadfastness of heart, of great charity towards all the sons of truth, of admirable purity which detests all unclean idols, of humble conduct sprung from an understanding of all things, and of faithful concealment of the mysteries of God. These are the counsels of the spirit to the sons of truth in this world.
>
> And as for the visitation of all who walk in this spirit, it shall be healing, great peace in a long life, and fruitfulness, together with every everlasting blessing and eternal joy in life without end, a crown of glory and a garment of majesty in unending light.

With these are contrasted the 'ways' of the spirit of falsehood:

> ... greed, and slackness in the search for righteousness, wickedness and lies, haughtiness and pride, falseness and

deceit, cruelty and abundant evil, ill-temper and much folly and brazen insolence, abominable deeds (committed) in a spirit of lust, and ways of lewdness in the service of uncleanness, a blaspheming tongue, blindness of eye and dullness of ear, stiffness of neck and heaviness of heart, so that man walks in all the ways of darkness and guile.

And the visitation of all who walk in this spirit shall be a multitude of plagues by the hand of all the destroying angels, everlasting damnation by the avenging wrath of the fury of God, eternal torment and endless disgrace, together with shameful extinction in the fire of the dark regions...

There are indeed striking similarities here to some features of the New Testament. For example, the Johannine literature mentions the contrast between light and darkness (John 1.5; I John 1.5), the 'Spirit of truth' (John 14.17; 15.26; 16.13), and even the difference between the 'spirit of truth' and the 'spirit of error' (I John 4.5).[9] Again, Paul can contrast 'the Spirit' and 'the flesh' in terms remarkably like the *Rule*'s description of the 'ways' of the two spirits:[10]

But I say, walk by the Spirit, and do not gratify the desires of the flesh. For the desires of the flesh are against the Spirit, and the desires of the Spirit are against the flesh; for these are opposed to each other... Now the works of the flesh are plain: Immorality, impurity, licentiousness, idolatry, sorcery, enmity, strife, jealousy, anger, selfishness, dissension, party-spirit, envy, drunkenness, carousing, and the like. I warn you, as I warned you before, that those who do such things shall not inherit the kingdom of God.

But the fruit of the Spirit is love, joy, peace, patience, kindness, goodness, faithfulness, gentleness, self-control; against such there is no law. And those who belong to Christ Jesus have crucified the flesh with its passions and desires. (Gal. 5.16-24)

At the same time, the perspective of Paul and John is by no means the same as that of the Scrolls. The fundamental difference is that the New Testament writers do not think primarily in terms of an ongoing struggle between equally balanced powers which will only be resolved at the end of time. They are convinced that the decisive turning-point has come with Jesus: the final conflict centres on the cross. Again, while the Scrolls do align the spirit of truth with God, over against the spirit of falsehood, both spirits are located on the same cosmic level, below and clearly set apart from God himself. The Spirit in the New Testament is unambiguously the Spirit *of God*, and John is careful to stress that the 'Spirit of truth' proceeds *from the Father* (John 15.26). Consequently, the eschatological note is even more pronounced in the New Testament than in the Scrolls: the Spirit is the power of the End-time which has broken in in Jesus and now drives to the consummation, whereas in the Scrolls the spirit of truth is more of an immanent force working through history, even though God will use it in a special way as his instrument at the final judgment. Another contrast stemming from these differences is that the New Testament does not portray the cosmic conflict as being between two spirits who are, as it were, mirror-images of each other. It speaks most characteristically of more asymmetrical contrasts between Spirit and flesh, or God and the world,[11] and even the Christ/ Antichrist antithesis, though it does more closely resemble that of the Scrolls, does not offset this general difference. Again, the thought that men belong *by their nature* to the one side or the other plays no great role in the New Testament, even though it does occasionally hint at the idea (e.g. John 8.44-47; I Cor. 2.14). Finally, the Spirit takes up a far larger space in the New Testament than in the Scrolls, where passages of the kind we have cited are relatively rare. Though clearly important for the world-view of the Qumran sect, they convey nothing of the New Testament sense of a fresh and decisive outpouring of the Spirit of God. The Scrolls are nevertheless relevant, for they do help to clarify and highlight features of the New Testament; and similar dualistic and predestinarian conceptions were to work powerfully among gnostic groups on the fringes of orthodox Christianity in the following centuries.[12]

2. Hellenistic Judaism and the Wisdom Tradition

In Hellenistic Judaism we find a very different world of thought from Qumran. The meeting with the language and ideas of Hellenistic culture fostered a style of religious thought and writing which was certainly Jewish and deeply concerned to remain loyal to the Old Testament, but which also took on something of the colouring of its environment. The messianic hope and the apocalyptic vision did not flourish as in Palestine; instead there was a move towards a more universal world-view which paved the way for the subsequent interaction of Christian and Hellenistic thought; indeed it was in Christianity rather than in later Judaism that the heritage of Hellenistic Judaism was exploited. In this movement, the idea of the Spirit, in Greek, *pneuma* of God developed along lines rather different from those we have so far mentioned.[13]

The Scriptures of Hellenistic Judaism were the Septuagint (LXX), the Greek translation of the Old Testament. In almost three-quarters of the places where *ruach* appeared in the Hebrew text, it was translated as *pneuma*, and *pneuma* was employed on at least some occasions for each of the various senses of *ruach*, including 'wind', 'breath', 'life', 'mood', 'self', 'supernatural spirit', and 'Spirit of God.'[14] Most of the cases where *ruach* was rendered by other terms are explained by the facts that Greek supplied alternative words for 'wind' (e.g. *anemos*) and, more importantly, that *pneuma* in pagan Greek at that time did not normally carry the psychological senses of 'mood', 'soul' or 'mind', which were frequently translated in the LXX by such alternatives as *thymos*, *psyche*, and *nous* respectively.[15] Further, the usual Greek term for a supernatural 'spirit' was not *pneuma*, but *daimon*. The fact that the LXX nevertheless sometimes used *pneuma* in these senses brought a new dimension to the word in Greek. It is, however, significant that Hellenistic Judaism on the whole preferred not to use *pneuma* of an *evil* spirit, applying in that sense words such as *daimon*. The same tendency can be traced in most of the New Testament, where only Mark has a noticeable fondness for speaking of an evil or unclean *pneuma*.[16] The kind of 'two spirit' dualism found in Qumran was not part of the Hellenistic vision, and *pneuma* was on the whole restricted to favourable senses.

More important still are the specifically theological associations of *pneuma* with prophecy or with God himself, which are to be attributed to the influence of the LXX through its translation of *ruach* by *pneuma*. Ecstatic prophecy and oracles were indeed well known in the Hellenistic world, but *pneuma* was not previously used in pagan Greek to name the power that inspired them. It was the LXX that imported this meaning into Greek. In fact, it inserted references to the *pneuma* of God in some cases where *ruach* was not mentioned in the Hebrew. In Num. 23.7 it added, 'and the *pneuma* of God came upon him' (that is, Balaam), and in Zech. 1.6 it modified the text to read, 'which I commanded *in my pneuma* to my servants the prophets.' Here is another reflection of the tendency of intertestamental Judaism to bind together prophecy and the Spirit in the fashion we have already noticed, now further reinforcing this new meaning of the Greek word as well.

The most distinctive and important new element, however, lay quite simply in the equation of *pneuma* with *God's* Spirit. In Greek of that period, *pneuma* was not normally used as a theological term at all, so that the LXX here introduced a completely new idea. The only (remote) analogue to the Old Testament thought was in the philosophy of the Stoics, who thought of the entire cosmos as animated and guided by a subtly diffused *pneuma*, which was understood as an exceedingly fine, but still *material*, fluid, and identified with 'god'. The connotations of the *pneuma* were thus very different from those of the *ruach* of Yahweh. While as we shall see, Hellenistic Judaism could speak of the *pneuma* of God in ways that bear some resemblance to Stoic conceptions, it nevertheless retained a strong sense of God's transcendence, and resisted the temptation to reduce him or his *pneuma* simply to a kind of pantheistic 'world-soul'.

These may seem very technical details, but they are a sign that we find ourselves here at a crossroads in the history of religious language and thought. Shifts of this sort in the meaning and use of words also signal profound alterations in theological and philosophical horizons. It is not going too far to say that the subsequent theological connotations of *pneuma* in Greek, or indeed of 'spirit' in English, *Geist* in German, or *esprit* in French, have been deeply influenced by this inflow of Jewish thought into the Greek-speaking culture of the Mediterranean in the centuries before Christ, and by that injection and modification of Old Testament conceptions in Greek garb.

Under the influence of the LXX, then, *pneuma* came to cover the same broad range of senses and to function in much the same style as *ruach*. It could be applied both to God and to man, and so operate as a linking term between them. Even when it was used, as it commonly was in Hellenistic Judaism, to mean the human mind or self, the thought was never far away that these were not independent or self-subsistent but given by God. This was very much in line with the Old Testament understanding; but the central theological applications were to be further developed in the Hellenistic Jewish tradition.

First there is the link of *pneuma* with prophecy. The conviction crystallised that not only Old Testament prophecy, but the sacred writings of the Old Testament generally, had been inspired by God's *pneuma*. In this lay their distinctive authority over against all pagan or later Jewish writings, and their inspiration was qualitatively superior to any other kind of illumination.

At the same time, the idea of the nature of that inspiration as presented in the Jewish writers of the first century AD, Philo and Josephus, shows the influence upon them of reflection on the subject among pagan religious and philosophical thinkers.[17] In the Hellenistic world, as in the earlier strands of the Old Testament, ecstatic frenzy was regarded as a symptom of divine possession, of 'enthusiasm' (*enthousiasmos*, the state of being 'filled with god'). In this state, one was understood to be the passive instrument of a power coming from without; and it was widely held that the very process of inspiration demanded the suppression of the rational faculties in order to permit the reception and mediation of a message transcending all ordinary reason or understanding. These ideas were assimilated by those Jewish writers, and in this they presumably reflect the general assumption. They qualified it, however, in two important ways. First, they drew a clear distinction between inspiration by the *pneuma*, inspiration *par excellence*, which was associated especially with the Old Testament prophets, and other, lesser experiences of 'inspiration' that others might attain. Second, they treated the process of inspiration as supra-rational rather than irrational, as mediating divine wisdom unattainable by unaided human reason. The effect of these qualifications was to prevent the danger of reducing inspiration to a kind of subpersonal possession—a danger which must always be guarded against if inspiration is not to be understood in an essentially pagan fashion.

The second major development was that the Old Testament hints at the creative and life-giving energy of the *ruach* of Yahweh began to be extended into a richer conception of his universally creating and sustaining *pneuma*. This is the particularly distinctive pneumatological thought of Hellenistic Judaism. It may to some extent have been helped along by Stoic ideas, but they were not the moving influence. Much more determinative was the link that came to be seen between God's *pneuma* and his *sophia*, 'wisdom', in Hebrew, *hokhma*.

In the Old Testament there is a distinct strand of 'Wisdom literature' (Job, Proverbs, Ecclesiastes, and some of the Psalms), whose chief burden is Wisdom, human and divine, rather than prophecy, cult, law, or sacred history. Wisdom binds together heaven and earth: God is wise; his Wisdom can be shared in by men; to live in accordance with it is to live wisely. Thus the idea of Wisdom operates there in a fashion not unlike *ruach* and other terms elsewhere in the Old Testament which link God and man. (In this light, the association of *pneuma* with *sophia* in the Hellenistic continuation of the Wisdom tradition was by no means purely arbitrary, though it also brought a certain transformation of both conceptions). Wisdom was understood as having a cosmic and creative role, most finely depicted in Prov. 8.22-31, where Wisdom herself speaks:

> Yahweh created me at the beginning of his way,
>> the first of his acts of old.
> Ages ago I was set up,
>> at the first, before the beginning of the earth.
> When there were no depths I was brought forth,
>> when there were no springs abounding with water.
> Before the mountains had been shaped,
>> before the hills, I was brought forth;
> Before he had made the earth with its fields,
>> or the first of the dust of the world...
> When he marked out the foundations of the earth,
>> then I was beside him, like a master workman;
> And I was daily his delight,
>> rejoicing before him always,
> Rejoicing in his inhabited world,
>> and delighting in the sons of men.

This probably should not be taken as meaning that the divine Wisdom is a separate 'being' from God, but as a poetic expansion of the thought of Ps. 104.24, 'Yahweh, how manifold are thy works! In wisdom hast thou made them all...' The creative Wisdom is God's *own*, and just as his *ruach* or word can be 'sent forth', so too can his Wisdom be spoken of as a kind of extension of himself, much as we might speak of the skill of an artist as being expressed (and giving him satisfaction) in what he makes.

These verses did however offer an obvious starting-point for further reflection. So, for example, the rabbis came to identify this pre-existent Wisdom of God with the Torah, the Law revealed through Moses. Other lines of interpretation of this passage helped to shape some of the most exalted descriptions of Christ in the New Testament—as the creative 'Word' of God (John 1.1ff), as 'the firstborn of all creation' (Col. 1.15), as 'the Son... through whom also he created the world ...

who reflects the glory of God and bears the very stamp of his nature' (Hebr. 1.2-3)—and it also figured prominently in the christological debates in the early church.[17a] It is not therefore surprising that some representatives of Hellenistic Judaism should have discerned a particular link between *sophia* and *pneuma* and sought to spell it out. This was achieved especially in the Wisdom of Solomon, probably composed in Alexandria in the first century BC. The main passage is ch. 7.21-30:

> And all such things as are either secret or manifest, them I
>   know;
>   for Wisdom, the fashioner of all things, taught me.
> For in her there is an understanding spirit, holy.
>   unique, manifold, subtle,
>   lively, clear, undefiled,
> plain, inviolable, loving of good, quick,
>   unhindered, beneficent, kind to man,
>   strong, secure, free from care,
>   all-powerful, all-seeing,
>   and passing through all spirits
>   that are understanding, pure and most subtle.[18]
> For Wisdom is more moving than all movement,
>   she passes and goes through all things because of her
>   purity.
> For she is the breath of the power of God
>   and the radiance of the pure glory of the Almighty;
>   therefore can nothing defiled fall into her.
> For she is the brightness of the everlasting light,
>   and the unspotted mirror of the energy of God,
>   and the image of his goodness.
> Being one, she can do all things,
>   and remaining in herself, makes all things new;
> and in all ages entering into holy souls
>   she makes them friends of God and prophets.
> For God loves none but him who dwells with Wisdom.
> For she is more beautiful than the sun,
>   and above all the rank of the stars.
> Compared with light, she is found superior;

for night succeeds the light,
but evil does not overcome Wisdom.

This *sophia/pneuma* is on the one hand universally present throughout the universe, but on the other distinctively present in 'the wise' who are also 'the righteous'. The note of discrimination comes out more clearly in ch. 1.4-8:

For Wisdom will not enter a wicked soul,
    nor dwell in a body that is given over to sin.
For the holy spirit of discipline will flee from deceit,
    and withdraw from foolish thoughts,
    and depart when unrighteousness comes in...
Because the spirit of the Lord fills the world,
    and that which contains all things has knowledge of the
        voice.
Therefore none that speaks unrighteously can be hidden,
    nor shall vengeance in punishing pass him by.

There is some resemblance here to the thought of Isa. 63, but also an obvious difference: the presence or absence of this holy *pneuma* is conditioned by the purity of the individual, and its chief gift is divine Wisdom imparted to him. 'Thy counsel who has known, except thou give Wisdom and send thy holy *pneuma* from above?' (Wis. Sol. 9.17) So Philo could say that God's *pneuma* is 'the pure wisdom in which every properly wise man participates.'[19]

This particular tradition has little or no direct influence on the New Testament understanding of the Holy Spirit, though as we have already hinted it is of considerable relevance for its christology. The reason is not far to seek: in this essentially universal, cosmic perspective there is room for *one* comprehensively mediating principle between God and the world, God and men, but it is not at all obvious that *more* than one is either necessary or desirable. It is therefore quite natural that in Alexandrian Judaism the *pneuma* and the *sophia* of God should have been united in this way, and that the initial Christian exploitation of that heritage should link them primarily with Christ as the Word or Son of God.

Consequently, some of the earliest approaches to a Christian reformulation of the doctrine of God were essentially binitarian rather than trinitarian, concentrating attention on God and his Word, on the Father and the Son. The place of the Holy Spirit was much more vague and uncertain. There was, however, another stream of Christian thought which maintained the link of the Spirit of God with his Wisdom; and once the matter of the divinity of the Son had been clarified in the fourth century, and the status of the Spirit had to be considered, it provided some of the necessary materials for a more fully trinitarian understanding.

One other point must be briefly mentioned. It has commonly been suggested that the notion of *pneuma* in Hellenistic Judaism takes on a certain distinctness and independence from God—that poetic personification leads on to the hypostatisation of the Spirit/Wisdom as a separate, intermediary entity between God and the world, comparable, for instance, with the spirit of truth in Qumran. This suggestion, however, goes beyond the available evidence.[20] The imagery of the Wisdom of Solomon—'breath', 'radiance', 'brightness', 'mirror' and 'image'—belongs in the same category as the Old Testament's 'glory' and 'presence'. It does not bespeak a 'being' other than God himself, but God's own active presence. What *can* be traced is a certain tendency to draw these disparate ideas together in a more unified fashion than in the diversity of Old Testament usage. Hellenistic Judaism nevertheless remained in touch with its Old Testament roots, as well as paving the way for the understanding which was to be hammered out with some labour in the early Christian centuries.

CHAPTER THREE

SPIRIT OF GOD—SPIRIT OF CHRIST

It is in the New Testament that the Holy Spirit really enters on the centre of the stage as 'the Spirit of your Father' (Matt. 10.20) 'the Spirit of his Son' (Gal. 4.6), 'the Spirit of Jesus' (Acts 16.7), 'the Spirit of Christ' (Rom. 8.9), 'the Spirit of life' (Rom. 8.2), 'the Spirit of sonship' (Rom. 8.15), 'the Spirit of Grace' (Hebr. 10.29), 'the Paraclete' (John 14.16). It also carries other names by now familiar, such as 'Spirit of truth' (John 14.17) or 'of wisdom' (Acts 6.3, 10). The bearer of all these titles is now seen and shown to be inherently involved in what God has done in Jesus Christ, and with the outworking of that divine action.

This is the message that sets the New Testament apart from the Old, and from the intertestamental writings. The Messiah has come; the age of the Spirit has opened; the Spirit itself is the power of the divine purposes centred in Jesus Christ, and radiating from him. All that the New Testament has to say about the Spirit points to that centre, and is ultimately controlled by it.

At the same time the diverse character of the New Testament writings is reflected also in a variety of ways of describing the Spirit.[1] This can best be seen by looking in turn at the main strands, beginning with the Synoptic Gospels and Acts, then travelling on to Paul, John, and other books.

1. The Synoptic Gospels and Acts[2]

These four books are knit together by the fact that Luke wrote Acts as well as his Gospel, while both Matthew and Luke seem to have used Mark as a source: hence the very similar passages we shall mention below. In addition, unlike the rest of the New

Testament other than the Fourth Gospel, they offer historical narrative, and it is by following the line of the story they tell that we can best trace their understanding of the Holy Spirit.

In the great majority of cases, the Spirit is referred to specifically in connection with Jesus or his followers, though mention is also made of its inspiration of the Old Testament prophets (Matt. 22.43; Mark 12.36; Acts 1.16; 4.25; 28.25). Luke speaks of it most frequently: in his infancy narratives the Spirit inspires John the Baptist (Luke 1-15, 17), Elisabeth (1.41), Zachariah (1.67), and Simeon (2.25ff), and Acts too regularly describes people as 'full of the Spirit'—e.g. Peter (4.8), Stephen (6.3ff; 7.55), Philip (8.29ff), Barnabas (11.24) and Saul and Barnabas (13.9).[3] Mark and Matthew by contrast say very little about the Spirit except in association with Jesus himself, and even there offer rather less than Luke. Indeed, the total number of references linking Jesus and the Spirit is not very great, though they tend to be particularly emphatic.

The key passages, all but the first of which appear in quite similar form in all three Gospels, describe:

(a) *The conception and birth of Jesus*   Matt. 1.18-20 and Luke 1.35 both ascribe this to the miraculous intervention of the Holy Spirit. Luke here also specifically connects this with the designation of Jesus as 'Son of God'; the same link appears in the baptismal narratives and also, in rather different form, in Rom. 1.4, 'designated Son of God in power according to the Spirit of holiness by his resurrection from the dead.'

(b) *Jesus' baptism*   Mark 1.10–11, Matt. 3.16-17, and Luke 3.22, in almost identical terms, describe the descent of the Spirit in the form of a dove, and thereupon the voice from heaven identifying Jesus as 'my beloved Son, in whom I am well pleased.'

(c) *The temptation*   Mark 1.12, Matt. 4.1, and Luke 4.1 follow the account of the baptism by describing how Jesus was 'driven' (Mark; Matthew and Luke soften the language to 'led') into the wilderness by the Spirit to face Satan. The sense of violence in Mark's language deserves notice, as does the patent desire of Matthew and Luke to tone it down. Elsewhere, however, Luke can describe Jesus as exulting in the Holy Spirit and breaking out into prayer (Luke 10.21).

(d) Victory over demons All three Gospels repeat, in various forms, the story of the accusation that Jesus was inspired by Beelzebub, and Jesus' denunciation of the blasphemy against the Holy Spirit (Mark 3.20ff; Matt. 12.24ff; Luke 11.15ff; 12.10). The point of Jesus' response in each case is the same: the power by which the evil spirits are compelled to submit is God's Spirit, by which the 'kingdom', the authority of God, is breaking into the world (Matt. 12.28; Luke 11.20).

(e) The promise to the disciples All three cite the saying of John the Baptist that Christ will baptise with the Holy Spirit (Mark 1.8; Matt. 3.11; Luke 3.16. Matthew and Luke speak of 'Spirit and fire'; this, as the context shows, is a symbol of judgment: cf. the similar combination in Isa. 4.4). Similarly, all three report Jesus' own assurance to the disciples that when they are on trial, the Spirit will tell them what to say (Mark 13.11; Matt. 10.20; Luke 12.12). Only Luke goes further to formulate a more general promise of the gift of the Spirit (Luke 11.13; the parallel in Matt. 7.11 refers to 'good things'), which is echoed again in Luke 24.49; Acts 1.5, 8; 11.16.

In addition, Luke emphasises that Jesus' whole ministry is empowered by the Spirit. After the temptation he returns 'in the power of the Spirit' to Galilee (4.14), and begins his preaching in Nazareth by quoting Isa. 61.1-2, 'The Spirit of the Lord is upon me...' (4.18). Acts 10.38 sums it up in the formula, 'Jesus was anointed with Holy Spirit and with power.' Such reiteration is lacking in Mark and Matthew: though Matt. 12.18 does cite Isa. 42.1-4 in full, it is to explain Jesus' enjoining of silence on those he cured rather than to underline his bearing of the Spirit.

It is striking that these passages are so few, and refer to the Spirit in such a limited variety of contexts. The writers, with the possible exception of Luke, were apparently not chiefly interested in presenting Jesus as a 'charismatic' figure, or in referring every aspect of his teaching and healing to the Spirit. The import of the references is primarily *eschatological*: Jesus is the promised Messiah in whom *the power of God's kingdom* has broken into the world.[4] Hence very little is said to fill out the picture of the Spirit: *it* is, so to speak, a known quantity, whereas *Jesus*' identity and destiny need to be interpreted and proclaimed.[5] Acts does, however, offer rather more detail, and shows, what Luke at least conceived to be the main aspects of the Spirit's activity.

Central to Luke's pneumatology is the account of Pentecost in Acts 2. Here, the greatest space is given, not to the dramatic events, the rushing wind, the tongues of fire, and the speaking in many languages, but to Peter's sermon (2.14-36), and the climax of the whole chapter comes in the words with which that sermon ends: 'Let all the house of Israel therefore know assuredly that God has made him both Lord and Christ, this Jesus whom you crucified.' The charismatic manifestations are explained as Joel's promised outpouring of the Spirit, which is in turn a sign of God's vindication of Jesus. More than that, it is *Jesus himself* who gives it: 'Being therefore exalted at the right hand of God, and having received from the Father the promise of the Holy Spirit, he has poured out this which you see and hear.' (v. 33) This is not merely a re-enactment of what happened in Jesus' baptism, a simple repetition among the disciples of what had once happened to him. The new outpourings of the Spirit has been made possible only through his death and resurrection. The Spirit came on him from the Father; it comes to his followers *through him*. So the activity of the Spirit is intrinsically bound up with Jesus Christ himself, and this double pattern of his reception and bestowal of the Spirit is constitutive of the whole fresh understanding of the matter in the New Testament. (It is hinted at by the Synoptic accounts of the Baptist's prediction, which they place before Jesus' baptism and reception of the Spirit. The Fourth Gospel reverses the order, and explicitly emphasises the connection— John 1.32-34.)

The coming of the Spirit is nevertheless depicted by Luke as quite visibly and audibly recognisable, both in the events of Pentecost and in the cases of the Samaritan converts (8.14ff), the household of Cornelius (10.44ff) and the group at Ephesus (19.6). A sense of the *unambiguity* of the Spirit's presence is generally characteristic of Acts, in spite of 2.13. This bears upon an issue on which Luke may seem inconsistent: is the Spirit given through baptism, through the laying-on of hands, or through the proclamation of the Gospel? Each of these can be presented as if it were determinative (e.g. 2.38; 8.16; 10.44-45), and those who wish to fasten on only one of them have sometimes been much exercised by Luke's untroubled shifting between them. But he was not concerned with that question; the giving of the Spirit carried its own identification and authentication, and because it could be recognised when it occurred it did not require to be specifically or exclusively bound to only one of these conditions. This does, however, signal a certain weakness in Luke's theology. Well before he wrote Acts it had become apparent that discerning the genuine presence of the Spirit was not quite so simple as he makes it out, as Paul had shown at length in I Cor. 12-14. Luke glosses over these difficulties, painting a somewhat idealised picture of the early church. This is not to say that he did not accurately preserve a great deal of older material; it is to counsel caution before accepting his account as the whole story, let alone a blue-print for the church today.[6]

What then are the special manifestations of the Spirit in Acts? While miraculous healings and exorcisms are mentioned, these are not specifically ascribed to the power of the Spirit. What are specially associated with it are, rather, speaking in tongues (2.4ff; 10.46; 19.6), praising God (10.46), bold proclamation (2.11; 4.8; 4.31), power in confrontation (6.10; 13.9), and, most prominent of all, new Christian prophecy (2.17-18; 11.28; 20.23; 21.4; 21.11), vision (7.55), and guidance for the church or for individuals (8.29; 10.19; 11.12; 13.2), with which belong special occasions when the Spirit 'sent' (13.4), 'forbade' (16.6-7), or 'bound' (20.22), or placed individuals as *episkopoi* ('overseers') in the community

(20.28). Related to this is a particular association of the Spirit with 'witnessing' (1.8; 5.32). The predominant motifs are those of communication, proclamation and guidance. Even speaking in tongues, which is only mentioned in accounts of Pentecost and later conversions, retreats into the background by comparison with prophetic messages to the church, while manifestations of sheer supernatural power are also quite rare (2.2-3; 4.31; 8.39). The Spirit appears chiefly as energising the church's worship and witness to Christ, and as guiding its life and mission.

This connection of the Spirit with the church, it may be added, is quite fundamental, so far as Acts is concerned. It is *in the church* that it is at work, and *through the church's mission* that it comes upon others. Its authority can be invoked for decisions made by the church's leaders (15.28), and to lie to them is to attempt to deceive the Spirit, which brings fearful retribution on Ananias and Sapphira (5.1-11). The Spirit is certainly not the church's *possession*, but God's *gift*, as the tale of Simon Magus illustrates (8.20); indeed 'gift' seems to be virtually a technical term for the Spirit (2.38; 8.20; 10.45; 11.17: *cf*. Hebr. 6.4 and John 4.10; 7.39). The Christian community lives by that gift, not by its own inherent power. But the gift *is given*, and given *in the church* rather than elsewhere. This theme is connected in particular with Luke's sharp antithesis between the church and the Jews: they are presented throughout as resisting God and his Christ, so that the church's mission, fulfilling Old Testament prophecy, turns increasingly to the Gentiles (*cf*. Acts 28.22–28). The Spirit is seen in terms of the Old Testament promise, the receiving and giving of it by Jesus Christ, and its continuing activity in the church, which has replaced the old Israel.

2. Paul[7]

In returning from the Synoptics and Acts to Paul, we find a richer conception and deeper exploration of the nature of the Spirit, of its activity, and of its inherent connection with Jesus Christ. Partly because his approach is theological rather than narrative/historical he probes more searchingly into the why and wherefore of the things of which he writes. That apart, he is profoundly aware of the centrality of the work of the Spirit, which is woven into the whole fabric of his theology.

Paul regularly speaks in terms of two realms of reality, two modes of existence. The contrast is formulated in many ways—light and darkness, faith and works, life and death, righteousness and sin, sonship and slavery, divine foolishness and human wisdom, Isaac and Ishmael, Jerusalem above and Jerusalem below, Second and First Adam, the new age and the old. All these antitheses pivot upon Jesus Christ himself. It is he who has opened up the sphere of light, life and faith, of righteousness and sonship; his cross is the divine foolishness which is stronger than the wisdom of the world; in him the new age has broken in, and our present life is set in the tension between it and the old. But the old is doomed, standing under the judgment of the cross, while our sharing in the new is the promise of salvation through him.

One of Paul's characteristic ways of expressing this all-pervading dialectic is in terms of flesh (*sarx*) and spirit (*pneuma*). Most extensively developed in Rom. 7-8, I Cor. 2-3, and Gal. 3 and 5, it also appears more summarily in such verses as Phil. 3.3, 'For we are the true circumcision, who worship in God's Spirit, and glory in Christ Jesus, and put no confidence in the flesh.' The real contrast here is not between the 'inner' or 'spiritual' side of human nature and the 'outward' or 'physical', though Paul can use *sarx* and *pneuma* in that way (I Cor. 5.3-5; II Cor. 7.1; Col. 2.5;[8] *cf.* the contrast of *soma*, 'body', and *pneuma* in I Cor. 7.34 and I Thess. 5.23): even then, however, the Old Testament sense that man's spirit depends on God is still clearly present.[9] This is, rather, the kind of contrast drawn in Isa. 31.3: *sarx* designates the earthly, human, and creaturely, *pneuma* the divine presence which encounters us in Jesus Christ, and into which we are drawn by him. (So Paul can use the formula, 'according to the flesh ... according to the Spirit', of Jesus himself in order to express what later theology would seek to describe in terms of his human and divine 'natures'—Rom. 1.3-4; II Cor. 5.16-17.) 'Flesh' stands generally for the world and man apart from

Jesus Christ, and 'Spirit' for the new reality established through him, the whole atmosphere within which 'life in Christ' is lived, and the power by which that life is formed. 'Spirit' comprehensively describes the totality of this newness: it does not merely name one elment in it, but designates the whole over against 'the flesh', life without Christ.[10]

Consistently with this, the Spirit is drawn into the closest possible connection with Paul's other favourite ways of stating the general antithesis—e.g. as 'the Spirit of sonship' (Rom. 8.14-15; Gal. 4.6) which is the source of liberty (Rom. 8.2; II Cor. 3.17) and stands over against the 'letter' of the Law as the giver of new life (Rom. 7.6; II Cor. 3.6), which makes us holy and righteous (I Cor. 6.11) and imparts truth that human wisdom cannot grasp (I Cor. 3.13). The sheer range of the Spirit's scope and activity is especially apparent in Paul's most extensive portrayals in Rom. 8.1-27 and Gal. 5.15-26: everything from justification to the final manifestation of the children of God, from faith to prayer, from ethical behaviour to calling God, '*Abba!* Father!', is enabled by the Spirit. This is a far wider canvas than in the Synoptics. Paul (a) discerns an integral connection of the Spirit's work with the activity of God in Christ, and (b) depicts it as extending across the whole spectrum of Christian life, and as driving dynamically towards the *eschaton*.

(a) God, Christ, and the Spirit. In Paul it is made much clearer than in the Synoptics and Acts that the Spirit is not only that power of God which was on Jesus and is sent by him: its nature and activity are stamped as intimately bound up with Jesus Christ himself. The connection between them is not external and accidental, but internal and necessary. What is opened up in Jesus Christ is nothing other than the life of the Spirit, and the work of the Spirit bears the indelible mark of Christ. So Paul can say not only that we are called to live and walk 'in the Spirit' (Gal. 5.25), but also that we are 'in Christ' (II Cor. 5.17). In one way, these descriptions are virtually interchangeable:

But you are not in the flesh, you are in the Spirit, if the Spirit of God really dwells in you. Anyone who does not have the Spirit of Christ does not belong to him. But if Christ is in you, although your bodies are dead because of sin, your spirits are alive because of righteousness. If the Spirit of him who raised Jesus from the dead dwells in you, he who raised Christ Jesus from the dead will give life to your mortal bodies also through his Spirit which dwells in you. (Rom. 8.9-11)

Clearly there is no material difference between 'if the Spirit of God dwells in you,' and 'if Christ dwells in you.' Yet Christ is not simply identified with the Spirit, for the Spirit is 'the Spirit of him who raised Jesus from the dead.' The Spirit is the power of God who raised Jesus; but as such it is also the power of Jesus' resurrection, and so too of his risen presence. Therefore it is both the Spirit *of God* and the Spirit *of Christ*. As God's Spirit, by its indwelling it constitutes us the temple of God's presence (I Cor. 3.16-17); as 'the Spirit of his Son' it makes us sons who can cry, '*Abba*! Father!' (Gal. 4.6). The Spirit as the active and transforming presence of God cannot be divorced from the crucified and risen Jesus on whom it rested, through whom it comes, and by whom it is defined. Paul cannot simply equate the Spirit with Christ, any more than he can dissolve away the difference between Christ and the Father. Rather, the fundamental distinction and relationship between the Father and Jesus Christ open up a field in which it is both possible and necessary to relate the Spirit to both without conflating it with either.[11]

Here, far more clearly than in Acts or the Synoptics, can we follow the motive and dynamic of the early Christian discovery that the Old Testament *ruach* of Yahweh was nothing other than the Spirit of Christ. Paul's writing reflects crystallisation and integration of awareness of the Father, of Jesus Christ, of the Spirit, which quite spontaneously generated the summary formulae in which all three are mentioned together—as, for instance, in the benediction he uses in II Cor. 13.14, or, for that matter, the baptismal formula in Matt. 28.19. These formulations capture and articulate a fundamentally new perception, in which the active divine presence, the 'Spirit', took on *Christ*ian shape as the essential third term in the pattern, as the activity of God which is centred in and reflects Jesus Christ himself, as a second focus in the ellipse of the divine operation. This is not to say that the doctrine of the Trinity in its later form is already stated by Paul; but the essential pattern is there, and in his sense of the connection and distinction of God the Father, Christ and the Spirit is sketched out the area which that doctrine would seek more formally to map.

(b) The Gifts and Activity of the Spirit. Paul makes it clear that he believes those to whom he writes have received the Spirit, and refers frequently to its having been given (e.g. Rom. 5.5; Gal. 3.2; I Cor. 6.11; I Thess. 1.6). It is not at all obvious, however, that this always refers to some patently 'pentecostal' gift. His tone sometimes seems to suggest that his hearers may not even realise that they have received it, nor what the appropriate response should be—'Do you not know that ... the Spirit of God dwells within you?' (I Cor. 3.16; *cf.* e.g. Gal. 5.25; I Thess. 4.8). The presence and impact of the Spirit are less superficially apparent than Acts would suggest; and while Paul by no means rejects striking charismatic manifestations—he himself speaks in tongues (I Cor. 14.18), and mentions 'signs and wonders' in his own ministry (Rom. 15.19; II Cor. 12.12)—he is concerned to open up a wider and deeper awareness of the Spirit's activity than an exclusive focus on such extraordinary phenomena would allow.

In the last chapter we quoted Paul's list of the 'fruits of the Spirit' in Gal. 5. The ethical note struck there is characteristic of him, but he does not mean by it simply to reduce the Spirit to a moral way of living. It has to do with 'sanctification', with the transformation of human life through Jesus Christ.[12] When he associates the Spirit with righteousness (Rom. 8.17; I Cor. 6.11; Gal. 5.5), peace (Rom. 8.17; 15.13; Gal. 5.22; Col. 3.15), joy (Rom. 8.17; Gal. 5.22; I Thess. 1.6), hope (Rom. 15.13) and, above all, love (Rom. 5.5; 15.30; I Cor. 13; II Cor. 6.6;

Gal. 5.22; Col. 1.8; 3.14), he is delineating the quality of the new, holy life which comes *from God*: it is *God's* love that has been 'poured into our hearts through the Holy Spirit' (Rom. 5.5), and by the Spirit we are gathered into a new relation to the Father:

> When we cry, '*Abba!* Father!' it is the Spirit himself bearing witness with our spirit that we are children of God, and if children, then heirs, heirs of God and fellow-heirs with Christ ... (Rom. 8.15-17; *cf*. Gal. 4.6)

> Likewise the Spirit helps us in our weakness; for we do not know how to pray as we ought, but the Spirit itself intercedes for us with sighs too deep for words. And he who searches the hearts of men knows what is the mind of the Spirit, because the Spirit intercedes for the saints according to the will of God. (Rom. 8.26-27)

> 'What no eye has seen, nor ear heard,
> nor the heart of man conceived,
> what God has prepared for those who love him,'
> God has revealed to us through the Spirit. For the Spirit searches everything, even the depths of God. For what person knows a man's thoughts except the spirit of the man which is in him? So also no one comprehends the thoughts of God except the Spirit of God. Now we have received not the spirit of the world, but the Spirit which is from God, that we might understand the gifts bestowed upon us by God. And we impart this in words not taught by human wisdom but taught by the Spirit, interpreting the spiritual truths to those who possess the Spirit. (I Cor. 2.9-13)

The thought here is in line with the Old Testament link between the Spirit of God and the human spirit, and indeed may also echo some of the themes of the Wisdom of Solomon, but now in a specifically Christian fashion. The Spirit is the inner dynamic of the life of faith, life which 'is hid with Christ in God' (Col. 3.3), and at its inmost core is formed by participation in a movement of communication, recognition and response issuing from the heart of God himself. It is the hidden centre of our own identity, the reflection and actualisation in us of Christ's relation of sonship to the Father, the reverberation in us of God's love, and the manifesting of his wisdom.

This profound awareness of the mysterious deeps of the Spirit, as well as his sense of its ethical outworking, readily explains why Paul resisted the reduction of the Spirit to a few obviously 'charismatic' gifts. So too does his conviction that the Spirit is the upbuilder of the Christian community. This comes prominently to the fore in I Cor. 12-14.[13] Against the exaggerated emphasis that some in Corinth were placing upon ecstatic phenomena such as speaking in tongues, he insists that the Spirit gives many different gifts, that those which benefit an individual in isolation are less valuable than those which edify the church, that incomprehensible utterances are of much less value than coherent prophecies, and, above all, that the highest gift is love, which strengthens the whole body instead of discriminating between an élite and the rest. Significantly, he finds it necessary to warn against 'prophecies' which 'curse Jesus' (I Cor. 12.3ff: cf. the similar warning against false prophecy in II Thess. 2.2), and to insist that any 'prophet' or 'spiritual person' who rejects the truth of what he writes should himself not be accredited (I Cor. 14 37-38). Quite matter-of-fact criteria were apparently needed to enable even the least 'charismatic' of the faithful to discriminate between authentic and inauthentic manifestations of the Spirit.

The Spirit thus reaches up to the presence of God, down to the deepest heart of man, and out to gather the community; but there is another dimension as well. Although the new has broken in Christ, and the church already lives in the power of the Spirit, the old has not yet been destroyed, and we are caught in the tension and conflict between the Spirit and the flesh. To the Spirit's praying in us what by ourselves we cannot pray corresponds its kindling a hope for what is not yet, for the completion of God's purposes, for the 'revealing of the sons of God' (Rom. 8.19). The present gift of the Spirit is a 'pledge' (*arrabon*—II Cor. 1.22; 5.5), a 'first-fruits' or 'downpayment' (*aparche*—Rom. 8.23). This hope points beyond the resurrection, 'the redemption of our bodies', (Rom. 8.23) when the whole creation 'will be set free from its bondage to decay and obtain the glorious liberty of the sons of God.' (Rom. 8.21) This eschatological dynamic is as fundamental to the work of the Spirit as everything else we have mentioned in Paul.[14] It is the power of God driving towards the end of history and carrying us forward to the destiny disclosed and anticipated in the resurrection of Jesus Christ.

3. The Johannine Literature[15]

Like the Synoptics and Acts, the Fourth Gospel speaks of the Spirit in Jesus' life and ministry, and of its imparting to his followers. Like Paul, it (and I John) presents the fruit of deep theological reflection on the Spirit's nature and activity. The Johannine perspective and language are, however, distinctive, and open fresh vistas, both in the general association of the Spirit with Jesus in the historical narrative, and in the extended treatment of the Spirit in the Farewell Discourses (chs. 14-16).

In the account of Jesus' life and ministry, the Spirit is first mentioned by John the Baptist (1.29-34). Jesus' baptism by him is not recounted, but he witnesses to the descent of the Spirit in the shape of a dove, and stresses that it *remained* on him, adding that this identifies Jesus as the one who will baptize with the Holy Spirit. By comparison with the similar material in the Synoptics, there is here a palpably stronger emphasis on Jesus' *possession* of the Spirit. Several of Jesus' reported sayings also go on to speak of the Spirit in a style not found in the Synoptics:

Unless one is born of water and the Spirit, he cannot enter the kingdom of God. That which is born of the flesh is flesh, and that which is born of the Spirit is spirit. (3.5-6)

For he whom God has sent utters the words of God, for it is not by measure that he gives the Spirit; the Father loves the Son, and has given all things into his hand. (3.34-35)

But the hour is coming, and now is, when the true

worshippers will worship the Father in Spirit and in truth, for such the Father seeks to worship him. God is Spirit, and those who worship him must worship in Spirit and in truth. (4.23-24)

It is the Spirit that gives life, the flesh is of no avail; the words that I have spoken to you are spirit and life. (6.63)

Similarly, Jesus' giving of the Spirit is promised in a rather different form:

On the last day of the feast, the great day, Jesus stood up and proclaimed, 'If any one thirst, let him come to me and drink. He who believes in me, as the scripture has said, "Out of his heart shall flow rivers of living water."' Now this he said about the Spirit, which those who believed in him were to receive; for as yet the Spirit was not (given?), because Jesus was not yet glorified. (7.37-39)[16]

Like Acts, John emphasises that it is only through the completion of Jesus' work that the Spirit will be given; indeed, Jesus must 'go away' if the Paraclete is to come (16.7). He locates that completion, however, not in a post-Easter exaltation, but in Jesus' 'glorification', that is, in his death and resurrection (17.1-5). Consequently, after several repetitions of the promise of the coming of the Spirit (14.17, 26; 15.26; 16.7, 13), Jesus breathes it upon the disciples on the first Easter Day (20.22). This shift in perspective is characteristic of John, who focuses the entire drama of salvation more intensively than the Synoptics in the person and history of Christ himself; it also coheres with a greater stress on the Spirit as *inhering in* Jesus and *flowing from* him. Just as Paul bound up Christ and the Spirit more intimately than Luke in his account of the operations of the Spirit in us, so John traces a comparable inner connection in the historical life of Jesus.

In view of this, it is not surprising that the terms in which the Spirit is spoken of in the Gospel and the Epistle draw on the same vocabulary used to describe Jesus Christ himself.

Indeed, the Farewell Discourses more than any other part of the New Testament identify the Spirit as the *counterpart* of Christ, the 'other Paraclete' (14.16), almost a separate 'individual' whose role is modelled on Christ's own. In the verses we have already quoted, two predominant associations appear—with 'truth' (and 'the words of God'), and with 'life' (and being 'born again'): both are central motifs in Johannine theology, signalled in the very opening words of the Gospel, 'In the beginning was the Word ... In him was life...' (John 1.1, 4), and repeatedly thereafter, as in 14.6, 'I am the way, and the truth, and the life.' Yet a third Johannine theme, colouring both its Christology and its pneumatology, is that of *conflict*—not so much, as in Paul, the conflict of Spirit and flesh, but of light with darkness (1.5; 3.19), truth with falsehood (8.44-45; I John 4.1-6), belief with unbelief (3.18; 6.35-40, 65; 12.37-50; 14.8-11; 20.26-29; I John 5.1-10), all reflecting a fundamental antithesis between God, Christ, the Spirit, even the disciples, and 'the world' (1.10; 3.16-21; 7.7; 14.30; 15.18; 16.33; 17.25; I John 5.4), which belongs to God, yet does not recognise his truth in Jesus, and consequently puts itself under judgment.

The motifs of life, truth, and the conflict with the cosmos largely mould John's presentation of the Spirit. Charismatic gifts of the more exotic type fade even further into the background than in Paul; the only time they are clearly hinted at is in I John 4.1-6, which is concerned, like I Cor. 12.1-3, to offer a criterion for distinguishing between prophetic spirits, described in language reminiscent of Qumran as those of truth and of error. The criterion is simply whether or not the spirit in question confesses that Jesus Christ has come 'in the flesh' (*cf.* II John 7): this probably reflects the need to counter docetic ideas known to the Johannine circle.[17] As in Paul, putative revelations must be tested by their coherence with the fundamentals of the faith that has been delivered. The verses explicitly connecting the Spirit with life have already been quoted: they all come from the earlier chapters of the Gospel. Their brevity should not lead us to overlook them, or to underrate their importance in the Johannine framework.

Being born of the Spirit is what is also described as being 'born of God' (1.13; I John 3.9), and the life thus mediated is that which is in the eternal Word (1.4) and was 'made flesh' in Jesus (1.14), so that, like the Father and by the Father's gift, he 'has life in himself.' (5.26). This life that is in him is given to us also by God (I John 5.11), and we live out of Christ as the branches from the vine (15.1-11). Directly related to this are the symbolic references in the passages from which we have quoted to both baptism (3.5) and the eucharist (6.51-65); these, and their connection both with Christ's death and with the Spirit, are again hinted at in veiled fashion in 19.34 (the water and the blood flowing from Jesus' pierced side on the cross) and I John 5.6-8, where Christ, water, blood, and Spirit are all mentioned together. The sacraments bespeak a new birth and a new life given through Christ and empowered by the Spirit.[18]

It is remarkable, however, that John does not explicitly attribute the ethical dimension of this life to the operation of the Spirit. I John speaks at length of righteousness and love, but these are not described in Paul's fashion as 'fruits of the Spirit'. Instead we can trace a certain parallelism: he who loves is 'born of God (I John 4.7), and by love we know that we are 'of the truth' (I John 3.19), just as our obedience assures us that we are 'in God' (I John 2.5). Similarly, we know that we are 'in God' and God 'in us' because he has given us the Spirit. (I John 3.24; 4.13). There is here, no doubt, an *implicit* connection of the Spirit with both life and righteousness, but it is not spelt out. The Spirit, whether spoken of as 'Spirit' or as 'the anointing of the Holy One' (I John 2.20-27), is chiefly appealed to as *evidence*. It has to do with the central Johannine themes of knowledge, witness and conviction. And these are clearly the dominant categories in the Farewell Discourses when they speak of the Spirit of truth, the Paraclete, and the conflict with 'the world':

And I will pray the Father, and he will give you another Paraclete, to be with you for ever, even the Spirit of truth, which the world cannot receive because it neither sees it nor knows it; you know it, for it dwells with you and will be in you. (John 14.15-17)

These things I have spoken to you while I am still with you, But the Paraclete, the Holy Spirit, which the Father will send in my name, he will teach you all things, and bring to your rememberance all that I have said to you. (14.25-26)

But when the Paraclete comes, whom I shall send to you from the Father, even the Spirit of truth, which proceeds from the Father, he will bear witness to me; and you also are witnesses, because you have been with me from the beginning. (15.26-27)

... if I do not go away, the Paraclete will not come to you; but if I go, I will send him to you. And when he comes, he will convince the world of sin, of righteousness and of judgment: of sin, because they do not believe in me; of righteousness, because I go to the Father, and you will see me no more; of judgment because the ruler of this world is judged. (16.7-11)

I have yet many things to say to you, but you cannot bear them now. When he comes, the Spirit of truth, he will guide you into all truth; for he will not speak on his own authority, but whatever he hears he will speak, and will declare to you the things that are to come. He will glorify me, for he will take what is mine and declare it to you. All that the Father has is mine; therefore I said that he will take what is mine and declare it to you. (16.12-15)

The Spirit is 'another Paraclete' because Jesus himself is 'Paraclete' (I John 2.1), i.e. 'advocate' or 'strengthener'. So it reflects the character of Christ and continues to convey his truth and vindicate him against the 'world'. It can indeed even be called simply 'the truth' (I John 5.7), but it is made clear in the same verse that it is 'witness', just as the Discourses stress that it does not speak on its own authority. Similarly, though Jesus himself is truth (14.6), he does not speak on his own authority, but on that of the Father (8.28; 12.49), and himself bears witness to the truth (18.37). The integral connection that John implies between 'the truth' and this 'witness' to it should not, however, be missed. The Father himself witnesses to Jesus (5.36-37; 8.18; I John 5.9), and the witness of the Spirit is the testimony of the Father, from whom it comes (15.26). Witness of this sort is to be distinguished from the witness to Jesus of John the Baptist (1.15; 32, 34; 5.33), the disciples (15.27; 19.35; 21.24; I John 4.14), the Scriptures (5.40) or even of Jesus' works (5.36; 10.25), for this is *God's own* testimony to his own truth in Jesus, his declaration, authentication and interpretation of it. This is not the testimony of an inferior: the Spirit witnesses to Christ by the necessity of inner consistency, not by imposed, external subordination.[19] In the same way, the controversy with 'the world' is Jesus' own, not a separate campaign of the Spirit's; it is the reiteration of the *krisis*, the 'judgment' or 'sifting' of the cosmos which Christ has provoked (3.19; 8.26; 9.39; 12.31), and it is because the cosmos does not know him (1.10) that it is incapable of recognising the Spirit—or indeed Christ's followers (I John 3.1) who are no longer 'of the world' (17.14-16). The Spirit mirrors Christ himself, but to the 'world' the mirror conveys no image.

These passages present what is, by comparison with Paul, a more sharply and narrowly defined outline of the figure of the Spirit;[20] but they also offer a nexus of bonds between the Father, Christ and the Spirit which were to have a profound influence in forming subsequent theological reflection. The Spirit 'proceeds from the Father' (15.26) and Christ himself 'comes from the Father' (16.28); not only will the Spirit come, but Christ himself and the Father will come and make their home with those who love him (14.23); similarly in I John 3.24 and 4.13 the presence of the Spirit is a sign of God's 'abiding' in us. This does not quite state the kind of mutual indwelling of the Father, Christ and the Spirit that is ascribed to the Father and the Son (14.10: 'I am in the Father and the Father in me'), but it points in that direction. So too does what we have called the Spirit's 'mirroring' of Christ. In all these ways, while by no means formulating the doctrine of the Trinity hammered out later, the Johannine writings set up further signposts along the road to it.

4. Other New Testament Writings

The remainder of the New Testament is well filled with references to the Spirit, but for the most part these run along similar lines to those we have traced in one or more of the previous sections. The Spirit inspired the Old Testament prophets (Hebr. 3.7; 9.8; 10.15; I Pet. 1.11-12; II Pet. 1.21), is given to Christ's followers (Eph. 1.13; 3.16; 4.30; II Tim. 1.7; Tit. 3.5-6; Hebr. 2.4; 6.4; 10.29), dwells in the church (Eph. 2.22; 5.18; II Tim. 1.14) and is the source of its unity (Eph. 2.18; 4.3-4). It brings about signs and wonders (Hebr. 2.4), the powers of the age to come (Hebr. 6.4), and is the inspirer of Christian ecstasy, prophecy and worship (Eph. 3.5; 6.18; I Tim. 4.1; Jude 20; Rev. 1.10; 2.7ff; 4.2; 14.13; 17.3; 19.10; 21.10; 22.17), by which God's promise is sealed (Eph. 1.13; 4.30). Two passages illustrate what by the end of the New Testament era was the well-established framework within which the Spirit was seen as the Spirit of Christ even in the Old Testament, and as the Spirit that brings about renewal through Christ:

> The prophets who prophesied of the grace that was to be yours searched and inquired about this salvation; they inquired what person or time was indicated by the Spirit of Christ within them when predicting the sufferings of Christ and the subsequent glory. It was revealed to them that they were serving not themselves but you, in the things which have now been announced to you by those who preached the good news to you through the Holy Spirit sent from heaven … (I Pet. 1.10-12)

> But when the goodness and loving kindness of God our Saviour appeared, he saved us, not because of deeds done by us in righteousness, but in virtue of his own mercy, by the washing of regeneration and renewal in the Holy Spirit, which he poured out upon us richly through Jesus Christ

our Saviour, so that we might be justified by his grace and become heirs in hope of eternal life. (Tit. 3.5-7)

There is, however, one distinctively new note that is struck, almost in passing, in the Letter to the Hebrews:

But when Christ appeared as a high priest of the good things that have come ... he entered once for all into the Holy Place, taking not the blood of goats and calves but his own blood, thus securing an eternal redemption. For if the sprinkling of defiled persons with the blood of goats and bulls and with the ashes of a heifer sanctifies for the purification of the flesh, how much more shall the blood of Christ, *who through the eternal Spirit offered himself without blemish to God*, purify your conscience from dead works to serve the living God! (9.11-14)

The Spirit does not merely come upon Jesus from the Father, flow to us through him, and enable our response to God. It is the motive and power of *his* dedication *to* the Father, which culminates and is sealed upon the cross. Here is opened up the profoundest meaning of his bearing of the Spirit, the purpose of his birth, the secret of his baptism, the true nature of his victory over temptation and the forces of evil. The decisive actualisation of the presence of God's Spirit in human life and history is encompassed in his offering of himself. There too is the source of the Spirit for us: the Spirit of God, by which we cry, '*Abba!* Father!', is the Spirit of the Crucified who reigns from the tree.[21]

5. Further Questions

By its very nature, the diverse witness of the New Testament points to further questions which it does not explicitly formulate or directly answer, but which the church had to face precisely because of its loyalty to its message. This involved tracing the direction of its testimony, following through its implications, and seeking to uncover the profound coherence of the realities of which it speaks. That endeavour did not only begin in the second century; it can be detected in the New Testament itself, as when Paul offers the Corinthians a deeper and wider vision of the Spirit's work, or John points up the link between the Father, Christ, and the Spirit of truth, or Hebrews discerns the power of the Spirit in the cross of Jesus. Later theology had to engage in that same task, not in order to move away from the New Testament witness, but to enter fully into it.

The further questions concerning the Spirit fall largely into three main areas, though all are interconnected:

(a) The Spirit and Creation. The reorientation and redefinition of the Spirit in terms of Jesus Christ lead in the New Testament to a virtually exclusive association of the Spirit with redemption, salvation, rebirth, eschatological hope. As in Palestinian Judaism generally, the Old Testament hints at a more general creative and life-giving power fall out of sight, while the cosmic role of the Spirit in Hellenistic Judaism is taken up into christology rather than pneumatology. Can we then properly describe the Spirit as Creator?

(b) The Spirit and the Church. The New Testament itself shows what problems could arise in this field: the problems of discernment of authentic gifts of the Spirit, problems of authority and truth. As the church consolidates into an ordered institution, there increases the danger of treating the Spirit as the possession of the church, which grows hardened and is no longer open to the Spirit's free energies. The resultant tensions between Spirit and structure have surfaced repeatedly through Christian history. This is not so much a theoretical question of theological formulation as a thoroughly practical challenge to the church—but one which also has a direct bearing on what it affirms about the Spirit.

(c) The Spirit in Relation to the Father and to Christ. Given all that is said in the Bible, and especially in the New Testament, about the character and activity of the Spirit, how are its status and identity to be expressed? Is it to be thought of as 'personal' or 'impersonal'—or is neither category wholly adequate? How

is its distinctness, brought out particularly by John, to be held together with its nature as the Spirit *of God*, as God's *own* presence and action? Is the Spirit God, even though the New Testament does not call it so, and though it does not speak of worship offered *to* the Spirit but *in* the Spirit? Finally, if the Father makes himself known through Jesus and by the Spirit, what does this mean about the nature of God himself? The need to face and struggle with questions of this kind eventually led to the doctrine of the Holy Spirit as the 'third person' of the Trinity.

PART TWO

PATTERNS IN PNEUMATOLOGY

CHAPTER FOUR

FIRST SKETCHES: THE SECOND AND THIRD CENTURIES[1]

The issues sketched at the close of the last chapter can be seen running through and shaping reflection on the Spirit in the early church. Not that most of the leaders of the church's thought consciously perceived themselves as facing yet unsolved conundrums posed by the New Testament. They were too aware of the continuity of a living tradition to see things quite like that. Indeed, the canon of the New Testament itself only came gradually to be established, and while most of the major writings were generally recognised in main-stream orthodoxy by about the end of the second century as 'apostolic' and authoritative, the process was not finally completed for another two hundred years. It was part of a general consolidation which also brought about the early catholic church structure, centred on monarchical bishops tracing their succession from the apostles (frequently on rather doubtful evidence), and the crystallisation of summary 'rules' or outlines of the faith, from which developed the later creeds.[2] This was all driven forward by controversy with sundry heresies which compelled the church to take up the task of clarifying and sharpening the distinctive doctrines. It was in this still somewhat fluid era that further thought began to be given to the place and function of the spirit.

Up to about the middle of the second century, there appears to have been a general decline both in charismatic manifestations and in the vital sense of the living presence of the Spirit. It is referred to in extant writings as an element in the faith, as having spoken by the prophets, as being given to the church—but usually in a rather formal way, lacking the freshness and vigour of the New Testament. It is as if awareness of it had been successfully domesticated, swallowed up in the emerging church institutions.

A powerful reaction in the opposite direction came with Montanism. The movement began in Phrygia with Montanus and his female followers, Maximilla and Priscilla, who were convinced that through them the Paraclete was delivering fresh revelations with new instructions for the life of the church, and announcing the imminent descent of the New Jerusalem at Pepuza in Asia Minor. The movement was rapidly and decisively rejected by the church at large, though it later won a notable sympathiser in Tertullian of Carthage († after 220), the first great Latin theologian.[3] By this time it seems to have shed some of its original features—the date for the advent of the New Jerusalem had passed in 177—but it appealed to him because of its moral strictness and its conviction of the active, communicating presence of the Spirit. The tension between the appeal to immediate, inspired authority and the government of the ecclesiastical establishment is very forcefully expressed in some of his later writings;[4] the same challenge was to be raised repeatedly by other movements in the history of the church.

Towards the end of the second century and into the third, more fully developed theologies of the Spirit begin to appear. Particularly important works were the *Adversus Haereses* of Irenaeus of Lyons († *ca.* 200), Tertullian's *Adversus Praxean*, and the *De Principiis* of Origen of Alexandria († 253/4). These cast a great deal of light on the questions that were being raised and the experimental answers to them in the generations before the period of more definitive doctrinal formulation that followed in the fourth century.

1. Irenaeus

Though he spent most of his active life in Gaul, Irenaeus originally came from Asia Minor, and it is likely that much of the material in his writings is drawn from a distinctive Asia Minor tradition of Christian theology which is now largely lost. The *Adversus Haereses* unfolds a positive statement of the faith and at the same time refutes in considerable detail the teaching of sundry gnostic groups, and of Marcion. Marcion rejected the Old Testament, and held that the Father of Jesus Christ, the God of love, was not to be identified with the Creator of the world, the God of the Old Testament, the jealous God. Many gnostics subscribed to even extremer views of this world as inherently evil, maintained that salvation was a matter of escaping from it, and believed in Jesus as a supernatural revealer of the secret knowledge (*gnosis*) which enabled the soul to rise into spiritual realms, but not as a man of flesh and blood. Against all these, Irenaeus firmly reasserted the identity of the one God as Creator and Redeemer, the nature of the world as God's originally good creation, and the genuine humanity of Jesus as the very foundation of our salvation. Within this framework—and at every main point in it—he also discerned the activity of the Spirit.

Irenaeus follows the thought of Hellenistic Judaism in identifying the divine Wisdom of Prov. 8 with the Spirit (IV.xx.3).[5] The Father has his Word, which is his Son, and his Wisdom, which is his Spirit, and these are his 'two hands' by which he created all things (IV.xx.1). The Spirit thus has a double role, in creation and redemption; in both respects it is given by the Word, which 'bestows the Spirit on all ... on some by way of creation, the gift of being; on some by way of adoption, the gift of rebirth as sons of God.' (V.xviii.1). Where Marcion and others snap the link between creation and salvation, Irenaeus sets each in the light of the other, and traces the same pattern in both. So he draws together the *Sophia-Pneuma* of earlier thought with the Spirit of Christ and of the Father disclosed in the New Testament. This is no merely arbitrary association, nor yet simply a mechanical fitting together of two pieces in a jigsaw. Rather he has been directed by the same insight that led Second Isaiah to proclaim Yahweh, the covenant-God of Israel, as both Creator and Saviour, and the New Testament to recognise in Jesus Christ the aboriginal creative power of God. Redemption through Jesus Christ is a new creative action which at the same time echoes and re-affirms God's original calling of all things into being, and the Spirit at work in the one is also active in the other.

Much more is to be said, however, than simply that the Spirit was active in creation. It has for Irenaeus a special connection with man as God created him 'in his image and likeness' (Gen. 1.26), for it is only through the gift of the Spirit of God that man, whose physical body is the 'image' of God attains to 'likeness' to God, and so to his own completeness (V.vi.1). Only by God's Spirit does man become really human and realise the intention of the Creator. By the Fall, however, 'we lost in Adam the privilege of being in the image and likeness of God' (III.xviii.1). The purpose of the incarnation was the reuniting of God with man and man with God (IV.xx.4) the undoing of Adam's disobedience and defeat by Christ's obedience and victory (V.xx.2ff), and so the restoration of man in him (*ibid.*). This at its heart involves the giving of the Spirit, which 'descended from God on the Son of God, made Son of man, and with him became accustomed to dwell among the human race, and to rest on man, and to dwell in God's creatures, working the Father's will in them, and renewing them from their old state into the newness of Christ.' (III.xvii.1) 'Already we receive some portions of his Spirit for our perfecting and our preparation for immortality, as we gradually become accustomed to receive and bear God. This is what the apostle calls a "first instalment" ... and makes us even now spiritual ... not by getting rid of the material body, but by sharing in the Spirit... If because we have the first instalment we cry, "*Abba!* Father!", what will happen when on rising we see him face to face? ... the whole grace of the Spirit ... will make us like him and will perfect in us the Father's will, for it will make man in the image and likeness of God.' (V.viii.1)

Several of the notes struck here were to be specially characteristic of the Greek fathers in general—the intrinsic connection of creation and redemption; the creative and re-creative energy of the Spirit; the restoration of human nature in God's image through the incarnation; the summing up of all things in Christ; the goal of salvation as *theosis*, 'divinisation', the making of man like God; the twofold action of the Word and Spirit throughout. So too is his sense of the circling movement of co-operation between the Father, the Son and the Spirit, discerned first in the inner dynamics of the Gospel, but opening out to display itself as the pattern of the whole cosmic activity of God: 'The Father supports creation and his Word; the Word, supported by the Father bestows the Spirit upon all as the Father wishes . . . So there is revealed one God the Father "above all, through all, in all." (Eph. 4.6) Above all is the Father, and he is the head of Christ; through all the Word, and he is the head of the church; in all the Spirit, and it is the "living water" which the Lord bestows on all that rightly believe and love and know him.' (V.xviii.1) 'The Father approves and commands, the Son carries out the Father's plan, the Spirit supports and hastens the work.' (IV.xxxviii.3) 'By the Spirit man ascends to the Son, through the Son to the Father.' (V.xxxvi.2) The entire activity of God is trinitarian, marked by the threefoldness of Father, Son and Spirit, yet harmonizing in a single patterned movement. Inevitably, this leads on to further questions which Irenaeus does not so directly tackle: what are the implications for God's own being and nature if this is the pattern of his action? Can one move in any way beyond the imagery of the 'two hands' of God? How in a doctrine of God are both the distinctness and the coherence of the Father, Son, and Spirit to be expressed?

2. Tertullian

Further progress on these matters was made by Tertullian.[6] His argument in *Adversus Praxean* is of interest less for its specific contribution on the Spirit than for the new ground it breaks in the more general area of the Trinity. 'Praxeas' (whose real identity is unknown) was a 'monarchian'. Monarchianism stood at the opposite pole to gnosticism: it insisted absolutely on the *oneness* of God. In the second and third centuries it took two main forms, each offering somewhat different solutions to the question of how that oneness was compatible with recognition of Father, Son and Spirit. *Modalist monarchianism* (or Sabellianism) held that the Father, Son and Spirit were simply successive 'modes' or 'manifestations' of God, as it were, 'masks' which he puts on.

Taken to its logical conclusion, this would mean that the same God who had been manifested as the Father was crucified on the cross in the form of Christ; it excluded any relation *between* the Father and the Son. *Dynamic monarchianism* was rather different: it described the Son and Spirit as 'powers' or 'energies' (*dynameis*) emanating from God, and believed that Jesus had been made Son of God by the descent of this Son-power upon him. Although it could appeal, for instance, to the Gospel accounts of Jesus' baptism to support this position, it represented a retreat from the teaching of the New Testament to a rather helpless artificiality. Both forms nonetheless show awareness of a genuine difficulty, though deeper analysis was required to enable more adequate models and formulations.

In order to answer monarchianism without toppling over into talking of three separate gods, Tertullian insists that the unity of God is balanced by what 'the Greeks call *oikonomia*,' and he renders *dispensatio* (2)—'distribution' is perhaps the closest English equivalent. So he holds together God's oneness with his threefoldness, his *trinitas* (a term which he seems to have been the first Latin theologian to use). The monarchians 'assume that the plurality and distribution of the *trinitas* implies a division of the unity; but the truth is that the unity in deriving a *trinitas* from itself is not thereby destroyed, but dispensed.'(3) To explain this more precisely, he introduces the words *substantia* ('substance') and *persona* ('person'):

> ... the one may be all in the sense that all are of one, that is, through unity of *substantia*; while this still safeguards the mystery of the *oikonomia* which disposes the unity into a *trinitas*, arranging in order the three *personae*, Father, Son and Holy Spirit, though these are three not in standing but in degree, not in *substantia* but in form, not in power but in manifestation ... because God is one and from him those degrees and forms are assigned in the name of the Father, Son and Holy Spirit. (2)

The formal analysis is further illustrated by three models: root-branch-fruit; spring-river-canal; sun-ray-point of focus (8): so he tries to show how there can be genuine organic oneness, living connection, and yet discernible distinction. In addition, the first stage in the unfolding, the generation of the Son from the Father, is interpreted as God's speaking-forth of his Word at the dawn of creation (7),[7] while the Spirit is 'in the Word' (12).

This work of Tertullian's was enormously influential in shaping Western trinitarian theology. The terminology of *trinitas, substantia* and *persona* rapidly became standard as did the models he offered to illustrate it. There was however still a strong note of *subordinationism* in his thought. The Father is the whole *substantia*, but the Son is 'derivative and a portion of the whole', the agent of the creation whereas the Father is the Creator (9), and his status *as Son* is given in the act of creation itself. In these respects, later orthodoxy was to find his views inadequate. Later still, further difficulties were to arise with the word '*persona*' as it gathered the psychological associations still preserved in the English 'person'. In Tertullian, however, it was a more formal label for a recognisably distinct individual, character, or role. So he could speak of three *personae* without thereby meaning 'three gods' comparable to three human 'persons'.

3. Origen

The same subordinationist note is to be heard in Origen, but within the framework of a vastly more subtle and comprehensive system of thought. His was the outstanding theological and philosophical mind in the early church; the *De Principiis*—which was only one of his innumerable writings—the first great systematic theology; and the lengthy third chapter of the first book, the earliest major treatise dealing specifically with the Holy Spirit. His treatment of it fits integrally into the wider pattern of his thought, about which a little must be said.

Central to the whole is the idea of 'participation' (*methexis*).[8] It stems originally from Plato, who used it to explain how what is temporal, impermanent, and of this world can yet have to do with what is eternal, unchanging, and above the world. Truth and reality rest in the eternal realm of the 'ideas' or 'forms' which are reflected in the world: everything 'participates in' the unchanging 'form' which makes it what it is and is recognised in it. But the two levels of being remain quite distinct: participation is not identification, but rather rests on and preserves the difference. Applied to the religious sphere, this offered a way of conceiving how men and the world can have to do with the eternal reality of God. They can participate in him and reflect his nature, but he himself remains unchangeably what he is. Whatever they receive by participation is inherent in him, whereas in them it is contingent, dependent, and derivative; in philosophical terminology, it is in God *substantially*, in them as an *accident*:

> There is no nature which is not receptive of good or evil, except for the nature of God, which is the fountain of all good things, and of Christ—for he is wisdom, and wisdom is quite incapable of receiving stupidity; and he is righteousness, and righteousness will certainly not accept unrighteousness (into itself); and he is the Word or reason, which of course can never be made irrational; and he is also light, and it is certain that 'darkness does not overcome the light' (John 1.5). In the same way also the nature of the Holy Spirit, which is holy, does not receive pollution, for it is naturally or substantially holy. If however any other nature is holy, it has this quality through the assumption or inspiration of the Holy Spirit, so that it may be made holy, not possessing this out of its own nature, but as an accident to itself—for which reason that which has come may also depart. (*De Princ.* I.viii.3)

This exemplifies the general pattern of thought, but there are further complexities to be considered. In spite of what is said here, Origen does not place the Father, Son and Spirit on one level, though collectively, so to speak, they stand over against everything else, as substantially and inherently good, wise and holy. There is also a hierarchy *within* the Trinity. Though the Son and Spirit 'excel all created beings to a degree which admits of no comparison,' 'they are themselves excelled by the Father to the same or even a greater degree.' (*Comm.*

John XIII.25) The Son is the image of God, and 'god' by participation in the Father, but he is not '*the* God'; God in the absolute sense (*Comm. John* II.2); he is the image of the Father's goodness, but not absolutely and unconditionally good, according to a fragment cited in Justinian's attack on Origen three centuries later (*Ep. ad Menam*). Similarly, he suggests that the Holy Spirit depends on the Son for the qualities of existence, wisdom and rationality, receiving them by participation in him (*Comm. John* II.10). While Origen advances beyond Tertullian in developing the idea of the *eternal generation* of the Son 'as the radiance of the eternal light' (*De Princ.* I.ii.2-6), the radical qualitative distinction between Father and Son remains.[9] He also proffers, albeit tentatively, the suggestion that the Spirit was 'the first of all that have been brought into being by God through Jesus Christ' (*Comm. John* II.10 (6)).

This hierarchical scheme is more than a little like that of the Neo-Platonist philosopher Plotinus, Origen's younger contemporary, who spoke of the three *hypostases*:[10] the Supreme One, the summit and source of all reality; the Divine Mind or Reason; and the World Soul. The goal of true philosophy was to rise in contemplation beyond the World Soul and Divine Mind to the mystical experience of union with the One. Origen, as a Christian, identifies the *hypostases* differently, but arranges them in a similar way. This leads him to assign increasingly narrower spheres of operation to each of the three, corresponding to their descending power, but at the same time enabling the expression in Christian terms of the equivalent to Plotinus' mystical ascent. The foundational pattern is outlined in another of the quotations preserved by Justinian: 'God the Father, since he embraces all things, touches each thing that exists, since he bestows on all existence from his own existence... The Son is inferior in relation to the Father, since he touches only things endowed with reason, for he is subordinate to the Father. The Holy Spirit is still lower in degree, pertaining only to the holy.' (*Ep. ad Menam*) The dynamic that it generates comes out in *De Principis* I.iii.8:

The grace of the Holy Spirit is added that those creatures which are not holy by virtue of their own being may be made holy by participation in the Spirit. Thus they derive existence from God the Father, rationality from the Word, sanctity from the Holy Spirit. Again, when they have once been sanctified through the Holy Spirit they are made capable of receiving Christ in the respect that he is the righteousness of God... Then when all the stains of pollution and ignorance have been removed and purged away, he receives such advancement in purity and cleanness that the being which was given by God becomes worthy of God, who bestowed it in order that it might attain its purity and perfection: so that the being is as worthy as is he who gave it existence.

By any reckoning, this was a brilliant achievement of theological and philosophical synthesis and integration, but the end result raises two radical questions. Is it adequate to delimit the work of the Spirit so narrowly, in effect restricting it to a *preliminary* process of sanctification? Irenaeus had pointed to a different road, and it was Irenaeus that the church was to follow. Again, for all its immense speculative and spiritual power, does this arranging of the Father, Son and Spirit in *descending* stages do justice to the deepest witness of the New Testament, or indeed to the implications of Isa. 63.9, 'In all their affliction *he* was afflicted, and the angel of his presence saved them'? These became major issues in the fourth century, when the heirs of Origen divided between the orthodox and Arian parties.[11]

It must however be stressed that these men were not simply spinning out abstract theories. In their theology sounds the rhythm of their faith; it coheres with spirituality, with worship, and with Christian life. The living heart of Origen's thought beats in such prayers as this from his predecessor, Clement of Alexandria† before 215):

Be merciful to thy children, O Teacher, O Father, charioteer of Israel, Son and Father, both One, O Lord. Grant that we thy followers, observing thy commandments, may make perfect the likeness of thine Image, that through his strength we may know the goodness of God and the kindness of his judgment. Bestow on us all good things, that we may live our lives in thy peace, and be brought to thy city, and sail over the waves of sin without storm, and be borne onward in serenity night and day by the Holy Spirit, the inexpressible Wisdom, until we attain to the perfect dawn.

That we may give praise and thanks to the Only Father and the Only Son; to Son and Father, the Son our Instructor and Teacher, together with the Holy Spirit; rendering all praise to the One in whom are all things, through whom all things are one, through whom is eternity, of whom all men are members, and the Ages are his glory; all praise to the Good, the Beautiful, the Wise, the Just; to him be glory now and for ever. Amen. (*Paedagogus* III.xii (101))

CHAPTER FIVE

THE LORD, THE LIFE-GIVER

The Arian controversy raged initially around the status of Jesus Christ as the eternal Son of the Father. The creed formulated at the Council of Nicea in 325 included a long, newly drafted second article, describing him as *homoousios*, 'consubstantial' with the Father, but followed that simply with the brief affirmation, 'And in the Holy Spirit.' Inevitably, however, the christological conflict led on to the question of the Holy Spirit, and when what is now known as the 'Nicene' Creed was approved—most probably at the Council of Constantinople in 381[1]— it included among several fresh formulations these clauses:

> And in the Holy Spirit,
> the Lord, the Life-giver,
> who proceeds from the Father,
> who with the Father and the Son is worshipped and glorified,
> who spoke through the prophets.

This is still much less full and precise than the second article, but it reflects the need to confront comparable questions: What is the Spirit's status? What its origin? What its relation to the Father? What the scope of its activity? The terms of the answers offered directly mirror the debates which began in the 350s.[2]

1. Cyril of Jerusalem
The general understanding of the Spirit before the new problems arose is well illustrated by the exposition of the creed used in Jerusalem in the lengthy *Catecheses* delivered to candidates for baptism by Cyril of Jerusalem about the year

350. The 16th and 17th of these deal with the words, 'And in one Holy Spirit, the Paraclete, who spoke by the prophets.' Cyril explains:

> There is only one Holy Spirit, the Paraclete; and as there is one God the Father, and no second Father, and as there is one Only-begotten Son and Word of God, who has no brother, so there is one only Holy Spirit, and no second Spirit equal in honour to it. Now the Holy Spirit is a power most mighty, a reality divine and unsearchable; for it is living and intelligent, a sanctifying principle of all things made by God through Christ. (XVI.3)

In a tone he shared with many of the fathers, Cyril warns his hearers against impudent prying into the Spirit's nature, or seeking to travel beyond the witness of Scripture (XVI.1-2). 'What is not written, let us not venture on; it is sufficient for our salvation to know that there is Father and Son and Holy Spirit.' (XVI.24) Warnings are also given against Marcion's separation of the Spirit in the Old Testament from the Spirit in the New (XVI.34); against tritheism and Sabellianism (XVI.4); against thinking that the Spirit is a mere power or energy without its own enhypostatic reality and agency (XVII.5) for it 'lives and subsists and speaks and works' (XVII.2); against the claims of heretics from Simon Magus through Montanus to Mani, the founder of Manicheeism, to possess the Paraclete (XVI.6-10); and against imagining that the Spirit takes *violent* possession of humans as evil spirits do (XVI.15-16). The point is also made, by no means unnecessarily, that not every reference to *pneuma* in Scripture is to the Holy Spirit (XVI.13).

On the positive side, Cyril expands at length on the Spirit's activity as Sanctifier. It is not only the power of God in the incarnation of Christ (XVII.6), and the source of all the innumerable gifts and graces of the Christian life, though all these are from it (XVI.12-22), but also the 'mighty ally and protector from God ... strong champion on our behalf' so that we need have no fear of evil 'for mightier is he who fights for us' (XVI.19). On this same sanctifying and strengthening power all earthly and indeed heavenly beings depend, and therefore 'the families of angels and all their hosts assembled together have no equality with the Holy Spirit. All these the excellent power of the Paraclete overshadows; they indeed are "sent forth to minister," (Hebr. 1.14) but it "searches even the deep things of God."' (I Cor. 2.10) (XVI.23) This activity of the Spirit completes the trinitarian 'economy of salvation towards us' which 'is from the Father and the Son and the Holy Spirit, and is inseparable and harmonious and one.' (XVII.5) Because 'our hope is in Father, Son and Holy Spirit,' (XVI.4) the Spirit 'is honoured together with the Father and the Son, and at the time of baptism is included with them in the Holy Trinity.' (ibid.)

> And the Father indeed gives to the Son, and the Son shares with the Holy Spirit. For it is Jesus himself who says ... (Matt. 11.27; John 16.13-14) ... The Father through the Son with the Holy Spirit is the Giver of all grace: the gifts of the Father are none other than those of the Son and those of the Holy Spirit; for there is one salvation, one power, one faith; one God the Father, one Lord, his Only-begotten Son, one Holy Spirit, the Paraclete. (XVI.24)

It is noticeable, however, that Cyril does not explore further fields which in retrospect can be seen opening just across the frontiers he maps. If the Son is 'begotten' from the Father, what is the origin of the Spirit? As a 'divine reality' whose action coheres with that of the Father and the Son, is the Spirit also God? What is the status of the Trinity whose identity Cyril so strongly affirms? Does his sketch of the role of the sanctifying Paraclete signal a need to break out of Origen's precise demarcation of the respective spheres of creation and sanctification? In sum, if what Cyril says about the Spirit is sound, must one not go on further, or else risk sliding back into such a relegation of the spirit to a lower level as would undercut those very affirmations? Cyril in Jerusalem may not have been aware of this challenge, but others elsewhere were about to raise it in a fashion permitting of no evasion.

2. *Athanasius*

During his third exile from Alexandria in one of the last periods of Arian ascendancy, probably about 358/9, Athanasius was contacted by bishop Serapion of Thmuis about the party whom he came to name the 'Tropici'—the 'Metaphoricals'. He never seems to have met them face to face, and it is unlikely that they were numerous or otherwise especially influential.[3] In answer to Serapion's plea for assistance, he wrote three separate letters,[4] which contain not only the sole evidence we possess for their teaching, but a fuller and more incisive vindication of the Spirit's divine status than any previously offered. The Tropici presented three arguments to show that it was a creature, an angel differing only in degree from other angels. First, Amos 4.13 in the LXX has God saying, 'I am he who creates *pneuma* ... and declares his *christos* to men.' (*Ad Serapionem* I.3) Second, Zech. 4.5 mentions 'the angel who spoke in me,' while I Tim. 5.21 combines in a single formula God, Christ and the 'elect angels' (I. 10-11). Third, the Spirit cannot be divine as the Father and the Son are, for then it must be a second Son or a grandson— which is, of course, inconceivable (I.15; IV, *passim*).

The first two of these arguments—which Athanasius had little difficulty in demolishing (I.3-14)—suggest that the Tropici were theological conservatives maintaining older traditions in which originally no very sharp distinction had been drawn between the Son, the Spirit, and the angels.[5] Now that the Arian controversy had highlighted the absolute difference between God and everything created they felt the line must be drawn between the Son and the Spirit. The third, which is negative rather than positive, shows the powerful influence of a binitarian mode of thinking, which could indeed see that the Father and Son are intimately related, but not how the Spirit could be drawn into the pattern. Here the gulf between Athanasius and the Tropici yawns widest, and to judge by the last letter, it was on this point that they remained unsatisfied. They sensed a genuine difficulty, whereas he, approaching the matter from the other side, found their question foolish and indeed blasphemous. 'Mock no more at the godhead!... It is sufficient for you to believe that the Spirit is not a creature, but is Spirit of God; and that in God there is a Triad,[6] Father, Son and Holy Spirit.' (IV.7) These remarks may not be entirely fair to the Tropici's intention, but they encapsulate both the main themes of Athanasius' response: (a) the Spirit is not a creature, and (b) there is in God a *Trinity*, not merely *Father and Son*.

(a) Arguments that the Spirit is not a creature are piled up in good number (esp. I.22-27; also III). It is from God; creatures are made by God out of nothing (I.22); it sanctifies and renews and quickens; creatures receive all these from it (I.22-23); as 'unction' and 'seal' it is qualitatively distinct from that which is 'anointed' or 'sealed' with it by the Word (I.23); it unites us to God and makes us 'sharers in the divine nature' (II Pet. 1.4), to which it therefore must belong (I.24); it is the 'image' of the Son, as the Son is the 'image' of the Father (I.24); like the Son, it is 'of the Father' and shares the being of the Father and the Son (I.25); as it unites creation to the Word, it cannot itself be a creature (I.25); it is immutable and omnipresent, and 'participated in' without itself 'participating' (I.26-27); it is *one*, whereas creatures are *many* (I.27).

Most of these evidences are not original to Athanasius; many are already in Cyril and earlier writers. Now however, they are brought to bear concertedly on a single focus: the absolute qualitative difference between what the Spirit is and does and the nature and activity of everything created. Several of them also echo and correspond to proofs he offers in *Ad Serap.* II and elsewhere of the divinity of the Son. Indeed, his sense of the coherence, parallelism and interaction of the Son and Spirit is crucial to the whole case, and is again apparent in his insistence on the trinitarian structure of the divine being and operation.

(b) Repeatedly, Athanasius appeals to the Trinity. 'Is God Triad or dyad?' (I.2) The 'very tradition, teaching and faith of the catholic church from the very beginning' (by which he means chiefly the faith expressed in the threefold baptismal

formula) shows that 'There is then a Triad, holy and complete, confessed to be God in Father, Son and Holy Spirit, having nothing foreign or external mixed with it ... in nature indivisible and its activity is one. The Father does all things through the Word in the Holy Spirit.' (I.28) To make the Spirit a creature is to unravel the Trinity itself, and Athanasius doubts whether those who do this can in fact retain a proper hold on the Son or the Father either (I.21). Everything is 'from the Father, through the Son, in the Spirit,' (I.30), and the 'unity of nature and order' that binds the Son to the Father also unites the Spirit to the Son (I.21). The Spirit 'is one with the Son as the Son is one with the Father, is glorified with the Father and the Son, is confessed as God with the Word, is active in the work that the Father works through the Son.' (I.31)

For those who 'ask, doubting, how these things could be,' (I.17) Athanasius has a blunt answer. 'Thus far human knowledge goes... For the things that have been handed down by faith ought not to be measured by human wisdom, but by the hearing of faith ... let them not say that what they cannot understand cannot be true... For all created beings ... find it impossible to speak adequately concerning things ineffable.' (*ibid.*) The tradition 'does not declare the godhead to us by demonstration in words, but by faith and by a pious and reverent use of reason.' (I.20) Against the Tropici's question about sons and grandsons, he sets Scriptural imagery—light/radiance/enlightening; fountain/river/drink; wise/wisdom/spirit of wisdom; essence and expression; original and image—as *illustrating* if not *explaining* the matter (I.19-20).

Athanasius' concern here is of course perfectly valid. In theology (or any other enquiry) it is vital to discriminate between productive and unproductive, appropriate and inappropriate questions, and not to allow the assumptions lurking behind a particular form of question uncritically to distort the discussion. He was all too well aware that there was in the air a good deal of superficial cleverness posing as profundity. At the same time, the Tropici's question, particularly if put less assertively than they seem to have framed it (I.15), marks an obscurity which his own answers do not wholly clear away. Is the 'person' of the Spirit modelled on that of the Son? Does it originate in similar fashion? Is its source in the Father or in the Son? Given the resources of Scripture, faith, and the reverent use of reason, might not some further advance on this front be possible? At this point, the Cappadocians were to take a further step.

3. The Cappadocian Fathers and Eastern Orthodoxy

So far as the doctrine of the Spirit was concerned, the Cappadocians found themselves fighting on two fronts. On the one hand were the extreme Arians, the Anomoeans, led by Eunomius, who insisted that God's very nature was defined as 'unbegotten', and who by appeal to John 1.3 sought to show that the Spirit had been created by the Son, who as 'begotten' was himself inferior to the Father. On the other were those on the left wing of the old Homoeousian party, to which they themselves had originally belonged. From about 360, most of this group had moved towards rapprochement with the Nicene Homoousians but a minority, led by Eustathius of Sebaste, had swung in the opposite direction, and it was among them that the Pneumatomachean tendency developed. They held that the Spirit was neither God nor creature, and offered such analogies as, 'God is master, creatures are servants, the Spirit is neither master not servant, but free.' Such incoherence had little hope of commending itself widely in a post-Arian era, but it forced the Cappadocians further to clarify their own stance, which was broadly in line with that taken earlier by Athanasius. Three main topics now came to the fore: (i) the addressing of worship to the Spirit; (ii) the Spirit's origin as contrasted with the generation of the Son; and (iii) the defence of the doctrine of the Trinity against the charge of tritheism.

(i) Worship of the Spirit

Both Cyril and Athanasius had emphasised that the Spirit is

venerated, revered and worshipped with the Father and the Son, and the implied acknowledgement of its divinity is made quite explicit by Athanasius. The same question erupted again when Basil was attacked by Eustathians for using in his liturgy a doxology which gave glory 'to the Father, and to the Son, and to the Holy Spirit'. They claimed that this was an innovation which was theologically and liturgically unsound: worship, they asserted, is not to be offered *to* the Spirit but *in* the Spirit, *through* the Son, *to* the Father. In answer to them Basil in 374 wrote his *De Spiritu Sancto*. He argued that his form of doxology was also traditional; and also, more centrally, that just as worship *through* the Son involves worship *of* the Son, so too does worship *in* the Spirit imply the Spirit's own worthiness of worship. The logic of this argument is similar to that of Karl Barth's 'By God alone is God known.' Basil, however, drew back—at least in his official, public statements—from calling the Spirit 'God' because such an explicit identification was not made in the Bible, and because it could cause offence. The same reticence is found in the Nicene Creed, which uses instead the divine title, 'Lord' (which could be supported by I Cor. 3.17). The final implication of his argument concerning worship is nonetheless clear enough, and was brought out openly six years later in the *Fifth Theological Oration* of Gregory of Nazianzus (*Or.* 31.12), while the Creed stresses that the Spirit is 'worshipped and glorified with the Father and the Son.'

(ii) The Spirit's Origin

Basil also pointed towards a solution of the Tropici's problem about the origin of the Spirit: it is '"from God", not in the sense in which "all things are from God," (I Cor. 11.12) but as proceeding from God, not by way of generation, like the Son, but as "the breath of his mouth" (Ps. 33.6).' (*De Spir. S.* 46) Gregory sharpened the point further in *Or.* 31.8: as the Spirit is neither Father nor Son, so it is neither *unbegotten* (as the Father is), nor *begotten* (as the Son is), but *proceeds* (John 15.26). Thus the affirmation of its divinity does not run into the 'second son or grandson?' dilemma, nor can that challenge be properly allowed to cast doubt on its divine status. The precise scope of this clarification is important. Gregory himself immediately goes on to qualify it: 'What, then, is procession? Do you tell me what is the unbegottenness of the Father, and I will explain to you the physiology of the generation of the Son and the procession of the Spirit, and we shall both of us be struck mad for prying into the mystery of God.' (*ibid.*) He does *not* mean— as a superficial reading might suggest—that there is no difference in sense between 'generation' and 'procession', or that their application to the Trinity is without meaning for us. He *does* mean that we cannot understand from God's side what it is that they refer to, or make such understanding a precondition for accepting them. What he has in mind here is the shallow rationalism of the Anomoeans, who believed that they could define the essence of God in terms of 'unbegottenness' and so rule out from the start the divinity of the Son and Spirit. Gregory has to make it clear that such arbitrary dictation of the terms in which God may or may not be spoken of is unacceptable, and that in offering 'procession' he is not playing the Anomoeans at their own game. He is not trying to explain how the Spirit 'proceeds' but to make clear that their assumptions and method can only distort the enquiry, and, by following a different approach, to fashion a terminology which will be controlled by the given realities of the Father, Son and Spirit and so point to them rather than obscure them. It is a measure of his success that 'procession' immediately became standard label for the distinct origin of the Spirit, its *tropos tes hyparxeos*, or 'mode of being', while 'who proceeds from the Father' found its way into the Creed.

This still, however, leaves the possibility of a further question: is there a bond between the Spirit and the Son? The fathers whom we have mentioned could speak of the Spirit as proceeding 'through the Son' or as 'being manifested in the Son', and such expressions also served to maintain the New Testament witness to the inseparable connection between the work of the Spirit and that of Christ. The Creed does not take this matter up, for the very good reason that it might have seemed to subordinate the Spirit to the Son. What had to be emphasised was the origin of the Spirit *from the Father*, parallel, so to speak, to the generation of the Son. The issues arising here were to cause wide future controversy, and led to a major divide between Eastern and Western theology as the West came to affirm the *filioque*—that the Spirit proceeds *'from the Father and from the Son.'* This disagreement also reflected divergences in the understanding of the triunity of God, in which the East was more deeply influenced by the line of thought of the Cappadocians.[7]

(iii) The Spirit in the Trinity

The increased insistence on the divine identity and activity of the Spirit led to the charge against the Cappadocians that they were in fact teaching 'three gods'. They set out to counter this by developing the formula, 'one *ousia*, three *hypostaseis*', which was broadly equivalent to the Western 'one *substantia*, three *personae*', but which they interpreted in a distinctive fashion. Basil laid the groundwork by explaining that the Father, Son and Spirit were one as three individuals share a common nature (*Ep.* 214.4), and his brother, Gregory of Nyssa, went so far as to draw an explicit analogy with three human individuals (*Quod non sint tres Dei*). It must be added that Gregory developed his case with considerable subtlety, put great weight on the *oneness* of the *ousia*, on the mutual 'indwelling' of the three *hypostases*, and on the *single* co-operating activity of the entire Trinity. In all these ways he broke through the *prima facie* tritheistic implications of the human analogy.[8] Nevertheless, Eastern theology thereafter generally inclined to emphasise the distinct individuality of the three *hypostases*, whereas the West was more inclined to start from the one *substantia*, and to interpret triunity with the help of models drawn from a *single* individual. Consequently, where the West traced a pattern of essential bonds uniting all three *personae*, the East found the guarantee of the divine unity in the respective and *distinct* origins of the Son and Spirit *in and from the Father*. The broad lines of the Eastern position are boldly drawn in the *De Fide Orthodoxa* of John of Damascus (*ca.* 675–*ca.* 749), which was largely composed of quotations from earlier Greek fathers, and came to serve as the standard text-book of Eastern theology:

> Likewise we believe also in one Holy Spirit, the Lord and Giver of life, which proceeds from the Father and rests in the Son, the object of equal adoration and glorification with the Father and the Son; since it is con-substantial and co-eternal, the Spirit of God, direct, authoritative, the fountain of wisdom and life and holiness; God existing and addressed along with the Father and the Son; uncreated, full, creative, all-ruling, all-effecting, all-powerful, of infinite power; Lord of all creation, and not under any Lord; deifying, not deified; filling, not filled; shared in, not sharing in; sanctifying, not sanctified; the intercessor, receiving the supplications of all; in all things like to the Father and the Son; proceeding from the Father and communicated through the Son; through itself creating and investing with substance and sanctifying and maintaining the universe; having subsistence, existing in its own proper and peculiar *hypostasis*, inseparable and indivisible from the Father and the Son, and possessing all the qualities that the Father and the Son possess, save that of being unbegotten or begotten ... derived from the Father, yet not after the manner of generation, but after that of procession... And we do not speak of the Spirit as *from* the Son, but yet we call it the Spirit *of* the Son ... manifested and imparted to us through the Son ... (I.viii)

Eastern theology thus came to be marked more deeply than Western by the sense, latent in the Nicene Creed, but also running through the Greek Fathers, that the Spirit has its own *complementary* role alongside and co-operating with the Son. It is in its own right the Lord, the Life-giver, Creator and Renewer, Discloser of the divine mystery, Transformer of creation by whose energy the cosmos is transfigured and man, renewed in the image of God, is called to his true vocation as the priest of creation. Characteristically, the focus of the eucharistic celebration was placed not, as in the West, in the words of consecration, but in the *epiklesis*, the invocation calling on the Father to send his Spirit upon the worshippers and upon the elements. Invocation of the Spirit itself, as in this prayer of St Simeon the New Theologian (949–1022), well displays its meaning for Eastern spirituality:

> Come, true light. Come life eternal.
> Come, hidden mystery. Come, treasure without name.
> Come, reality beyond all words. Come person beyond all understanding...
> Come, all-powerful, for unceasingly you create, refashion and change all things by your will alone.
> Come, invisible, whom none may touch and handle...
> Come, for you continue always unmoved, yet at every instant you are wholly in movement; you draw near to us who lie in hell, yet you remain higher than the heavens.
> Come, for your name fills our heart with longing and is ever on our lips; yet who you are and what your nature is, we cannot say or know.
> Come, Alone to the alone.
> Come, for you yourself are the desire that is in me.
> Come, my breath and my life.
> Come, my joy, my glory, my endless delight...[9]

This did not, however, mean that an absolute disjunction was drawn between the activity of the Son and Spirit. Instead, Eastern theology developed a distinction between the *essence* and the *energies* of God.[10] In his essence, God remains the unattainable, incomprehensible mystery; and at the heart of that mystery lie the generation of the Son and the sending forth of the Spirit, both issuing in their different modes from the Father. But God also reaches out by activity of his uncreated energies to create and to involve the creation in participation in the movement of his triune being. At the level of the energies, as opposed to that of the hidden essence, the Spirit shines out in the Son, reflects the Son, and manifests the glory incarnate in him. Yet what enables and underlies this activity of imaging and displaying the Son is the primal springing of the Spirit *from the same One who is Father of the Son*, not a procession of the Spirit *from both*. The abyss of the divine nature overflows doubly in the begetting of the Son and the sending forth of the Spirit, the Lord, the Life-giver, who proceeds from the Father.

CHAPTER SIX

GOD'S LOVE, GOD'S GIFT, THE SOUL OF THE CHURCH[1]

In the West through the Middle Ages the Spirit was usually spoken of in a rather different fashion from what we have seen in the East. Certainly the heritage of earlier teaching was preserved, and with it the broad pattern of established trinitarian doctrine. Certainly, too, theology and piety could combine in magnificent invocations of the Spirit, from the 9th century *Veni, Creator Spiritus*,[2] to the perhaps even finer *Veni, Sancte Spiritus* of some four centuries later.[3] Yet doctrine and worship alike acquired a distinctive Western flavour. The keynote is struck in the 12th century hymn that begins by calling upon the Spirit as *Amor Patris et Filii*, 'Love of the Father, love of the Son'. The Spirit is identified above all as *love*, the love of the Father for the Son and of the Son for the Father, and therefore also as their common *gift*. So, at the very height of the Middle Ages, Thomas Aquinas († 1274), following the earlier lead of Peter Lombard (*Sent.* I.xvii.6), could ascribe to the third person of the Trinity three proper names: 'Holy Spirit', 'Love' and 'Gift' (*Summa Theologica* I, *qu.* 36, 37, 38).

These themes, dominating Western thought particularly from Augustine († 430) onwards, lent special colouring to medieval and subsequent Roman Catholic teaching, and go far to explain its interpretation and defence of the *filioque*. Bonaventura (1221–1274) seized the point precisely when he observed in his *Commentary* on Book I of Lombard's *Sentences*, *Dist.* xi, *qu.* i, 'The Greeks have compared the Spirit to the breathing forth of an *outer breath*, the Latins to the breathing forth of an *inner love*.' Not only does Western medieval thought describe the Spirit chiefly in terms of love; it also displays a pronounced drive towards *interiorisation*—the Spirit is the *inner* love of the Trinity, the *inner* animating principle of the church, the source of the *inner* life of the soul—and towards *unity* and *union*—the unity of the Trinity, the unity between Christ and the Spirit, the union of Christ with the church, the unity of the church itself, the ultimate union of the soul with God. All this is signalled in Augustine's celebrated description of the Spirit as *vinculum caritatis*, the 'bond of love' between the Father and the Son;[4] and it was his reflections, especially in his great *De Trinitate*, that guided his Western successors for a thousand years and more.

1. Augustine on the Trinity

Augustine worked, on and off, for some twenty years on the fifteen books of the *De Trinitate*, and only finally published it *ca.* 419, although still dissatisfied with it, because unauthorised copies of earlier sections were already in circulation. Four aspects of its subtle and complex thought deserve special mention here.

First, there is the very perception of the issue which Augustine poses at I.4, and which runs through the whole enquiry: how 'the Trinity is the one and only true God, and the Father, the Son, and the Spirit are rightly said, believed and understood to be of one and the same substance or essence.' *The* metaphysical question which fascinates him is how one can be three, and three one; or to put it more accurately, the object of his reverent enquiry is the simultaneous oneness and threeness of God. The same dialectic is reproduced in the (thoroughly Augustinian) formulations of the *Quicunque vult*, the misnamed Athanasian Creed, which dates from about the end of the fifth century:[5] '... we worship one God in Trinity and Trinity in unity, without either confounding the persons or dividing the substance. For the Father's person is one, the Son's another, the Holy Spirit's another; but the Godhead of the Father, the Son and the Holy Spirit is one, their glory equal, their majesty co-eternal ... not three Gods but one God ... not three Lords but one Lord ... And in this Trinity there is nothing before or after, nothing greater or less ... both Trinity in unity and unity in Trinity must be worshipped.'

The boundaries thus marked set the stage for the development of Trinitarian thinking through the Middle Ages, and pose what was to be a perenially fascinating object of theological speculation.

Second, Augustine developed further than had been done before the idea of *relation* within the Godhead. It had been a commonplace in the controversy with the Arians that the very name 'Father' implies a relation to the Son, and that the relations implicit in these terms must be seen as constituting the structure and pattern of the divine being itself. (By contrast, Arianism sought to define that being in terms which would deny alike the divinity of the Son and the Fatherhood of the Father.) In Book V of the *De Trinitate* Augustine extended this mode of argument to the Spirit: as the *Gift* of God, the Spirit is inherently related to the *Giver* (V.12). Here lies the root of what became axiomatic in Western Trinitarian theology: that the divine *persons* are defined by their *relations* to each other, that indeed *persona means* 'a subsisting relation' (Aquinas, *Summa Theol.* I, *qu.* 29, *art.* 4), and that it is by their relations that the three persons are also distinguished. He went on to develop the further thought that the Spirit itself is nothing other than the relation of love and communion between the Father and the Son, and therefore to be named 'Love' as well as 'Gift' (VI.7).

Third, in the Spirit's role as the 'bond of love', Augustine traced the ground of the fact that it is of the Son as well as of the Father, and accordingly concluded that it proceeds 'from both'. This does not mean that it proceeds *separately* from each; rather, there is a single simultaneous procession from both which is a function or immediate implication of the generation of the Son, and in which therefore the primacy of the Father is maintained:

> ... God the Father alone is he from whom the Word is born, and from whom the Spirit principally proceeds. And therefore I have added the word 'principally' because we find that the Holy Spirit proceeds from the Son also. But the Father gave this too to the Son, not as to one already

existing and not yet possessing it; but whatever he gave to the only-begotten Word, he gave by begetting him. Therefore he so begot him that the common Gift should proceed from him also, and the Holy Spirit should be the Spirit of both. (XV.29; *cf. 47, where the a-temporal simultaneity of the generation of the Son and procession of the Spirit is heavily underlined.*)

Finally, the second half of the work was largely taken up with the exploration of possible *vestigia Trinitatis,* 'traces of the Trinity', which could serve as models to assist our understanding. Book VIII focused upon the triad of one who loves, the object of that love, and the love itself; this Augustine felt to be certainly a kind of *vestigium* of the Trinity, but only of a preliminary sort, pointing the way to further exploration. In Books IX and X he drove further into the analysis of the human self, and uncovered there two sets of three, in each of which each member in a manner contains and involves the other two: the mind, its knowledge of itself, and its love for itself (*mens, notitia, amor*); and memory, intelligence, and will (*memoria, intellectus, voluntas*). After considering some alternative models in Books XI-XIII, he returned again to these two in XIV-XV, and located the 'image of God' in man's capacity to remember, understand, and love God (XIV.15), these three dimensions of the human person reflecting the three persons of the Trinity—the Father as the divine 'mind' or 'memory', the Son as his expressed or articulated 'knowledge' or 'understanding', the Spirit as the 'will' or 'love' of the Father and the Son. He was careful to remark on the limitations of the analogy: it should not be taken to mean that the Father is pure 'memory' but not 'understanding' or 'love', and similarly with the other two (XV.28); but there remained a certain fittingness in using the three terms to name the three persons (XV.29), and in particular in designating the Spirit as 'love' alongside the Son or Word as 'knowledge' (*ibid.*).

2. Medieval Trinitarian Theology and the Filioque

To a very great degree, the Trinitarian and pneumatological thought of the Western church throughout the Middle Ages ran more or less consistently along the lines Augustine had designated. The twin analogies of mind, knowledge and love (*mens, notitia, amor*) and memory, intelligence and will (*memoria, intellectus, voluntas*) regularly reappeared, and could indeed commonly be appealed to not simply as *illustrating* but as *demonstrating* the nature of the Trinity and the order in which the three persons are necessarily arranged. So, for example, Alexander of Hales († 1245) drew on them to support the *filioque*: '... while the generation of the Son is *per modum naturae* ("by the mode of nature"), the procession of the Holy Spirit is *per modum voluntatis* ("by the mode of will"). Just as in the natural order *natura* precedes *voluntas*, even so the generation of the former is before the procession of the latter.' (*Summa Universae Theologiae* I, *qu.* 46,) Aquinas saw the matter similarly (*Summa Theologica* I, *qu.* 27, *art.* 4), although later the Nominalist thinkers, who were generally sceptical about the capacity of creaturely rationality to 'prove' or 'demonstrate' the mysteries of the faith, were to criticise this mode of argument—notably Durandus († 1334) in his *Commentary* on the *Sentences* I, *Dist.* 2, *qu.* 4.[6] Modern neo-Scholasticism has also been known to place great weight on the model of knowledge and love as supplying the framework within which the Son and Spirit are to be placed.[7]

Again, even when other models or analogies were drawn upon, they tended to be those which fell neatly into the same pattern, and in particular pointed to the Spirit as the 'unity' of the Father and the Son. Pope Leo III († 816) wrote, 'In the Father there is eternity, in the Son equality, in the Spirit the *connexio* ('binding together') of eternity and equality.' (*Ep.* 15) With the introduction of Aristotelian categories into theology in the High Middle Ages, other similar possibilities became available. So Alanus of Lille († 1203) treated the *unity* of *matter* and *form* constitutive of every thing that exists as an illustration of the Trinity (*De Arte* I, *Sent.* 25). Speculation of this kind, seeking to trace an essential three-foldness in the highest and ultimate unity of the source of all things, reached its height in the work of Nicolas of Cusa (1401–1464),[8] which forms a bridge between medieval thought and the sense of a

threefold dynamic as the very rhythm of reality in the
Hegelian Idealism of the 19th century.

The impulse given by Augustine had a further outworking
in the fondness of Scholastic theology for what can perhaps
best be termed the 'mathematical' interpretation and
exposition of the Trinity. Few thinkers went quite so far as the
philosopher and mathematician Roger Bacon († 1294), who
entitled the fourth part of his *Opus Maius* 'The Usefulness of
Mathematics in Divine Matters', and symbolised the Trinity
as an equilateral triangle each of whose angles is distinct,
equal, and yet embraces the entire area of the whole.
Nevertheless mathematical models and modes of thought
became widely influential from the eleventh century onwards;[9]
a good example is the final, sixteenth chapter of the *De
Processione Spiritus Sancti* of Anselm († 1109), which begins,
'Now there are six distinctions among the Father, Son and
Holy Spirit ... (1) to have a Father, (2) not to have a Father,
(3) to have a Son, (4) not to have a Son, (5) to have a Spirit
proceeding from oneself, (6) not to have a Spirit proceeding
from oneself. Each of the two persons has one property from
among these distinctions by which he is different from the
other two persons, and he has two common properties, so that
by what he shares with one person he differs from the
other...' This goes far beyond Augustine in its formalisation,
but is essentially in tune with his unity/Trinity dialectic.

Further exploration of these matters lies outside the scope of
our study here, but these patterns of trinitarian thought had a
direct bearing on the development of pneumatology in the
strict sense. The primary dogmatic concern was the *filioque*,
and the clarifying and consolidation of Western thought over
against that of the East.[10]

In the centuries following Augustine's death, the *filioque*
gradually emerged as a settled conviction through the Western
church, and from the Council of Toledo in 589 it began to be
affirmed in official statements as an article of faith.
Controversy with the East erupted towards the beginning of
the ninth century when Charlemagne tried to have it formally
inserted in the Nicene Creed. Pope Leo III resisted this

demand; though believing that the *filioque* was theologically correct, he did not feel that the Creed formulated by an Ecumenical Council could be unilaterally altered. Later in that century Photius, Patriarch of Constantinople, went on the offensive, insisting that the Spirit proceeds 'from the Father *alone*'. The West did not accept this, but the final break did not come until the eleventh century. Pope Benedict VIII officially sanctioned the addition to the Creed, probably in 1014, and the schism between East and West occurred in 1054. The *filioque* became (and has remained to the present) a major bone of contention between East and West. The controversy provoked further defences of the clause in the West, and also its reaffirmation in the Councils of Lyons (1274) and Florence (1438–9).

The main lines of the defence were developed by Anselm in his *De Processione Spiritus Sancti* (1102) and rearticulated by Aquinas a century and a half later (*Summa Theologica* I, qu. 36). Numerous complex evidences were adduced, but the really decisive consideration was that if the Son and Spirit are to be properly distinguished from each other, there must be a 'relation of origin and opposition' between them which both links and separates their two persons, comparably to the relations between each of them and the Father. Within the general horizon of Western trinitarian theology, dominated as it was by the equation of *persona* with *relatio*, and by the sense of the unity, co-equality and virtual equivalence of the three persons of the Trinity, no other conclusion was possible; the *filioque* also served powerfully to undergird the message of the New Testament that God's Spirit is indeed the Spirit of Jesus Christ.

To the East, however, with its very different approach to the triunity of God, the *filioque* appeared necessarily either to introduce two distinct 'sources' into the Trinity, or to dissolve away the distinction between the Father and the Son. Nor was the Eastern church willing to be persuaded by the definitions and clarifications offered by the medieval councils. Lyons stated,

... that the Holy Spirit proceeds eternally from the Father and the Son, yet not as from two origins, but as from one origin, not by two breathings, but by a single breathing ... (*DS* 850)

Florence reiterated this point, adding that the patristic formula, 'from the Father through the Son', 'tended to this meaning', which it further explained in terms drawn from Augustine: by begetting the Son, the Father also bestows upon him that the Spirit should proceed from the Son as well as from himself (*DS* 1300–1302). Florence indeed intended to achieve a reconciliation between East and West, and there were Eastern representatives present; but the agreement was immediately repudiated by the Eastern Orthodox authorities. At bottom, the East did not share the perception of the whole issue which was taken for granted by the West.

Some of the underlying reasons for the Eastern attitude have emerged more clearly in the general criticisms of Western pneumatology advanced in the twentieth century by Lossky and others.[11] They believe that in the whole drive of Western trinitarian theology from Augustine onwards there runs an unbalanced emphasis on the divine unity which tends towards Sabellianism; that the *filioque* itself reflects the pressures generated by that imbalance; and that it results in a perceptible subordination and depersonalisation of the Spirit. By this is meant that its role and activity have been overshadowed by those of Christ, and consequently swallowed up in the ministrations of the church. This is not yet the place to attempt to assess how valid these charges maybe; but they do show that the *filioque* has wider ramifications, and point to other aspects of Western medieval pneumatology which must also be taken into account. Here again, it was Augustine whose thought largely influenced the development—in particular, his view of the connection between the Spirit and the church.

3. The Spirit as Soul of the Church
Another of Augustine's sayings that reverberated down the

centuries was, 'What the soul is in our body, the Holy Spirit is in the body of Christ, which is the church.' (*Sermo* 267.iv.4) The same theme has been powerfully expressed in two of the most important Roman Catholic ecclesiological statements of modern times—Leo XIII, *Divinum illud munus* in 1897 (*DS* 3328) and Pius XII, *Mystici corporis* in 1943 (*DS* 3807–3808)— though Vatican II put the matter rather less absolutely in *Lumen Gentium* I.7.[12] Such an explicit identification of the *Spirit* as the animating power of the church is not to be found in the New Testament, though it can be argued that it represents a consistent development of the description of the church as Christ's body. Clearly there is a sense in which it is perfectly valid: if the church is not vitalised by the Holy Spirit, it ceases truly to be the church. If however the critical element implicit in this way of putting the matter is submerged and lost to sight, the Spirit may be taken for granted as simply given in the ecclesiastical institution, or as present in *THIS* body but not in *THAT*. One obvious danger is then of the domestication of the Spirit in the interest of the claims of one ecclesiastical body over against others. And it can scarcely be overlooked that the roots of this conception of the Spirit as the soul of the (true) church lie partly in the problems the early church faced in confronting the issue of unity and disunity, of the catholic faith over against heresy, of the one church over against schismatic churches. Already in the second century it was with a critical eye on gnostic communities that Irenaeus formulated his dictum, '... they have no share in this Spirit who do not join in the activity of the church (i.e. the catholic church, descending from the apostles) ... For where the church is, there is the Spirit of God; and where the Spirit is, there is the church and every kind of grace.' (*Haer.* III.xxiv.1) Similarly, both the positive and the negative force of Augustine's description of the Spirit as the soul of the church emerge most clearly in the context of the question of division, particularly as bearing on the matter of the recognition of baptism.

In the middle of the third century there had been a heated controversy between Cyprian of Carthage and Stephen of Rome about the treatment to be given to those who had been baptised in heretical or schismatic communities, and now wished to be admitted to membership of the catholic church. Cyprian held that their previous baptism was void, and that they must now be baptised properly; Stephen treated the earlier baptism as valid. Augustine, who was faced 150 years later with the existence in North Africa of the large and aggressive Donatist church (which denied the authenticity of the catholic priesthood and the validity of the catholic sacraments) took up the question afresh in his *De Baptismo* and offered a more differentiated answer. Essentially, he maintained that an heretical or schismatic baptism might indeed be *valid* but not *efficacious*. The true meaning of baptism, even when administered by a non-catholic, was in fact incorporation into communion with the catholic church; it marked the baptised person indelibly with the brand of Christ; but only on admission to the one true church did it become, as it were, effectively activated. Rebaptism was therefore not required, as entering into the unity, charity and peace of the catholic church made the previous baptism for the first time fully operational. There in the one true church was the living reality of the community of the Spirit, to which heretical or schismatic communities and ministrations witnessed only in fragmentary, broken, partial and incomplete fashion.

It would certainly be quite wrong to accuse Augustine here of falling into sectarian thinking. He had an incomparably richer, deeper and fuller conception of the universality of the church than had the Donatists, and that is what underlies and emerges in his reflections upon baptism. But there is another and much subtler temptation which now arises. If it is right and proper to insist over against the sectarian claims of the Donatists (or indeed the Montanists or any other group) that the full presence of the Spirit is only to be found within the richness of the universal, catholic church, it is equally necessary to recognise the distinction between the activity and presence of the Spirit and those of the church as a given, empirical, visible institution. If that boundary should be blurred, the church might easily and even unconsciously substitute itself for the Spirit, or assume that the Spirit is automatically inherent in its own structure. Alternatively, acute awareness of the difference between things divine and human could evacuate the sense of the presence *of the Spirit* of genuine content, and lead to the formulation and systematisation of other doctrinal categories which might appear better fitted to express the nature of the divine activity in the church. The end result again would then be the effective displacement of the Spirit from the centre.

Both of these tendencies came to work very powerfully in the medieval Western church, encouraged by the imposing authority of ecclesiastical tradition, by the intensifying claims of the papacy, and above all by the enormous development of the doctrine of grace as an objective, supernatural power mediated through the sacraments to nourish the spiritual life of the church and of the individual soul.[13] Divine grace dispensed through the ministrations of the church tends now in effect to replace the Spirit, which is located and spoken of primarily in the context of the eternal Trinity as the common source with the Father and the Son of the uncreated grace which in turn effects created grace in human life. A wedge is thus driven between the mystery of the triune God on the one hand and the pattern of divine activity in the world on the other.[13a] The end result is apparent in the famous statement of a modern Roman Catholic theologian: 'I experience the action of the living God through Christ realising himself in his Church.'[14] The question inevitably arises whether the Augustinian identification of the Spirit as gift, as love, and as soul of the church, does not issue in the substitution of another and rather different Trinity for the Father, Son and Holy Spirit. Even if that way of putting the matter seems too heavily biassed, it can at least serve to focus an unresolved tension in the main line of medieval Western ecclesiology and pneumatology.

It must of course be added that the rich diversity of medieval thought also threw up movements which in one way or another reacted against that main line. Mystical theology, for example, sought the reality of God, the power of the divine love and of ineffable union, in inner experience and devotion, and can be seen as countering any too external, too legalistic or mechanical conception of the nature of the church itself. More radical streams, such as that represented by Joachim of Fiori († 1202) and the Spiritual Franciscans, anticipated a new, apolyptic Age of the Spirit, in which the corrupt church would be finally destroyed and superseded.[15] Nor were there lacking powerful voices to criticise the juridical presumptions of ecclesiastical authority or the hallowed claims of established theological tradition. None of these protests, however, issued in a coherent and viable alternative grasp of the relation of the Spirit to the church. That remains a central problem in the medieval and later Roman Catholic cultivation of the Augustinian heritage.

CHAPTER SEVEN

THE ENLIGHTENER AND SANCTIFIER[1]

The volcanic upheaval of the Reformation precipitated a shift in pneumatological interest fully as dramatic as that ushered in by Augustine. Mainstream Protestant theology preserved and maintained the established Western *doctrine* (including the *filioque*), but at the same time concentrated with a new intensity on what the Spirit *enables* and *performs*. There is a good deal of justice in the claim of the Princeton theologian of the turn of the century, B. B. Warfield: 'The developed doctrine of the work of the Holy Spirit is an exclusively Reformation doctrine.'[2] Certainly the kind of understanding of the Spirit's activity that Warfield had in view was more richly developed in various strands of Protestant theology than elsewhere, and took on a prominence there which contrasts sharply with the tendency in the medieval period. The new note is sounded by many writers; typical is the seventeenth century English Puritan Richard Baxter, who on this point at least well expresses the conviction of the great Reformers of the century before:

> ... to believe in the Holy Ghost is to take him for Christ's Agent or Advocate with our souls, and for our Guide, Sanctifier, and Comforter, and not only to believe that He is the third Person in the Trinity.
> (*Christian Directory* I.iii.3)

The presence and action of the Spirit in the life of the believer to represent Jesus Christ, to convey forgiveness, to illuminate and renew by divine spiritual energy—these themes take on a new centrality owing directly to the fundamental insights of the Reformation.

1. *Luther and Calvin*

At first sight, this may seem a surprising claim. Most
Protestants today, if asked what the Reformation was
primarily about, would not immediately think of the Holy
Spirit. The rectification of abuses in the church, the battle-cry
of justification by faith alone, the uniqueness of Jesus Christ as
Redeemer and Saviour, the authority of Scripture—these
would more commonly come at once to mind. Yet the
Reformers themselves were well aware that faith, redemption
by Christ, justification by faith, the authority of Scripture,
were all necessarily bound up with the Holy Spirit. As Luther
put it in the third chapter of his *Short Catechism* when speaking
of faith,

> I believe that it is not of my own reason or my own strength
> that I believe in Jesus Christ my Lord. It is the Holy Spirit
> that by the Gospel has called me, with his gifts has
> enlightened me, through genuine faith has sanctified and
> sustained me, just as he calls, gathers together, enlightens,
> sanctifies and sustains, by Jesus Christ, in true and proper
> faith, all Christendom.

Were this not so, were faith itself not the gift of the Spirit, it
would be a 'work', an achievement of our own—something
quite the opposite of what Luther understood it to be, and
implying a radical inversion of his doctrine of justification by
faith. To be justified by faith is to be justified solely by the free
grace of God; it is to depend on Christ alone for salvation; it is
therefore something that only God can perform, realise, and
make effective. Certainly Protestantism has by no means
always remembered this fundamental message of Luther's. If
the temptation to medieval Western theology was to substitute
the church for the Spirit, Protestantism has often enough been
inclined to substitute the individual's 'act' or 'decision' of
faith, propounding its own ersatz Trinity of 'God, Jesus, and
my faith'. This was far from Luther's intention. He was clear
that it is only by the Spirit that we can hear in faith God's
Word to us, that we are given to share in the 'alien

righteousness' of Jesus Christ, that *justification* is accompanied by *sanctification.*

While Luther could express this in quite traditional language, he was in fact making a decisive break with the framework of thought that had dominated medieval theology and religiosity, and which can not unfairly be termed '*caritas* idealism'.[3] According to that scheme, divine grace operated in the soul to awaken love for God, responding to his love in Christ; this in turn evoked faith which issued in good works pleasing to God; and so prevenient grace brought about an onward and upward advance in holiness. The Spirit tended to be reduced to (or replaced by) the historical outworking through the church of the grace emanating from Jesus Christ and enabling the progress of the soul towards God. The *justificatio impii*, 'justification of the ungodly', could therefore be described by Aquinas under the general heading of the 'effects of grace', and as brought about by the 'infusion of grace', by which sin is forgiven and man freely wills to respond to God (*Summa Theologica* I/II, *qu.* 113). Luther understood both sin and justification in more radical terms: man's will is not free but enslaved by sin, and justification can only consist in the declaration of God that the sinner is righteous—in *Christ*, not *in himself*. Faith hangs always and solely on 'that child in the stable, that man on the cross', whose righteousness is mediated and appropriated only by the immediate activity of the Spirit of God; the *justificatio impii* means that *even as sinners* we are righteous in God's eyes—*simul justus et peccator*. There is no departing from this foundation: faith is continually returning to its ground in Christ, continually absolutely and totally dependent on him, continually beginning afresh. The work of the Spirit accordingly came again to be recognised as profoundly coherent with that of Jesus Christ himself and as displaying the same pattern of sovereign divine action—as is forcefully brought out in the *Scots Confession* of 1560:

And so, as we confess that God the Father created us when we were not, as his Son our Lord Jesus redeemed us when we

were enemies to him, so also do we confess that the Holy
Spirit does sanctify and regenerate us without respect to any
merit proceeding from us be it before or after our
regeneration. To put this even more plainly, as we willingly
disclaim any honour and glory for our own creation and
redemption, so do we willingly also for our regeneration and
sanctification; for by ourselves we are not capable of
thinking one good thought, but he who has begun the work
in us alone continues us in it, to the praise and glory of his
undeserved grace. (Ch. xxi)

This fresh appreciation of the Spirit, the new awareness of
the vital centrality of its work in complementing and answering
to what God has done in Jesus Christ, corresponded far more
closely than the established patterns of medieval thought and
piety to the message of the New Testament, and held out hope
that theology could be recast in a mould more biblical, more
personal, more historical and eschatological, and more
radically christocentric than in the past. The activity of the
Spirit was seen to be inherently bound up with each of the
three great foci of the Reformers' concern—*God's Word* in
Scripture; *the unique work of Christ* for our salvation; and *the
sovereignty of grace*, not now understood in the medieval sense,
but rather as God's active mercy, favour and love.

Of all the great Reformers it was Calvin who undertook the
most systematic exploration of the Spirit's work—notably in
the third book of his *Institute*, which reached final form in
1559.[4] There were indeed differences between him and Luther,
reflected in the divergence from the mid-sixteenth century
onwards of the separate Lutheran and Reformed traditions;
but the main points of disagreement had to do with christology
and eucharistic doctrine rather than with the Holy Spirit.
Calvin was, however, less fond than Luther of abrupt paradox.
In his writing, Luther's *simul justus et peccator*, though by no
means denied, tends to give way to closer analysis of the
various aspects of the Spirit's activity in regeneration and
sanctification. The fundamental recognition that all this
depends wholly on the once-for-all redemption wrought by

Jesus Christ remains decisive, as does the message that our righteousness before God lies in him, not in ourselves; but Calvin sets out to explore and unfold their implications and to map the shape and dynamics of life in Christ as empowered by the Spirit. The hinge on which all turns is that it is the Spirit that unites us to Christ himself:

> ... so long as we are without Christ and separated from him, nothing which he suffered and did for the salvation of the human race is of the least benefit to us. To communicate to us the blessings which he received from the Father, he must become ours and dwell in us. Accordingly he is called our Head and the Firstborn among many brothers, while on the other hand we are said to be ingrafted into him and clothed with him ... And although it is true that we obtain this by faith, yet since we see that all do not indiscriminately embrace the offer of Christ which is made by the Gospel, the very nature of the case teaches us to ascend higher, and inquire into the secret efficacy of the Spirit, to which it is owing that we enjoy Christ and all his blessings. (*Inst.* III.i.1)

This union between Christ and us (which lies at the very heart of Calvin's theology) corresponds and answers to the union between God and man in the incarnation, described by Calvin in terms strongly reminiscent of Irenaeus and other Greek fathers: '... we trust that we are the sons of God because the Son of God by nature assumed to himself a body of our body, flesh of our flesh, bone of our bone, that he might be one with us; he declined not to take what was properly ours that he might in turn extend to us what was properly ours that he might in turn extend to us what was properly his, and so might be in common with us both Son of God and Son of man.' (*Inst.*II.xii.2) So,

> ... until our minds are intent on the Spirit, Christ is in a manner unemployed, because we view him coldly without ourselves, and so at a distance from us. Now we know that he is of no avail save only to those to whom he is a Head and

the Firstborn among many brothers, to those, in short, who are clothed with him. To this union alone it is owing that in regard to us the Saviour has not come in vain. To this is to be referred that sacred marriage by which we become bone of his bone and flesh of his flesh, and so one with him, for it is by the Spirit alone that he unites himself to us. By the same grace and energy of the Spirit we become his members, so that he keeps us under him, and we in turn possess him. (*Inst.* III.i.3)

The twin doctrines of the headship of Christ and our union with him by the Spirit lead into Calvin's detailed account of the Spirit's work and of the Christian life as a sharing with Christ in his life, death and resurrection for us. So in Book III he deals with such themes as faith, regeneration, repentance, self-denial, meditation on the future life, justification, Christian liberty, prayer, election, and the final resurrection, going on in Book IV to the 'external means or helps, by which God allures us into fellowship with Christ, and keeps us in it'—chiefly the church, ministry and sacraments. This order thus gives a certain systematic priority to the activity of the Spirit within the individual, whereas medieval and Roman Catholic teaching placed first its work in and through the church; and this shift has remained broadly characteristic of Protestantism.[5] Calvin himself was, however, far from the extremes of individualism to which some strands of Protestantism have veered, as his powerful presentation of the place of the church in *Inst.* IV.i shows. He would have rejected as false any absolute antithesis between the two approaches, or any notion that the church occupied a merely secondary or incidental place in the divine scheme. Much more indicative of his true position than the setting of the individual believer over against the community of the church is the insistence running through both of these books that church and individual alike depend wholly upon Christ, and that any idea of personal merit, any self-obsession which leads us to look away from him or to put our trust anywhere other than in him, is a snare and a delusion. The Spirit does not raise up the individual over against the church but directs both to Christ, unites them with him, and refashions them in his likeness.

These are the lines along which Calvin relates the Spirit to *the work of Christ* and depicts it as *the Spirit of grace* by which we are renewed and restored through him. There remains the third central Reformation theme: *the activity of the Spirit in relation to the Word in Scripture.* Luther, following the suggestions of Augustine in his *De Spiritu et Littera*, had powerfully maintained that the Bible conveys the living Word of God to us only as the Spirit makes us able to hear it; otherwise it is but a dead letter, a purely external word which cannot save because it does not evoke a living faith. His own discovery of the message of justification *sola gratia, sola fide* made this no mere theoretical matter: this was what he had received and been gripped by as the very Gospel of God. In the 1520s, however, he found it necessary to distance himself from more extreme reformers, the 'heavenly prophets', as he ironically called them, who believed the inspiration of the Spirit in their own visions and revelations made the Bible redundant, and who claimed that they were simply following through the true direction of his own earlier teaching with greater consistency than he himself had done. Against them he vigorously declared that the 'inner witness' of the Spirit is to nothing else than *the Word* presented in Scripture: it is *that* Word and none other that it makes resonate in our hearts and brings as the Word *for us*. The 'outward Word' of the Bible is accompanied by the 'inner testimony', and only so is the message of grace, forgiveness, and redemption conveyed, received, and realized.

Calvin's position, outlined in *Inst.* I.vi-ix, is essentially in accord with Luther's. The authority of the Bible can only be recognised by the *testimonium internum Spiritus Sancti* because only God can authenticate his own Word (I.vii.4); but it is to the Bible and not elsewhere that we must go if we would hear that Word (I.ix, *passim*). This is not, as 'the fanatics' imagine, to subordinate the Spirit demeaningly to the 'dead letter'; it is to recognise the inner consistency of the Spirit, who both inspired the Scriptures and now convinces us of their truth (I.ix.2). There is a certain parallel here between Calvin's account of the relation between the 'internal testimony' of the Spirit to the Word and his acute sense of the union established by the Spirit between Christ and ourselves. In each case, the Spirit enables the reception and appropriation of the given, objective reality of Christ or of the Bible because it is itself by its very nature the bridge over the divide, uniting and bonding both sides together. The power by which we hear the Word of the Bible is the same power by which Scripture was inspired; the Spirit that unites us to Christ is the same Spirit with which Christ himself was endowed on our behalf (*Inst.* II.xv.2). The Spirit is the uniter of inner and outer, past and present, written Word and faith's hearing, Christ and ourselves. As he put it in speaking of the Lord's Supper, 'the Spirit truly unites what is separated by space' (*Inst.* IV.xvii.10).

2. *Post-Reformation Protestantism*

It was Calvin more than any other who laid the basis for the attention to the work of the Spirit which Warfield had in mind when he spoke of it as a specifically Reformation concern. The double theme of enlightenment and sanctification signals the primary emphases, the axis along which the activity of the Spirit was discerned. So on the one hand its inspiration of Scripture and enabling of the reception of the Word in faith, on the other its applying to faith of the benefits purchased by Christ and issuing in new spiritual life, came to be central themes in Protestant theology and piety through the following centuries. It is no accident that Protestantism brought forth such diverse fruits as, for example, the classic seventeenth century Puritan treatises, John Owen's *Pneumatologia, or A Discourse Concerning the Holy Spirit*, and John Goodwin's *Pleroma to Pneumatikon, or A Being Filled with the Spirit*; the (very different) Quaker doctrine of the 'inner light'; the emphasis on the inward work of the Spirit so central for German Pietism; the sense of the vital activity of the Spirit in conversion, conviction, witness, and 'Christian perfection' in the eighteenth century Methodist and Evangelical revivals; the new concern in the nineteenth and twentieth centuries with 'pentecostal gifts', associated first with Edward Irving and the

Catholic Apostolic Church, and more recently with Classical and Neo-Pentecostalism. To say the least, there has been a recurrent awareness that without the active presence of the Spirit of God there must be a desperate vacuum at the heart of Christian life.

At the same time, the sheer variety of these movements—themselves reflecting the wider diversities within the Protestant traditions—shows how hard the heirs of the Reformation found it to hold to the centre to which the great Reformers had pointed. (i) Many slid back into a posture remarkably similar to what had preceded the Reformation, altered only by the substitution of the authority of Scripture, doctrinal confession, or individual conscience for that of Pope, tradition, and church. (ii) Other movements sought to be more radical than the Reformers had been in criticising and rejecting established doctrine, including the dogmas of the Trinity and the Incarnation, and thus also the teaching on the Spirit as well. (iii) All this took place within a wider stream of questioning and exploring which has brought enormous advances in all kinds of fields of knowledge, has supplied theology with new tools and fresh material, but has also raised the most searching questions about the place, the rationale and the justification of theology itself. This needs to be kept in mind in any review of the course of modern Protestant thought, though it is a story we cannot pursue here.[5a] To conclude this chapter, however, we may summarily note some major issues raised by developments following the Reformation in these three main areas.

(i) Inner Tensions

Calvinism, like Lutheranism in Germany, rapidly settled into an established 'orthodoxy', represented in the English-speaking world by Puritan Federal Theology as expressed, for example, in the *Westminster Confession*.[6] This places great emphasis on the work of the Spirit in effectual calling, justification, adoption, sanctification, saving faith, repentance unto life, good works, perseverance, and assurance of grace and salvation (chs. x-xix),[7] but the overall framework is determined by the divine decrees of election and reprobation, and by the two covenants of works and of grace. All men stand condemned by Adam's failure to observe the covenant of works, but the elect (and only they) have a share in the covenant of grace established in Christ. While Federal Theology had immense strengths, there were also drastic weaknesses in this narrowing down of the Spirit's work to an activity of regeneration in the elect, and so to only one side of a scheme primarily determined by the double decree; in a sense that it evoked of distance between the finished work of Christ and the present action of the Spirit; and also in a perceptible shift towards an overly rationalist type of theological thought which risked reducing the inward illumination of the Spirit to a largely formal assent to the authority of Scripture or of the teaching of the *Confession*.

One of orthodox Calvinism's prime aims was to preserve the sovereignty of God's free grace, which, however, it inclined to understand in a very deterministic fashion. It had hardened on this point in opposition to the form of Arminianism which was rejected at the Synod of Dort in 1619, and came to be looked upon as the most fearful heresy. Arminius sought to soften the doctrine of predestination by reducing it to God's eternal *fore-knowing* who would in fact repent, come to faith, and so be saved. This gave Arminians a genuine evangelical concern: they could preach in the conviction that *now* all was at stake for the eternal destiny of their hearers, that *now* the Spirit was at work to convert; but to strict Calvinists their position seemed Pelagian, substituting the human response of faith for God's eternal election. The same criticism was made of the new Evangelical movements of the eighteenth century. Evangelicalism nevertheless became a powerful influence within Calvinist churches as well as elsewhere, and a driving force behind the modern missionary movement.

In some forms, however, the Evangelical concern could result in a type of discrimination as dubious as in the doctrine of the double decree, though very differently expressed. It commonly came to be held in some branches of Protestantism that only those with a certain 'experience of conversion' were

If the Spirit is what links us to Christ – either this explicit conversion is required for us to be Christians or it is not necessary?

genuine Christians. So the activity of the Spirit was in effect restrictively defined in terms of one particular style of piety. Essentially similar questions were to arise with those branches of Pentecostalism which believed the Spirit had only been given to those manifesting specific 'gifts'. On one level, the problem here has to do with discerning the gifts of the Spirit; more profoundly, however, the difficulty lies in overlooking Calvin's point that the Spirit is our link with Jesus Christ. This results in its virtual reduction to an element within our own personal psychological, intellectual or spiritual history.

Very much the same issue arose in the seventeenth century within Calvinism itself. The weight placed upon God's hidden decrees of election and reprobation generated a terrifying personal and pastoral problem: how could one be confident of one's own election? An answer came to be given in terms of the 'doctrine of evidences' and of the 'practical syllogism'.[8]

By self-examination one might detect the signs of the Spirit's work in sincere faith, in due repentance, in the fruits of good works, and so attain assurance (or at any rate reasonable confidence) of one's election to salvation. It would be hard to imagine a more drastic inversion of the teaching of Luther or Calvin; for while they did indeed give a place to self-examination, they insisted that *for assurance of salvation* we must look only to Christ. A theology which was not centred on Christ but on the divine decree had that path barred to it, and consequently also found it hard to hold his work and the Spirit's together.

Similarly, the balance and correlation between the inspiration of Scripture and the inner testimony of the Spirit was not always successfully maintained. In the generations following the Reformation, the authority of the Bible came widely to be understood simply in terms of literal divine dictation. The Word lay visibly there before the eyes of all in its pages, and the Spirit's testimony reduced to mere recognition of that simple fact. While this conception of inspiration did play a part, for instance, in Calvin's theology,[9] it was accompanied there by the sense of living communication by the Spirit's agency; but that sense seems to have faded from the minds of many of his successors. The authority of Scripture could then become an axiomatic, dogmatic assertion rather than an experienced conviction. This was paralleled by a strong tendency to emphasise the objective, finished work of Christ so exclusively that the activity of the Spirit as sanctifier receded into the background: it was often presented simply as 'applying' the fruits of Christ's 'satisfaction' offered to the Father for our sins, and so largely in negative rather than positive terms. Over against these strongly objectivist tendencies there not surprisingly emerged a series of reactions which sought to redress the balance: notably the Quaker doctrine of the 'inner light'—a transposition of the *testimonium internum* which in effect (if not in intention) eventually threatened to reduce it to something purely subjective—and the less extreme but still very powerful emphasis on inwardness and devotion in Pietism and Methodism. An uneasy oscillation between objectivism and subjectivism has marked a good deal of Protestant theology and piety ever since, as indeed it has also marked wider Western culture. Here again it is hard to evade the conclusion that somewhere in all this Calvin's profound awareness of the Spirit as the unifier as our link with Christ, as the energy of God's self-communication to us, had been largely lost.

In this connection it is worth noticing that it was within Calvinism, but in strong reaction against these tendencies, that the first strikingly 'pentecostal' theology of modern times emerged, with Edward Irving (†1834). Irving, like his friend John McLeod Campbell (†1872), was expelled from the ministry of the Church of Scotland for teaching incompatible with the *Westminster Confession*. He was convinced that the present activity of the Spirit needed again to be brought into the centre of the church's preaching; that signs and wonders, tongues and healing, were not (as they had generally come to be regarded) simply restricted to the age of the apostles as authenticating the original revelation, but should continue to mark the life of Christians; and that Christ himself must be seen anew as the one in whom *sinful* humanity had been sanctified by the indwelling Spirit, and so as the abiding ground of our sanctification now. This was in fact an attempt to recover the sense we noticed in the Greek fathers of the dynamic activity of the Spirit in Christ and in his people, and to integrate christology and pneumatology. Irving himself ended his days in the Catholic Apostolic Church, which had grown out of his London congregation, and which went on to develop its own unique character, combining charismatic and eschatological expectation with high ritual and elaborate structures of ministry. After a period in which it flourished and spread widely, it has suffered a long decline, while the 'pentecostal' torch has been more widely carried by other movements, differing very greatly from it. The current search for a more adequate pentecostal theology than those so far on offer could nonetheless benefit by paying Irving more attention that it has generally done.[10]

(ii) Anti-trinitarianism

The sixteenth century had also seen the beginnings of a frontal assault on trinitarian dogma as a whole in the writings of Michael Servetus, who was burned at the stake in Geneva in 1553. Shortly after, there developed the movement known from its chief leader, Faustus Socinus (1539–1604) as Socinianism. Socinus maintained that the New Testament witnesses only to one divine 'person', the Father; that Jesus was not eternal or divine, but a man who was begotten by the Father through the Spirit, endowed with the Spirit at his baptism, and raised to glory at his resurrection; that the Spirit is simply the active power and energy of the Father; and that the whole pattern of classical trinitarian doctrine was an elaborate ecclesiastical invention which wrongly treated the Spirit as a distinct 'person', and accordingly ran into insoluble difficulties over the threeness and oneness it incoherently ascribed to the divine nature itself. The rather simplistic biblicism of the Socinians did not meet with widespread success except in Poland: elsewhere it served chiefly as a target, an object-lesson in heresy, for orthodox writers. In Britain in the late seventeenth and eighteenth centuries, however, something fairly similar emerged in modern versions of Arianism—a development which was indebted to the rise of deism in the same period—and led to the establishment of the Unitarian Church, into which English (but not Scottish, Irish or Welsh) Presbyterianism virtually dissolved, leaving the banner of English Calvinism to be carried by Baptists and Congregationalists. The controversy between these latter-day Arians and their orthodox opponents covered much the same ground as had the fourth century debate, but with one major difference. Now there was abroad a suspicion of a yawning gulf between the teaching of the New Testament and the dogmatic theology that had only later been formulated—a suspicion that owed much to the Reformation insistence on *sola Scriptura*, and was heightened rather than lessened by the further expansion of critical biblical studies in the following centuries. One consequence of this has been that the classical dogmas, even when not actually denied, have commonly been relegated to the edge of theological interest and have frequently played very little part in shaping thought, worship and spirituality across broad reaches of Protestantism.

(iii) Reinterpretations of 'Spirit'

Against this background, it is not perhaps surprising that Protestant theology has also known sundry attempts to redefine the nature and activity of the Spirit along lines rather different from those we have so far mentioned. Already in the seventeenth century Owen's *Pneumatologia* was in part directed against the idea that God's Spirit should be regarded simply as an ethical quality of human life, a 'spirit' of natural morality, rather than as a 'spiritual principle' engendering new spiritual life in us. Such ethical or humanistic reductions of the Spirit have been very common. An outstanding instance is supplied by the extremer forms of the Liberal Theology advanced a century ago by Albrecht Ritschl († 1889) and given popular expression in Adolf Harnack's *What is Christianity?* (ET 1901).[11] This followed the lead of Immanuel Kant in linking religion directly with 'practical reason', with morality and behaviour; interpreted the Kingdom of God in ethical rather than eschatological terms as an ideal society built upon the

Fatherhood of God and the brotherhood of man; and criticised the entire structure of trinitarian and christological dogma as obscuring the primitive simplicity of Jesus' original message concerning the Father, the infinite worth of the individual soul, and the 'higher righteousness' of love. In such a vision there was little or no real place for the Holy Spirit except as a cipher for the realm of moral and spiritual values. Certainly, by no means all adherents of the Liberal approach went so far in this direction as did Harnack; certainly too there was some ground for their protest against the introverted piety which is content to seek after inward holiness and cares nothing for outward justice. Nevertheless, Liberalism in this extreme form threatened entirely to domesticate the Spirit of God in the highest human religio-ethical ideals. It was none too acutely aware of the need to make what P. T. Forsyth described as his own transition 'from a lover of love to an object of grace.'[12]

Rather different perspectives were opened up by the two earlier thinkers who, more than any others, offered theology in the nineteenth century distinctively fresh approaches— Schleiermacher (†1833) and Hegel (†1831). Schleiermacher gave a new centrality to *experience* in theology, was sharply critical of the reduction of faith to mere *knowledge* or mere *activity*, and pointed to a sense of inner depth, of '*God-consciousness*', as the distinctively religious dimension of our awareness. He did not aim to characterise 'God-consciousness' primarily in terms of the Spirit, instead basing his account of it on an analysis of human self-consciousness as such; but he did then go on to describe the Holy Spirit as communicated by Jesus and working to form the community of believers, redeemed by receiving a share in Jesus' God-consciousness, and thereby also 'regenerated' and brought into 'a state of sanctification'. The Spirit could thus be defined as 'the union of the divine essence with human nature in the form of the common Spirit which animates the corporate life of believers.' (*The Christian Faith*[2], §123) In effect, this was a Protestant restatement of the thought of the Spirit as *anima ecclesiae*, expressed in terms of Schleiermacher's Romantic philosophy of history as a living, moving, incorporating power acting to unite God with men, Christians with Christ and with each other.

From his own day to this, Schleiermacher's thought has evoked widely differing reactions. It has been held that he was the first thinker properly to identify the distinctively religious dimension of human experience; that he rightly showed how it must be given its own space instead of being squeezed out between the falsely polarised alternatives of an excessively rationalist objectivism and an ethical reductionism; and that while his analyses may need modification and improvement, he has pointed theology in the necessary direction towards what might today be called a 'theocentric anthropology'. Experiential awareness of God, on this account, is the essential ground of all theology, and talk of the Spirit must be explicitly related to it. On the other hand, Ritschl and his followers believed that Schleiermacher was altogether too 'mystical', and that theology should not be built on God-consciousness but on the 'historical revelation' in Jesus' preaching and example, and issue in the building of the Kingdom he proclaimed. Such criticisms were even more sharply intensified in the reaction against Liberal Theology itself, led by Karl Barth, Emil Brunner and Rudolf Bultmann in the 1920s. They stressed with a new urgency the 'radical otherness' of the Word of God in Jesus Christ, the eschatological Word which creates faith in the 'moment of encounter' between eternity and time. Consequently, they criticised Schleiermacher as trying to start his theology from the wrong end, beginning with man rather than with God and producing an 'anthropocentric theology'. These diverse attitudes to Schleiermacher are bound up with equally different overall conceptions of the nature and activity of the Spirit and its relation to religious and spiritual experience.

Hegel's philosophy (very different in tone and aim from Schleiermacher's theology) made *Geist*—'Spirit' or 'Mind'— its fundamental category and opened up a view of the entire history of the universe as the unfolding and returning to itself of Spirit, with the emergence of the human spirit and its multifarious expression in culture and civilisation, art and religion, as a necessary intermediate stage in the whole cosmic process. Hegel's 'Spirit' was not exactly identical with the Holy Spirit, though he believed his philosophy to give the true conceptualisation of what was less adequately pictured in religious ideas. The system was practically pantheist: 'Spirit' produced 'Nature' as its own opposite, through which it moved in order to realise and return to itself on a higher level as 'Absolute Spirit'. Nevertheless, Hegel deserves special notice here for at least three reasons. First, he was a leading representative of a wider movement in post-Kantian philosophy which sought to describe ultimate reality in terms of Spirit, and by tracing the triple movement of Spirit in thesis, antithesis and synthesis to reconcile the oppositions between subject and object, mind and matter, ideal and real which run through much modern thought and are directly related also to tensions that can be felt in theology as well. This philosophical tradition has fed powerfully into both philosophy and theology ever since; it has also provoked plenty of criticism in both, in that movements such as Existentialism and Marxism stood Idealism on its head, while anglo-saxon Empiricism rejected it outright. Yet much of the heritage remains in the use by other schools of 'Spirit' or essentially related concepts—'Being', 'Existence', 'Historical Dialectic', 'Life', 'Process' have been especially widely canvassed—to express the nature of reality; and all of these have been taken up by some theologians in one way or another, in order to speak of God's presence and activity in the world.

Second, and quite apart from such metaphysical constructions, Idealism also opened up the possibility of a new understanding of man as 'spiritual' or as 'possessing spirit'. 'Spirit' could be seen, not as a 'substance' but as a 'dynamic', not as an element of the person, but the personal totality of the self, and as having or indeed being the capacity for self-awareness and so for self-transcendence, for aspiration to the universal and eternal, as what makes man permanently restless, not content simply to be at home in the world, but reaching out by the impulse of his very nature, as the inner secret striving which is at once the mystery of his own identity and a direction towards God.[13] It was Kierkegaard in particular who fastened on the Idealist categories—though inverting the 'System', ridiculing the 'Method', and referring the whole scheme to the individual in the sheer stark recognition of the overwhelming otherness of God rather than to the serene dialectic of a Spirit both transcendent and immanent—to explain the nature of the self; on this, in *The Sickness Unto Death*, he framed his analysis of 'despair'. The basic definitions are stated in the opening chapter:

> Man is spirit. But what is spirit? Spirit is the self. But what is the self? The self is a relation which relates to its own self, or it is that in the relation [which accounts for it] that the relation relates itself to its own self; the self is not the relation but [consists in the fact] that the relation relates itself to its own self. Man is a synthesis of the infinite and the finite, of the temporal and the eternal, of freedom and necessity, in short it is a synthesis. A synthesis is a relation between two factors. So regarded, man is not yet a self.

> In the relation between two, the relation is the third term as a negative unity... If on the contrary the relation relates itself to its own self, the relation is then the positive third term, and this is the self.

> Such a relation ... must either have constituted itself or have been constituted by another.

> If this relation which relates itself to its own self is constituted by another, the relation ... is in turn a relation relating itself to that which constituted the whole relation.

> Such a derived, constituted, relation is the human self, a relation which relates itself to its own self, and in relating itself to its own self relates itself to another ... the self cannot of itself attain and remain in equilibrium and rest by itself, but only by relating itself to the Power which constituted the whole relation ... by relating itself to its own self and by willing to be itself the self is grounded transparently in the Power which posited it.[14]

This account has been immensely influential in more recent theology, not least because such a relational idea of the self or spirit seems much closer to biblical emphases than the idea of an 'immortal spirit' as a 'component' of man alongside body, soul and mind.

Finally, while Hegel's description of the dialectic of thesis, antithesis and synthesis in the movement of Spirit has by no means been universally accepted as giving the true, 'philosophical' meaning of the religious doctrine of the Trinity, his restatement of the older theme of an ultimate triplicity-in-unity did nevertheless offer the opportunity to take it seriously once more. It did not have to be looked upon simply as a datum of revealed faith to be blindly accepted, nor as a self-contradictory incomprehensibility to be appropriated only by the sacrifice of the intellect, or rejected as dogmatic obfuscation. Instead it could express the dynamic of the divine life, and the movement of God into history in the incarnation. In this way, the attempt could be made to uncover again the frequently obscured and forgotten ground of the doctrine itself, and the Trinity drawn back into the centre of Christian theology.

PART THREE

CURRENT ISSUES

CHAPTER EIGHT

PENTECOST AND EXPERIENCE

This title may immediately bring to mind the pentecostal and charismatic movements and their impact in many churches through the last two decades. Yet 'experience' does not only mean 'charismatic experience', and there are other questions to be faced than whether particular 'pentecostal gifts' are distinctive or decisive manifestations of the presence of the Holy Spirit. Indeed the whole topic of 'Christian experience' became prominent very largely independently of specifically pentecostal or charismatic encouragement, and the debates it provoked offer bearings upon these movements as well.

1. Liberal and Dialectical Theology

An excellent starting-point is H. Wheeler Robinson's widely influential book, *The Christian Experience of the Holy Spirit*, first published just over fifty years ago.[1] Robinson, in common with several of the leading Protestant theologians of his day, belonged to the broad stream of Liberal Theology. Like many of these others, he found his place in that current within it which combined a strong emphasis on religious experience with the aim of preserving the broad pattern of catholic, orthodox Christian doctrine by restating its intention in the categories of 'personality', 'value' and 'communion'.[2] His approach was to posit an essential affinity between God and man, between 'Spirit' and 'spirit', 'Spirit' being the prime description of the divine nature, and 'spirit' the quintessentially personal in human life. The main arguments and chief conclusions are distilled in a series of brief paragraphs (p. 285):

(1) The intensive approach of the New Testament—Spirit,

Son, Father—together with the fact that both the Son and Father are described in terms of Spirit, affords an ultimate conception of the Godhead as Spirit; that which is last in revelation becoming first in principle, and that which is initial in experience becoming also final in interpretation.

(2) Spirit is interpretable in terms of personality, our highest category; our knowledge of God as Spirit must always be based on the assumption that there is real kinship between the human spirit and the divine.

(3) The nature of spirit in ourselves is chiefly seen in its unifying, socializing, transforming and sacramentalizing activities; all these are suggestive of the nature or activity of God.

(4) The most important analogy is that of the communion with God in which man realizes his own personality in God; the supreme case of this is in regard to the human personality of Jesus. Individuality is realized by its own moral and religious surrender.

(5) A 'Social' Trinity taken seriously is pluralistic and destroys the unity of God, but our experience of Spirit does suggest a unity differentiated, though not individualized, in which there is the co-existence of that which our thinking cannot combine ontologically.

(6) Spirit affords the necessary conception of God as dynamic and redemptive. In this connection, the true equivalent of the temporal in the eternal is not simultaneity but purpose. It is creational, redemptive, and sanctifying purpose that best displays the unity of the Godhead.

The force of these concentrated statements can perhaps best be drawn out by some further passages from Robinson's closing pages (pp. 286–288). In their warm and evocative language they express the Liberal approach at its finest:

To keep the mind steadily and reverently fixed on this subject is to open the way for a new experience of God. The interpretation of his ways with us makes possible a new fact, indeed the ultimate fact—the fellowship of spirit with Spirit. This is the doctrine of the Life-giver, the vitalizing doctrine to all other portions of Christian truth...

This is the doctrine of a dynamic God. His limitless resources roll in on the shores of human life like the waves of the sea, ceaseless and unnumbered, terrible in wrath, majestic in their encompassing might, mysterious by their far horizon. Yet for all that immensity of the 'sea of the Spirit' (a better metaphor than the wind for an island-race), it does not disdain to enter into our little lives, rippling its way into the tiny pools, lifting the pink shells and floating the fronds of weed; nothing is too small for the dynamic activities of the Spirit, as nothing is too great...

This, too, is the doctrine of divine personality which brings God near in all the intimacies of spiritual companionship, The basal kinship of God and man is lifted to a new level by this growing friendship, this conscious kinship of mind and heart ... the externality of religion is transformed into a new relation... Religion becomes faith in a Burden-bearer, Who carries us and saves us, a God Whom no imagery can ever portray, because He is Spirit...

The God of Christian faith is himself a unity, Who reveals Himself in unifying the universe, both in nature and in grace—One God, not three—but God Who is Spirit, and Whose unities are always inclusive and recapitulatory, giving as they receive... Life in the Spirit ... means new life, and the primary content of that new life is in a new relation to other persons, a new ethical relation, which is best expressed in the Spirit of the Cross of Christ. The actual world we know is a world half-spoiled in the making... Yet we see a miracle of transformation wrought in the meaning of things by the attitude of individual spirits, and we dare to believe in an ultimate transformation of the meaning of it all by the Spirit of God...

We may summarily (if less elegantly) paraphrase: God himself is Spirit; human personality is the primary analogue for the divine nature; to speak of 'the Holy Spirit' is to speak of the divinely-enabled communion and fellowship with God in a redemptive and transforming inward relationship of trust, surrender and love, supremely achieved and exemplified in Jesus Christ himself; entering consciously into this relationship brings the recognition that the divine purpose is threefold, creative, redemptive and sanctifying; this is the meaning and justification of the 'consecrated terms' (p. 284) of Father, Son and Holy Spirit; they therefore may and should continue to be used to express God's nature, but not interpreted or explained in ways that would obscure the fundamental unity of the God who is essentially Spirit, and as such unifies this threefold purpose in himself.

To much of what Robinson here says, we can only add 'Amen!' Yet there are certain weak points in the overall pattern—weaknesses which even as he wrote were being devastatingly exposed in the Germanic homeland of Liberal Theology under the withering onslaught of the new Dialectical Theology. A few years later they were criticised in Britain by Frederick Camfield's strongly Barthian *Revelation and the Holy Spirit*.[3] Of the many charges laid by the new thought at the door of the older school, three in particular recall the primary concerns of the Reformers. First, it was accused of paying too little heed to the 'otherness' of God, of inclining too easily to domesticate his transcendence. Second, it did not do justice to the radical uniqueness of Jesus Christ, tending to portray him as the supreme heroic example of humanity at its best—a 'best' whose depiction owed more to the serene humanitarian ideals of Liberal Theology than to the radical eschatological emphasis of the New Testament. Third, it was insufficiently sensitive to the need to *listen* to the Bible, to the force and carrying-power of God's self-revelation, to the encounter with his challenging Word of judgment and mercy. Camfield accordingly insisted on *dis*continuity between God and man, heavily underscored the transcendence of the Holy Spirit, and challenged Robinson's axiom of a natural kinship between divine Spirit and human spirit. He replaced it with the revitalised concept of revelation, thus aiming to awaken a sense of height and depth, of contrast and antithesis, of the sovereign freedom of God's grace and of the Spirit's working above and beyond our natural capacities and expectations, for it is *Holy* Spirit, not merely the divine counterpart and answer to our spirit.

The critical questions which Camfield brought into the open did not have to do solely with pneumatology: they turned upon the underlying conceptions of God, of Jesus Christ, of revelation, as well as on the connection and distinction between Spirit and spirit. This highlights the full scope of the disagreement; but it may also offer us some leverage upon it. Such leverage is certainly needed, for it is hard not to feel that there is important truth on both sides, but that neither position is wholly adequate. The appeal of Robinson's account lies above all in his desire to discern an authentic presence of God's Spirit in the life of mankind, to evoke awareness of a living experience of communion with God. The weakness lies in the grounding, and consequently also in the terms by which this presence and experience are characterised. By contrast, Camfield was surely right to stress that God cannot be projected simply as the ground and goal of human personality. His position is, however, vulnerable on the other side, in its repeated insistence on God's sheer, stark otherness, which—in spite of his struggles with the matter—leaves it very uncertain what real link there may be between the Spirit and the realm of human concerns, what authentic manifestation of it to our experience of awareness, or how, even from God's side and by divine initiative, human beings could be drawn into an authentic relationship with him. If Liberal Theology risked sliding from a theocentric anthropology to an anthropocentric theology that undercut what Kierkegaard had termed 'the infinite qualitative difference' between God and man, Dialectical Theology was so anxious to eliminate that risk that it threatened to cut off anthropology from theology altogether. The complaint somewhere attributed to C. S. Lewis that 'Barthianism' amounted to 'the flattening out of all things into common insignificance before the majesty of the Creator' was certainly a gross caricature—but a caricature that nonetheless had some basis.

A viable alternative to both extremes cannot be found by

oscillating hopefully between them, nor yet by trying to negotiate some uneasy compromise in the fields of pneumatology and anthropology alone. Reconsideration is needed of the deepest implications of the faith. Here, Barth's own later thought points a way forward.[4] He came to hold that the early, Dialectical emphasis had been valid but one-sided. It had been right and necessary to 'let God be God', not simply man writ large. Yet that could not be the last word. In the light of the incarnation it must be said that God's *deity* includes his *humanity*: in Jesus, God defines himself as *God for man*, and affirms human nature as his own. In other words, there is a foundation deeper and more solid than Liberal Theology had thought to lay by working from an analysis of human personality. Human nature *is* grounded in God—in Jesus himself. The Son of God made Son of man is the centre enabling both a genuinely theocentric understanding of man and a properly anthropocentric doctrine of God.

The sense of otherness, of distinction and difference, characteristic of Dialectical Theology is not indeed suppressed in this new setting; but it is maintained in significantly altered form. Our relation to the Father is mediated through Jesus Christ: it is a reflection of and a sharing in his sonship. The action of the Holy Spirit is not located simply in the meeting of the human self with God, in the encounter of spirit with Spirit, but in the bringing of that self into communion with the Father through the incarnate Son. This opens, deepens and enriches the pattern of Liberal Theology by making it pivot unambiguously on Jesus himself. Equally, however, it modifies the perspective of Dialectical Theology as well. It is not only to the unutterable strangeness of the transcendent Word in Jesus that the Spirit directs us, but to the *man* Jesus who is himself both God's Word and the answer to that Word, spoken in him from the heart of humanity. He represents us all; in him, our human nature is lifted up to the Father; in him, our identity as the children of God is promised, declared, and confirmed. That identity is and can only be given to us from beyond ourselves as we know ourselves; yet it is given to us as the Father knows us in him. This note of gracious displacement, of 'I, yet not I, but Christ', is struck at the very heart of the Gospel; interpretations of the Spirit or of the experience that elide it out echo from the surface rather than the depth, and to that extent threaten to clash discordantly against the ground-tone of Christian faith. In speaking of the Spirit we also speak, implicitly or explicitly, of the foundation laid in Jesus Christ himself.

The other side of this coin, however, is that in order to speak of Jesus we must also speak of the activity of the Spirit in him. It has been a weakness of much Protestant theology that—in spite of the place ascribed to the Spirit—it has commonly inclined to describe it simply as applying the fruits of Christ's work to our souls, or as enabling the awakening of saving faith, acknowledging what Christ has done for us.[5] This effective subordination of the Spirit unobtrusively paves the way for its equation with our experience—an equation which in turn smooths the path for its accommodation to what are conceived to be the highest reaches of human spiritual personality. Attempts to recover and express a more vital sense of the Spirit's power, presence and fullness can only succeed if they are carried beyond such cramping restriction of the space and room that the Spirit creates, but not if they accept that limitation and concentrate solely on evoking a more intense experience and awareness *within ourselves*. If the Spirit is the power of God working to renew us in the likeness *of Jesus* Christ, that divine action must answer to and echo the Spirit's work *in Jesus*.

This sounds a warning not only against possible short-circuits in Liberal (or Pentecostal) Theology, but also against trends in some other recent thought, including even that of Barth himself. Berkhof notes with approval that Barth energetically strives to overcome the limitations of a purely noetic or applicative understanding of the Spirit's work, and in the later volumes of the *Church Dogmatics* richly and fully depicts the Spirit as the living power of the risen Christ.[6] This is true, but it may be doubted whether even Barth goes far enough. Certainly Berkhof's own development of the same idea results in his attempt to rehabilitate a Marcellan doctrine of the Trinity in which the Spirit is effectively conflated with the action of Christ.[7] To see the Spirit as Christ's reaching out to us is indeed a necessary corrective of the inclination to regard it simply as empowering our response to him—but the correction remains at best partial. According to the New Testament, Jesus is not only the giver but also the *receiver* of the Spirit. If that is not kept in view, it is all too easy to absorb pneumatology in christology, and so to reduce the very name 'Holy Spirit' to a mere cipher. Room must be left to discern and describe the activity of the Spirit in the person and history of Jesus. This means, however, that the questions of anthropology and its connection with theology, of the relation of the Spirit to human existence, arise afresh as *christological* questions. This is not to imply that a separate pneumatological focus is required to counterbalance the one-sidedness of christocentrism, as Barth's critics have often suggested. Rather, christology itself requires pneumatology, not in order to be 'less christocentric', but precisely in order to be *christo*logy, the doctrine of Jesus as the Christ, the one anointed with the Spirit.

In what terms, then, is that activity of the Spirit in Jesus to be described? Liberal Theology as represented by Robinson tended to project upon Jesus a markedly idealised conception of human personality. Consistently with that, it believed it could discover in the New Testament witness sufficient evidence to illuminate Jesus' self-understanding; by tracing his inner dispositions, convictions and attitudes it portrayed him as the outstanding example of human personality in unbroken relation to God, of communion with the Father, of devotion and self-surrendering sacrifice. Jesus' consciousness and experience constituted the field in which the presence and action of the Holy Spirit were supremely disclosed; by the same token, they also became paradigmatic for the Christian experience of communion with God, and so the circle was completed.

Dialectical Theology proceeded to break that circle open again. It had become embarrassingly apparent towards the end of the nineteenth century that this kind of portrait of Jesus could only with difficulty be maintained in the face of advancing New Testament study. Jesus was turning out to be a stranger figure altogether. More seriously still, the Gospels did not offer a window into his innermost soul: they proclaimed him as the crucified and risen Christ, and presented his earthly life as understood from the standpoint of the post-Easter church. Insofar as experience was opened up for us in the New Testament, it was that of certain individuals and communities in the early church rather than Jesus' own. Analysis in those terms thus ran up against an insuperable barrier which effectively disqualified it as a christological instrument. These convictions were followed through with particular consistency by Rudolf Bultmann, notably in his sharp distinction between the objective Word of the cross, which is God's revelation in Jesus, and the response of faith, which he interpreted as a form of *self-* understanding in the encounter with that Word. *Jesus must stand over against us rather than alongside us so long as experience, consciousness and awareness supply the lines of the enquiry*: that is one chief implication of the reaction against Liberal Theology. The kerygmatic Christ, we may say, is one in whom God *addresses* us rather than one who invites us to share his experience.

How, along these lines, might we describe the activity of the Spirit in Jesus? Clearly not in terms of his awareness of the Father, for we have no direct access to that. The Spirit could, however, be related to the *total* history of Jesus, centred in his cross and resurrection. This, it must be said, certainly does greater justice than Liberal Theology to one whole dimension of the New Testament evidence. The Spirit is specifically associated with such cardinal moments as Jesus' conception, baptism, defeat of demons, crucifixion and rising from the dead. Most of this evades any straightforward translation in terms of his psychological experience. The Spirit, as spoken of there, has to do primarily with the whole purpose of God worked out in the preparing, claiming, sending, sacrifice and vindication of Jesus as Messiah. The searchlight is not turned chiefly upon his teaching or example, but on the victory won through apparent defeat, the divine foolishness that is stronger than the wisdom of the world, the *kerygma* that proclaims him risen, and presages in him the restoration of creation and the manifestation of the children of God. *That* is the canvas on which the work of the Spirit is displayed: it does not have to do simply with Jesus' experience, but with his whole person, destiny and significance. Similarly, the Spirit in us cannot be dissolved and swallowed up without remainder in *our* experience: rather it opens us up and sets our lives in the broad horizon of God's redemptive purposes in Jesus Christ.

This swing away from Liberal Theology and its particular form of experiential emphasis was certainly justified, and theology today would be ill-advised to seek to reverse it. Yet it should also be sensitive to the dangers of overkill. There were elements in the Liberal approach which should not be dismissed, however defective may have been their exegetical and theological execution. It is very easy indeed to hold forth as the Christ of faith a figure whose humanity seems almost irrelevant, a dramatic, even mythic *Christus Victor*, whose human life and human death, whose hunger and tiredness and anger and testing and fear—to which certainly Liberal Theology paid far too little attention because of its obsession with the heroic—simply fall out of the picture, jettisoned like the first stage of a rocket when it has reached escape velocity and broken out of the strongest pull of the earth's gravitation. If that happens, the humanity of Christ may indeed continue to be affirmed as an article of faith, yet be effectively denied in practice. On the other side, our own human experience in the broadest sense necessarily accompanies and informs all of our engagement with him: there is no way by which it can be tidily or untidily eliminated from the equation. If this is consciously or unconsciously ignored, if his experience and ours are dismissed openly or tacitly as unworthy of serious interest, we shall in all probability end up proclaiming an unreal Christ whose human awareness and consciousness are as irrelevant to our salvation as in the heresy of Apollinaris of Laodicea, who denied that Christ possessed a human mind.[8] Experience, particularly as understood in the Liberal tradition, certainly cannot be made *the* fundamental category to which all others are referred, but the experiential and personal dimension of the whole matter nevertheless remains. Christology cannot be built on the exploration of Jesus' consciousness of the Father alone, but it can scarcely treat that awareness as if it were of no account. It is the Spirit of the Son that cries in us, '*Abba!* Father!' and forms in us the mind of Christ, searching through him the depths of God. If Liberal Theology tended to put this back to front, seeing Jesus through the prism of its own analysis of personality and experience rather than vice versa, it was nevertheless right to witness to the connection between the two.[9]

So far we have not taken up several other major issues raised by Robinson's account—particularly the nature of human 'spirit' and the meaning of God's being 'Spirit'—but concentrated chiefly on the matter of the place of experience, as it is of immediate importance for the pentecostal and charismatic topic. The others will concern us in the last two chapters: while they are by no means in principle irrelevant to the pentecostal theme, they tend not to loom very large in writing upon it, especially from the Classical or Neo-pentecostal side, which on the whole is able to use biblical or traditional theological categories without any desire for radical, let alone 'modernising' reinterpretation.

2. *The Pentecostal Challenge*

The beginnings of what is now generally called Classical Pentecostalism date from the first year of this century; by mid-century Pentecostal churches were widely planted and vigorously spreading, especially in Latin America and the Third World.[10] They were distinctive especially in the place given to 'the gifts of the Spirit', by the weight laid on 'baptism in the Spirit' as a 'second blessing' manifested in glossolalia, and by an inclination to dismiss the older churches as lacking the living presence of the Spirit. The attitude was largely reciprocated. For decades, other churches and theologians generally saw in Pentecostalism nothing more than a modern upsurge of long familiar forms of 'enthusiasm' or 'illuminism', marked by credulity, and naively literal application to the present day of arbitrarily selected portions of the New Testament. Some critics judged more harshly still, finding in the alleged spiritual gifts evidence of demonically-inspired delusion rather than merely excessive zeal and misguided exegesis. More recently, however, a very different climate has begun to form, though the newer attitudes are far from being universally approved or accepted.

First of all, theologians in the older churches began to wonder aloud whether the pentecostal witness was not a justified reminder of something the other churches had too long forgotten, indeed repressed—that Christian life is life in the Spirit, and ought by its very nature to display manifest signs of its transforming and invigorating energy. One of the earliest such diagnoses was offered a generation ago by Bishop Lesslie Newbigin. In *The Household of God*[11] he traced three broad forms of ecclesiology—the *sacramental*, exemplified in Roman Catholicism; the ecclesiology of the *Word*, found in traditional Protestantism; and the ecclesiology of the Spirit, represented afresh in our times by Pentecostalism, but promising the recovery of an understanding as valid, biblical, traditional and authentic as the others. Each had its own contribution to make to a complete understanding of the church while the absence of any of them resulted in an unbalanced (and to that extent also defective) appreciation of its nature and calling. An exclusively sacramental conception presented the church in static, substantial and hierarchical terms, swallowing up the Spirit in the church's official organs and ministrations. An exclusively kerygmatic subordinated the Spirit to the Word, reducing living experience and vital participation to the bare hearing of the proclamation. This did indeed preserve an element of dynamism lacking in the purely sacramental understanding, but tended to reduce the church to a 'mere event of proclamation'. Both needed to be corrected and completed, not just by each other, but by the third, by the sense of the church as the living community filled and guided by the free and sovereign Spirit of God. Newbigin's work proved prophetic, and in the following decades many other voices came to be heard calling both for a new openness and sensitivity to the movement of the Spirit in the church, and for a fresh appreciation of the Spirit in Christian theology.[12] At the same time, ecumenical contacts were extended between the older churches and the new Pentecostalist denominations which thereby moved further out of the relative isolation of earlier decades.

Later came the explosion (from the 1960s onwards) of Neo-pentecostalism in the various charismatic groups and movements in the Roman Catholic and several Protestant churches.[13] The various strands are somewhat diverse, and the very terms 'pentecostal' and 'charismatic' are sometimes applied in a rather bewildering range of senses. Particularly in the Roman Catholic Church, 'charismatic' sometimes seems to describe little more than a certain freedom and informal spontaneity in worship—something whose impact and significance in a community as liturgically formal as the Roman Catholic has traditionally been should by no means be underplayed, but which amounts effectively to the rediscovery within that communion of styles of worship long familiar to many Protestants who would never have dreamt of dignifying them with the 'charismatic' label. These invite comparison more with an old-style evangelical prayer-meeting than with the glossolalic worship of Classical Pentecostalism. Yet there have also emerged both in the Roman Catholic and in other churches much more recognisably pentecostal groups, with the accompanying signs of tongues, healings, prophecies, visions and revelations. While this has led in some instances to the formation of new communities and organisations alongside the established churches, it has been remarkable how many of the new movements have remained firmly anchored within them.[14] This indeed has been the most striking feature of Neo-pentecostalism, and the most obvious contrast with the Classical form.

One important result of this denominational spread is that the new charismatic movements to a large degree retain the theological and devotional colouring of their own ecclesiastical traditions. This in turn is reflected in their exposition and interpretation of the fresh awareness of the activity of the

Spirit. So, to the surprise (and by no means always approval) of Protestant observers, Roman Catholic charismatics frequently witness to a deepened devotion to the church, to the sacrifice of the Mass, and to the figure of Mary.[15] By contrast, the Reformed theologian, Thomas Smail, was led by his charismatic experience into a renewed exploration of the christological ground of pneumatology, and has more recently travelled further along that same road by advocating a new concentration upon the person of the Father.[16] Both in their different ways perhaps demonstrate the aptness of Robinson's observation that 'the doctrine of the Life-giver' is 'the vitalizing doctrine to all other portions of Christian truth' rather than a separate and wholly independent theme, one which stands simply by itself, or which can be made the foundation of all others. It would seem also to follow from this that shared charismatic experience cannot of itself resolve all the other differences in doctrine and devotion separating the churches, though it may well help in the same fashion as other forms of common worship and action to assist a profounder fellowship and mutual understanding.

What then, is to be made of charismatic experience itself, of tongues and healings and prophecies? This is on the face of it the primary question raised by both forms of Pentecostalism: are these 'supernatural', 'miraculous', 'patent manifestations of the Spirit', forms of experience or activity which by themselves unambiguously demonstrate its presence and power? Yet this can be admitted to be the primary question only if a simple, unambiguous 'Yes or No' answer can be given to it. Significantly, however, some of the Neo-pentecostal writers mentioned above seem to feel that such a straightforward affirmative answer would be wholly misleading, for it would put the material focus of interest in the wrong place—in certain 'gifts' rather than in the Spirit, in the work of the Spirit in itself rather than in that to which the Spirit directs us, in a narrow band of 'supernatural' occurrences rather than in the whole range of God's redemptive and transforming action.[17] Their caution confirms the need for the kind of criteria hinted at above: experience of the Spirit must be related to the work of Christ, and the work of the Spirit in us connected with its action in him.

This reserve comes out very clearly in their handling of glossolalia,[18] on which Classical Pentecostalism laid such considerable weight. Speaking in tongues was treated there as *the* biblical evidence for 'baptism in the Spirit'. Recent studies, however, suggest that the phenomenon is essentially a *natural* one, though there is as yet no entirely satisfactory description of the mechanism by which it is brought into operation or of the pattern of its working.[19] It seems to involve a kind of sub-linguistic articulation which brings a certain healing integration of the conscious and subconscious levels of the personality, and as such may also have positive therapeutic psychological and religious value. This is not to say that it has nothing to do with the work of the Spirit; it is to suggest that the activity of the Spirit must be conceived of more broadly and fully as having to do with the whole person rather than with its invasion on one waveband by a force from beyond which 'takes it over'. Much the same may well also apply to cases of healing.[20] Some of Cyril of Jerusalem's remarks are worth quoting here:

> For the unclean devil, when he comes upon a man's soul ... comes like a wolf upon a sheep... His coming is most fierce; the sense of it most oppressive; the mind becomes darkened. His attack is an injustice, and so is his usurpation of another's possession. For he makes forcible use of another's body and another's instruments, as if they were his own... Such is not the Holy Spirit, God forbid! For his doings tend the contrary way, towards what is good and salutary. First, his coming is gentle; the perception of him is fragrant; his burden most light; beams of light and knowledge gleam forth before his coming. He comes with the kindness of a true guardian, for he comes to save and to heal, to teach and admonish, to strengthen and to exhort, to enlighten the mind, first of him who receives him, and afterwards of others also through him. (*Cat.* XVI.15-16)

While it is exceedingly doubtful whether Cyril was a

'charismatic' in the modern sense, these words of his would certainly be applauded by a significant proportion of the present Neo-pentecostal movement. According to their testimony, and to that of sympathetic observers, while speaking in tongues is a normal feature of their worship, and healings do also occur, neither of these is the primary object of attention. What really matters is the rich and deep awareness of God's presence, the sense of the liberating power of his love, the upsurging response of joy and praise, the discovery of a new freshness in the words of the Bible, and the consciousness of communion with the Father through Jesus Christ. This does not render such phenomena as glossolalia incidental or insignificant; but they are valued not as ends in their own right, but as means which mediate and express the shared and living experience of communion and celebration.

Where this view of the matter is taken, the Classical Pentecostal doctrine of the 'second blessing' of 'baptism in the Spirit' has clearly been very considerably qualified. How far such qualification should go is admittedly a much debated point. Leaving aside the criticisms of the doctrine from those outside the movement,[21] we find some of its members critical of talk of 'baptism in the Spirit',[22] but others both within and without arguing for its retention in some sense.[23] This raises all the complexities of sacramental theology, and especially of the nature and significance of baptism in water, as well as the exegetical question of what the scattered references in the New Testament to 'baptism in the Spirit' actually mean. These cannot be pursued here, but to those who do not themselves belong to any branch of the charismatic movement, the position advanced by Smail may well seem sound and sensible. He refuses to lay down any 'law' of what constitutes 'baptism in the Spirit' not even 'a law of tongues', but insists that what really matters is 'that God the' Holy Spirit is working in people with a love and power and freedom they have not previously known.'[24] If this is so, then the stock criticism of Pentecostalism may perhaps be stood on its head. Is it not so much that Pentecostalism in both its forms interprets the gifts of the Spirit too narrowly (though it may well be in some danger of doing that), but that non-charismatic Christianity may be insufficiently open to the movement of the Spirit on experiential levels other than those that have been safely institutionalised, sacramentalised, intellectualised, or otherwise comfortably domesticated in the household of faith?

> Father of light, from whom every good gift comes,
> send your Spirit into our lives
> with the power of an irresistible wind,
> and by the flame of your wisdom
> open the horizon of our minds.
> Loosen our tongues to sing your praise
> in words beyond the power of speech,
> for without your Spirit it is not given to man
> to raise his voice in words of peace
> or announce the truth that Jesus is Lord.[25]

CHAPTER NINE

SPIRIT, SELF, AND WORLD

'Spirit' in Wheeler Robinson's description was bound up with the ideas of personality and of an essential affinity between God and ourselves. Two questions arise here. The first calls for clarification: what is actually *meant* by speaking of 'spirit' in God or man? Second—and now much more than definition is at stake—does it identify something *common* to God and man? What is the resemblance, affinity, or correlation implicit in the use of 'spirit' language in theology?

These are already suggested by the Old Testament's application of *ruach* to God and humans, by Paul's awareness of God's *pneuma* witnessing with ours, by Irenaeus' affirmation that it is only through participating in the Spirit of God that man becomes fully human in God's image. 'Spirit' as applied to God is also inevitably freighted with human meanings and associations. The implicit issues have, however, been brought into the open by the prominent role ascribed to 'spirit' in much theology and philosphy since the Enlightenment.

So too has a further matter. Especially in the stream of thought influenced by Hegelian Idealism, 'Spirit' and similar terms have been widely used as ontological categories, as labels for the nature of reality, or for a fundamental element or essential dimension of the constitution of the universe. So another question confronts us. What might such a Spirit have to do with the God of Christian faith, or with the Holy Spirit? Can such conceptions assist in tackling the theological problem of God's nature and relation to the world?

1. Spirit in Man

A major influence on substantial theological reflection in this century has been Kierkegaard's equation of the spirit with the self, and his definition of the self as a relation to oneself and will to be oneself that disclose the self's transcendent ground.[1] Behind this lie on the one hand the thought of Augustine, on the other that of Dialectical Idealism in the style of Schelling and Hegel. From Augustine derive the sense of the triple structure of the human person, the understanding of the person as existing in relation rather than as an atomistic individual substance, and the sense that man is determined and directed by an inherent striving towards God, a striving that is somehow, albeit confusedly and obscurely, present in his inmost relation to himself.[2] Idealism breathed fresh life into these patterns by applying them to the dialectical movement of Spirit through its self-posited opposite to its own absolute realisation. Kierkegaard in turn set out to destroy Idealism, to force down admiring eyes from dizzy contemplation of the transcendental synthesis of Spirit and the world to the lonely promontory of the self where each individual stands isolated and utterly exposed to the overwhelming presence of eternity. Nevertheless, it was from the Idealist armoury that he wrested many of his categories and methods of argument, including those that chiefly concern us here.

At the risk of considerable simplification—and certainly without pretending to reproduce the whole sweep of Kierkegaard's penetrating insight—we must attempt to summarise his essential perceptions. The truest self-awareness necessarily involves a sense of the self as both subject and object of that awareness. This in turn points to a third term in which the two are united; and that is the relation to oneself which then emerges as the key to the very nature of the self as such. The self exists in self-realistion; it consists in the capacity to bridge the subject/object distinction, not by *merging* the two sides, but by *relating* them. Both the moment of otherness and that of the living, acting relation are inherent in what is to be a self. Further, as the self experiences itself, not simply as constituting itself as a self by its own power or choice, but as already being inescapably *endowed* (whether it will or not) with selfhood, this self-relation points yet further beyond, to Another by whom the self is established and to whom it is related. When, then, *spirit* is defined in terms of *self*, this means that spirit is to be understood in terms of relation, of meeting with otherness, of the identity of the self as the dynamic of self-relation, and of the relation of the self-related and other-related self to God.

One central fibre in this strand of thought is drawn out further by Martin Buber:

> Spirit in its human manifestation is man's response to his You ... it is the response to the You that appears from the mystery and addresses us from the mystery... Spirit is not in the I, but between I and You. It is not like the blood that circulates in you, but like the air in which you breathe. Man lives in the spirit when he is able to respond to his You... It is solely by virtue of his power to relate that man is able to live in the spirit.[3]

Spirit as the power of relation between the 'I' and the 'You' transcends the confines of the self as ego; yet precisely as such power to relate, it is of the essence of that self. There are thus two dimensions to the matter, and greater weight may be laid proportionally on the one or on the other. We may on the one hand stress the innate and inherent striving towards 'the other', 'the universal' or 'the transcendent', this may be treated as constitutive of man's humanity, and it may be said that in this respect, as one who essentially reaches after self-transcendence, man *is* 'spirit'. This gathers up a recurrent motif in the whole tradition of idealistic philosophy from Plato onwards, and is also directly connected with what we earlier described as the *'caritas* idealism' of medieval theology.[4] It is well expressed by George Thomas.

> The spiritual activity of an individual is that which is directed towards *universal* truth and value. It is by his identification of himself with the universal that a person enters the spiritual life. The reason for this lies in that capacity for 'self-transcendence' which is the glory of mind. The most profound thing in Plato's theory of love is his statement that it indicates at once a defect of being on the

part of the soul and an aspiration to overcome that defect by seeking to possess the perfection it lacks. Similarly the Scholastics hold that, though the human soul is finite, it has an aspiration that can be filled with nothing short of the infinite. Spirit involves a kind of union of the individual with the universal.[5]

Alternatively, however, one may insist that the 'spirit' thus described is *more* than the self, refuse to identify the self simply as 'spirit', and choose rather to say that man may *have* (but not actually *be*) spirit insofar as he is opened up to participate in it. This approach has affinities with the teaching of Luther and the Reformation rather than with that of ancient or modern idealistic thought.[5a] It has more recently been pursued, with echoes of Kierkegaard by Emil Brunner, and even more radically, by Karl Barth. Brunner puts it like this:

> Man can be person because and in so far as he has spirit. Personal being is 'founded' in the spirit; the spirit is, so to speak, the substratum, the element of personal being. But what is spirit?... God *is* spirit, man *has* spirit... The spirit of man is not to be understood from below but 'from above'... We claim that this final point of reference, for which and from which our spirit as spirit exists, is the God who reveals himself to us in his Word. And, more than this, it is the Spirit of God who reveals himself to us in his Word, and in it creates us as spirit. This is the point from which we must start if we wish to understand 'the spirit in general' or 'the spiritual'. If even the philosophical concept of spirit is not purely psychological but one that can only be understood in 'transcending', this is still more true of the theological concept.[6]
>
> The natural man is always either an Idealist or a Materialist; an Idealist who regards his spirit as part of the divine Spirit; a Materialist, who, owing to his corporeal nature, regards himself merely as a 'more highly developed animal', and denies his higher destiny... The spirit ... is that aspect of human nature by means of which man can perceive his divine destiny, and, knowing and recognising

this, can receive it ... The spirit receives the Word of God.[7]

With the proviso that the human spirit is to be understood 'from above' as answering to the Word and Spirit of God rather than 'from below' as a spark flying upwards, Brunner was nevertheless still willing to speak of man as 'body and spirit' or as 'body-soul-spirit'. Barth went a step further, virtually disposing of all idea of a distinct 'human spirit'.

In an extended discussion in his *Church Dogmatics* III/2 §46.2, 'The Spirit as Basis of Soul and Body', Barth began by stressing, like Brunner, that man *has* (rather than *is*) spirit, and that this 'means that he is grounded, constituted and maintained by God as the soul of his body.' (p. 344) 'This relation and fellowship cannot proceed from man himself, for God is his Creator... The Spirit is identical with God.' (p. 356) Further—and here the contrast with Brunner really becomes apparent—'Spirit in his being *ab extra* is neither a divine nor a created something, but an action and attitude of the Creator in relation to his Creation. We cannot say that Spirit is, but that he takes place as the divine basis of this relation and fellowship. Spirit is thus the powerful and exclusive meeting initiated by God between Creator and creature.' (p. 356) So,

> Man has Spirit. By putting it this way we describe the Spirit as something that comes to man, something not essentially his own but to be received and actually received by him, something that totally limits his constitution and thus totally determines it. As he is man and the soul of his body, he has Spirit. We must perhaps be more precise and say that he is, as the Spirit has him. Man has Spirit, as one who is possessed by it. Although it belongs to the constitution of man, it is not, like soul and body, and as a third thing alongside them, a moment of his constitution as such. It belongs to his constitution in so far as it is its superior, determining and limiting basis. (p. 354)[8]

Barth does not mean this to apply only to the believer, but to the constitution of man as human. Even 'the natural man also lives in the same way,' (p. 359) in dependence on the creative presence of God's Spirit. Without it, 'man cannot in any sense be man, nor in any sense soul of his body... In this sense, Spirit is the *conditio sine qua non* of the being of man as soul of his body.' (p. 359) All humans are held in being by the immediate relationship grounded on God's side in the event which is the Holy Spirit. So, indeed, is all created reality (p. 359).

By contrast with Brunner and Barth, positions more of the first type have been adopted in particular by Roman Catholic thinkers seeking to develop their own form of theocentric anthropology in dialogue with post-Kantian thought. An outstanding instance is the enormously influential Karl Rahner. His first major book, *Spirit in the World*,[9] saturated with Rahner's subtle (and heady) blend of Thomism with Heideggerian Existentialism, distilled as a transcendental anthropology, 'uses a Thomistic metaphysics of knowledge explained in terms of transcendental and existential philosophy to define man as that essence of absolute transcendence towards God insofar as man in his understanding and interpretation of the world respectfully "pre-apprehends" towards God.'[10] Its conclusion, 'Man as Spirit in the World' (pp. 406-408), sums up his view:

> ... strictly speaking, the first-known, the first thing encountering man, is not the world in its 'spiritless' existence, but the world—itself—as transformed by the light of the spirit, the world in which man sees himself. The world as known is always the world of man, is essentially a concept complementary to man. And the last-known, God, shines forth only in the limitless breadth of the pre-apprehension, in the desire for being as such by which every act of man is borne, and which is at work not only in his ultimate knowledge and in his ultimate decisions, but also in the fact that the free spirit becomes, and must become, sensibility in order to be spirit, and thus exposes itself to the whole destiny of this earth. Thus man encounters himself when he finds himself in the world and when he asks about God; and when he asks about his essence he always finds himself already in the world and on the way to God. He is

both of these at once, and cannot be one without the other...

Insofar as we ask about the world known by man, the world and the man asking are already placed in question all the way back to their absolute ground, to a ground which always lies beyond the boundaries within man's grasp, beyond the world. Thus every venture into the world shows itself to be borne by the ultimate desire of the spirit for absolute being; every entrance into sensibility, into the world and its destiny, shows itself to be only the coming to be of a spirit which is striving towards the absolute. Thus man is the midpoint suspended between the world and God, between time and eternity, and this boundary line is the point of his definition and his destiny...

Thus for Rahner, man is quintessentially spirit, for spirit is nothing other than the subject whose very nature impels him to reach out to experience, act and know, who finds himself by engaging with his world, and in the process consciously or unconsciously seeks after the unknown yet 'pre-apprehended' ground and horizon alike of his world and of himself, the encompassing mystery of absolute being, which is God. This is not of course in any way to identify man's spirit with God's Spirit; it is to distinguish the two, and to treat man's spirit as his identity as a striver after the Absolute but in that sense and 'from below' to present it as man's dimly-perceived but really existing directedness towards God.

The difference between Barth and Rahner does not lie chiefly in their understanding of 'spirit', for both speak of it as defining man as man, and as involving his relation to God. It is in the different conceptions of that relation, which in turn are reflected in their presentation of it. Rahner works, as it were, 'up' and 'in' from 'spirit in the world' to God's concrete revelation in the world in Jesus Christ (p. 408). Barth travels 'out' in the light of that revelation and traces a movement 'down' in the Spirit by which man is constituted as 'body and soul'. So Rahner focuses on a movement of man towards God, Barth on a movement of God towards man; Rahner speaks of man as *being* spirit, Barth of him as *receiving* it; Rahner presents man as the seeker after God; Barth as the one whom God has already found.

In Barth's support it could be argued that to talk of a distinct human spirit risks breaking off prematurely the thought that spirit constitutes *relation* rather than merely *orientation*, and that it raises the further problem of the connection between this spirit and God's[11]—a problem which the category of Spirit itself cannot resolve in the way Barth's approach enables because for him Spirit *is* meeting and relation between God and creature. On Rahner's side it can be urged that Barth's position amounts in the end to a denial of man's independence and freedom because of a one-sided understanding of the God-man relation,[12] and also that without some more full-blooded idea of the human spirit, talk of God in terms of Spirit risks becoming abstract and empty. This was the view of Paul Tillich, developed most fully in the fourth part of his *Systematic Theology*, 'Life and the Spirit'.[13]

> Spirit can be defined as the actualization of power and meaning in unity. Within the limits of our experience this happens only in man... Man, in experiencing himself as man, is conscious of being determined in his nature by spirit as a dimension of his life. This immediate experience makes it possible to speak symbolically of God as Spirit and of the divine Spirit... no doctrine of the divine Spirit is possible without an understanding of spirit as a dimension of life. (p. 111)

Tillich's position is not, however, identical with Rahner's. The points made here reflect the distinctive pattern of his own theological system, which may not unjustly be regarded as the most brilliant sustained endeavour in the last generation to crystallize the fruits of Idealism and its offshoot, the 'philosophy of life' that flourished in the late nineteenth and early twentieth centuries, in a Christian theology of the Spirit and of God as Spirit. In some respects the fourth part of the *Systematic Theology* is the culmination of the whole, and we shall return to it again in the last chapter in connection with the question of the Trinity. Here it is his understanding of the human spirit that must be briefly sketched.

'Life'—a term which he prefers to 'Process' (p. 11)—is a *universal* concept covering all that is (p. 12), but it has several 'dimensions': inorganic, vegetable, animal, psychological, followed by spirit and history. Each arises out of a 'constellation of conditions' (p. 25) in the previous one, but is qualitatively distinct and constitutes a fresh multidimensional unity. Spirit is the dimension of personal subjects capable of cognitive and moral activity (pp. 17–18), and so transcends the merely psychological.

The actualisation of Life is always ambiguous because it combines essential and existential elements, and the existential involves estrangement from essential unity with the ground of being (pp. 30–32). This is reflected in three functions which may be traced in every dimension (and not only in that of spirit): self-integration, self-creativity, and self-transcendence, which are always threatened by disintegration, destruction, and profanization (*ibid.*). In the dimension of spirit these functions generate respectively morality, culture, and religion. In religion, the function of self-transcendence in the dimension of self-aware spirit, consciousness of Life's ambiguity leads to the quest for unambiguous life, for which there are 'three main symbols ... Spirit of God, Kingdom of God, and Eternal Life.' (p. 107)

Thus far, in accordance with his 'method of correlation',[14] Tillich has been developing the question opened up by analysis of the nature and ambiguities of Life. The answer cannot, however, be produced by man, nor by the description of his search, but solely 'through the creative power of the Spiritual Presence' (p. 112), the theme of his second main section (pp. 111–161). 'The Spirit, a dimension of finite life, is driven into successful self-transcendence ... grasped by something ultimate and unconditional ... it remains what it is, but at the same time it goes out of itself under the impact of the divine Spirit. "Ecstasy" is the classical term for this state of being grasped by the Spiritual Presence.' (p. 112) It is experienced *fragmentarily* and *anticipatorily* yet *unambiguously* (pp. 138–141) in the 'transcendent union' which 'appears within the human spirit as the ecstatic movment which from one point of view is called "faith", from another, "love".' (p. 129) Faith is 'the state of being *grasped* by the transcendent unity of unambiguous life—it embodies love as the state of being *taken into* that transcendent unity ... faith logically precedes love, although in actuality neither can be present without the other.' (p. 129) This makes it possible to resolve the long-standing controversy between Roman Catholics and Protestants about the relation of faith and love:

> We have already indicated that faith logically precedes love, because faith is, so to speak, the human reaction to the Spiritual Presence's breaking into the human spirit ... This view affirms Luther's statement that faith is receiving and nothing but receiving. At the same time, the Catholic-Augustinian. emphasis on love is asserted with equal strength, by virtue of the insight into the essential inseparability of love and faith in the participation in the transcendent unity of unambiguous life. In this view, love is more than a consequence of faith, albeit a necessary one; it is one side of the ecstatic state of being of which faith is the other. A distortion of this relation occurs only if the acts of love are understood as conditioning the act by which the Spiritual Presence takes hold of man. The Protestant principle—that in relation to God everything is done by God—remains the weapon against such a distortion. (p. 135)

The repeated phrase, 'transcendent unity', offers the key to Tillich's distinctive arrangement of the ideas rather differently organised in the others we have considered. He does not define 'spirit' in terms of 'self-transcendence', for that is a function in *every* dimension of Life. 'Spirit' is understood rather as *unifying within the human dimension*. It 'transcends the duality of body and mind ... It is the all-embracing function in which all elements of the structure of being participate.' (Vol. I, p. 250) Therefore it also supplies 'the symbolic material which is used in the symbols "divine Spirit" or "Spiritual Presence".' (p.

111) On the other hand, the divine Spirit is not another 'dimension' in the same *metaphorical* sense of the 'dimensions of Life': it *could* be described *symbolically* as 'the dimension of depth' in which 'all dimensions are rooted and negated and affirmed', but this would be confusing and should be avoided (p. 113). It is the *transcendent* unity for which the human spirit in its unifying character supplies the symbol. 'Transcendent' here affirms what Tillich calls 'the Protestant principle' and underlines the priority of faith over love; 'unity' echoes the 'Catholic-Augustinian emphasis on love' as the necessary obverse of faith, or what elsewhere he was fond of calling 'Catholic substance' (p. 6). Beyond that, Spirit, thus understood, is the 'inclusive symbol' for the divine life itself: 'God as Spirit is the ultimate unity of both power and meaning.' (Vol. I, p. 250)

Whether Tillich's resolution of the ecumenical disagreement can succeed depends on the solidity of its basis in his whole system—about which perhaps few today would be highly confident. Later we shall have some comment to make on it. For the present, the material presented from him and others (including Wheeler Robinson in the previous chapter) may serve at least to introduce the stock of ideas that have been much employed in recent theological reflections upon 'spirit' in God and in man, and illustrate the diversity of patterns in which they can be set.

2. *Spirit in the World*
That stock of ideas has also been drawn upon by philosophies envisioning a wider dynamic of Spirit in the world of nature and history. Whether the panoramic philosophies of Spirit, Life, Being or Process that have been spun out since Hegel can be made fruitful for theology has, however, proved somewhat contentious. They can indeed seem vulnerable on several scores.

There is, for example, the suspicion commonly voiced by more empiricist philosophers that Idealism in every ancient or modern form generates and feeds upon the illegitimate projection upon the universe at large of conceptions properly relevant only to man and his conscious experience. Again, it is hard to overlook the political menace of claims to detect and follow the inevitable movement of History—a menace which one prominent critic has attributed to tendencies lurking in idealist thought from Plato onwards.[15] On a more mundane level, it is naturally easy to sympathise with such complaints as one struggles with convoluted accounts of Spirit poured out by writers so apparently intoxicated by it that comparison with glossolalia springs unforced to mind.

Theology here also has its own questions to face. How far can such all-embracing metaphysical systems be validly employed in its own work? It is one thing to appropriate ideas, insights or concepts that help to express and illuminate the Gospel, but quite another to abdicate in favour of a philosophy that proposes to lay down what theology really ought to be about, and how it must define and describe it. The sense of danger is scarely lessened when one observes how some forms of Idealism issued in virtual pantheism, or in the reduction of God to a purely immanent Spirit working through the evolution of the cosmos.[16]

These warnings must be heeded; but there is another side. To leave matters here could easily serve to entrench a twofold isolation of theology from the rest of human experience and understanding, and of man from the wider realm of nature. Such dichotomies are venerable, prevalent, and multifarious in manifestation. One example in theology is the inclination, characteristic of deism but by no means only indulged there, so sharply to emphasise the otherness of God that he is understood to stand in no real relation to his creation, or to have only to do with the inner life of man at the tangential point of encounter between time and eternity, or to be uniformly related to the universe as a whole in a fashion that excludes the possibility of his incarnation because 'the scandal of particularity' it would involve militates aginst his universal concern.[17]

The root of the trouble here does not merely lie in the theological assumption as such. It has a further ground in the underlying pattern of thinking by which it is moulded and which can take such a firm hold that its theological expression is acquiesced in as if it were elementarily self-evident. That pattern is itself impressed upon us by the duality of mind and body, which easily issues in the presumption of an unbridgeable gulf between matter and mind, nature and spirit, and in the projection of an analogous dualism upon the world and God. Proper awareness of otherness, duality and distinction is subtly transformed into the dubious proposition of an absolute separation.

Against such pervasive dualism, the concept of spirit proffers the lens to focus a radically different perception. One of the primary aims of the Idealist dialectic was precisely to vanquish such dichotomies between subject and object, self and world, God and nature, not by negating real distinctions, but by tracing the third moment of encounter and interaction that both presupposes distinction and enables the bridging of the divide in a reconciling movement of mutual participation and indwelling. Implicit in all the descriptions of spirit as the unity of man as body and soul, as man's relation to his world, as his personal meeting and engagement with his 'You', as his original and ultimate orientation towards God—descriptions which all echo Augustine's motif of the *vinculum caritatis*—is that it is the very nature of spirit to make possible, indeed to consist in, such a meeting, relating and uniting of the really distinct and 'other'.

John Taylor's *Go-Between God*[18] takes up this theme. God's Spirit is his capacity to involve himself with and participate in what is other than himself—to call it into being, set it in motion, endow it with form and meaning, spontaneity and freedom, life and consciousness, emotion and understanding, and so to entice and evoke responsive awareness of his presence. His Spirit *is* his reaching out to ground and engage with his creation, a reaching out which is at the same time the inner depth and energy of creation's answer, the infinitely mysterious 'beyond' that is yet 'in the midst', the transcendence in which (without abandoning or surrendering it) he can and does make himself present and call us into his own presence. This brings us to the vision not only of man's but of nature's indwelling by the divine Spirit, a vision which, as in Hopkins' splendid lines, also draws out a cry of protest against the alienation of man from his world:

> The world is charged with the grandeur of God.
> It will flame out, like shining from shook foil;
> It gathers to a greatness, like the ooze of oil
> Crushed. Why do man then now not reck his rod?
> Generations have trod, have trod, have trod;
> And all is seared with trade; bleared, smeared with toil;
> And wears man's smudge and shares man's smell: the soil
> Is bare now, nor can foot feel, being shod.
>
> And for all this, nature is never spent;
> There lives the dearest freshness deep down things;
> And though the last lights off the black West went
> Oh, morning, at the brown brink eastward, springs—
> Because the Holy Ghost over the bent
> World broods with warm breast and with ah! bright
> wings.[19]

In a recent article,[20] Jürgen Moltmann has underscored the contrast between this sense of presence, deeply rooted in the mystical tradition, and the simple disjunction between creation and Creator. Of the mystical theologians he observes,

> ... we can find in many of them a pantheistic vision of the world in God and God in the world. 'All is one, and one is all in God', says the *Theologia Germanica*, while for the poet monk Ernesto Cardenal the whole of nature is nothing but 'tangible, materialised divine love', 'reflection of his beauty' and 'full of love-letters to us'. Certainly the mystical theologians recognise the Old Testament doctrine of creation as maintained in the dogmatics of the Church. But for their vision of the *world as from God* they prefer the images of 'outpouring' and 'flowing', of the 'spring' and the 'fountain', of the 'sun' and its 'shining'. And for their vision of the *world in God* they speak of 'returning home', of 'entering', of 'submerging' and 'dissolving'. In terms of the history of thought, this is the neoplatonic language whicn

speaks of the emanation of all things from the One and All, and their return to it. In terms of theology, however, it is the language of *pneumatology*. (pp. 517–518)

Is this not, however, to dissolve away the distinction between Creator and creation, to substitute pantheism for the doctrine of creation itself? Are the mystical theologians even consistent in apparently affirming both? Moltmann recognises the challenge and proceeds to meet it:

By contrast to the world of creation and the historical 'works' of God, the Holy Spirit is 'poured out' upon all flesh (Joel 3.1ff; Acts 2.16ff), 'into our hearts' (Rom. 5.5)... In the history of the Holy Spirit a different kind of divine presence is made known from that in the original creation... This history of the Spirit that is poured out upon all flesh, and this new world that is glorified in God, are what the mystical theologians mean with their neoplatonic-sounding doctrine...

Herein lies a new and specifically Christian vision of reality which is stamped by faith in the *incarnation* of the Son of God and the experience of the *indwelling* of the Spirit of God. The ecclesiastical reiteration of the doctrine of creation in the jahwistic and priestly writings in Genesis cannot be regarded as a creative achievement of Christian theology. This understanding of creation can be Christian or non-Christian. In it is conveyed a distance between Creator and creature which does not correspond to the Christian experience of God. If it is true that the Israelite doctrine of creation was a reflex of Israel's experience of the Exodus, then the Christian doctrine of creation must be a reflex of Christianity's experience of Christ and the Spirit. From a theological standpoint the 'pantheism' of the mystics was not a particularly successful step in this direction; but it was nonetheless a step. (pp. 518–519).

While it is more than doubtful whether all the Christian mystics were as clear about the ground of their vision as Moltmann suggests we need to be, he is surely right to map out the logic of the situation as he does. It is not a matter of having to choose between creation and pantheism, between absolute dualism and dissolution of the distinction between God and the world, but of the radically new orientation alike of vision and of understanding enabled, indeed demanded by the incarnation, and consequently by participation in the Spirit poured out on and through Jesus Christ, the Spirit in which all things are from God and toward him.

Just here, however, a further question is raised by Moltmann's sharp contrast between 'the original creation' and 'this new world that is glorified in God', between the 'historical works of God' and the Spirit 'poured out upon all flesh'. This rightly makes everything pivot upon the incarnation, the gift of the Spirit, the new creation. But it *could* also suggest that the Spirit thus poured out was not present in the world before, and even that the vision of the 'world in God' is, properly speaking, 'eschatological' in the extreme 'gnostic' sense that it does not really have to do with *this* material world at all. A rather different conclusion is, however, suggested by Moltmann's comparison of the Christian and Israelite doctrines of creation. The experience of the Exodus did not issue in the conviction that Yahweh was Creator simply in the sense that he had brought Israel out of Egypt, but that he who had brought Israel out of Egypt had thereby manifested himself in the salvific act as Creator *in the beginning* of the heavens and the earth. The Exodus both actualised and disclosed the intention and nature of the Creator. Similarly, the author of the Fourth Gospel proclaimed *the man* Jesus as the one who *in the beginning* was the Word, while Col. 1.15ff hymns him as 'Firstborn of all creation... Firstborn from the dead'—and these two affirmations are concentric. *What ever was is now achieved,* and *it is because it is now achieved that it ever was.* Paradoxical though that must sound, it is the logic of 'Before Abraham was I am.' If the incarnation is seen (as it must be if taken seriously), not merely as an episode *within history and time,* but as real *for God,* then history and time themselves have present within them in Jesus Christ their beginning and end.[21] Even before his coming, the Spirit was moving through and to him, and if in one sense it was not given, in another it was already active. 'The original creation' itself is to be set in the light of the incarnation and the Spirit's presence, and not merely contrasted with them.

In that case, without at all abandoning the centrality of the incarnation or the reality of the history of 'before' and 'after' which Moltmann rightly underlines, we may yet look for echoes and anticipations, not only in earlier history but in the world of nature, of the Spirit's working in and through Christ. At the same time, we may also be alert to possible analogies between 'matter' and 'mind', which could help to break down the absolute dichotomy between them and open up a wider (though necessarily differentiated) field of the Spirit's action.

Hence the advances of science in the last few generations have been greeted by many Christian thinkers as opening mines of rich promise yet undreamt of when the older Idealism spoke of a movement of Spirit in nature. Fascinating vistas have been disclosed by the biological track of evolution, by cosmology stretching back the perspective to the very beginnings of the universe, by the shaking of the foundations of classical Newtonian physics and their reconstruction in the light of relativity and quantum theory. The vast field of theological and related writing on these themes cannot be explored here,[22] and it must also be admitted that there are as many differences as similarities between, for example, the cosmic-spiritual vision of Teilhard de Chardin,[23] the neo-Thomism of Eric Mascall,[24] the personalism of Karl Heim,[25] the view of an evolving 'sacramental universe' of Arthur Peacocke,[26] the application of Process philosophy and theology to the discoveries of biology by Charles Birch,[27] and the profound probing of Thomas Torrance into the theological and scientific encounter with reality.[28] But these and others have laid weight in various ways on ideas of relationality, spontaneity, rational structure, purpose, and awareness, and insisted that, however anthropomorphic they may seem, it is impossible to make sense of the material universe now opening before our eyes without appealing to some of them. The pattern of reality at the subatomic level seems more to resemble a movement of creative thought than a jostling jumble of inert bits and pieces; the emergence from matter of life, awareness and mind invites comparison with the creation of a living work of art or the composing of a symphony rather than either an haphazard series of accidents or the running of a pre-programmed machine; the rationality of the world so awesomely evoking and aswering to the rationality of the mind exploring it suggests that even such 'distinctively human' characteristics as identity, relation, perception, intellection and intention are not alien products of an indifferent universe, but both correspond to a transcendent creative purpose, and represent the flowering of potentialities already latent or even realised in analogous fashion lower down the evolutionary scale—perhaps, indeed, right down at the very lowest levels. Certainly these claims are by no means either proven or undisputed;[29] but the accumulating evidence may well suggest that the sense of the whole creation as suffused with divine presence and purpose is by no means so outlandish as might at first appear.

Such a presence and purpose might not indeed be described by all these writers in terms of 'Spirit', let alone 'the Holy Spirit'. Yet it is surely of the Holy Spirit that their suggestions must remind the Christian theologian—not simply because of the influential understanding of 'spirit' as uniting and relating in the modern strands of thought we have followed, but because that understanding in turn takes us back to Augustine's relational interpretation of the Spirit, and, beyond him, to the source for all such interpretations, the sense of the indwelling in us of the Spirit of God which is the Spirit of Christ. Although Protestant theology has very often inclined to restrict the activity of the Spirit to the spiritual, psychological, moral or religious life of the individual (and Roman Catholic to locate it simply in the church), Calvin, at least in occasional brief hints saw matters differently, and managed to combine the experienced presence of the Spirit in us with awareness of its universal creative power. Discussing the deity of the Spirit in *Inst.* I.xiii.14, he argued

... that the Spirit of God was expanded over the abyss of shapeless matter ... shows not only that the beauty which the world displays is maintained by the invigorating power of the Spirit, but even before this beauty existed the Spirit was at work cherishing the confused mass... In this his divine majesty is clear. But ... the best proof to us is in our familiar experience. *For nothing can be more alien from a creature than the office which the Scriptures ascribe to him, and which the pious actually feel him discharging—his being diffused over all space, sustaining, invigorating and quickening all things, both in heaven and in earth.*[30]

Clearly, distinctions must then be drawn between, say, the presence of the Spirit in the whole fabric of the cosmos; in living beings; in man; in those who in faith and with the community of the church consciously participate in the mystery of the grace of God in Jesus Christ; in the consummation when God will be 'all in all' (1 Cor. 15.28). The classical schema of creation/redemption/consummation can be drawn upon here. So, too, may the images which supplied the titles for our historical chapters. As Lord and Lifegiver God's Spirit is God's mastery over chaos, his creative and sustaining power, his living energy which is the inner mystery of created life itself. As God's Love and God's Gift, it is the actualisation of God's own nature, expressed and achieved in our time and space, our world and history, in Jesus Christ, and reaching out through him to meet, claim and empower us in our human creatureliness as the children of God. As the Enlightener and Sanctifier, it is God's making of himself known to us in the face of Christ, and his renewing us in Christ's image. In each, a victory is won, and a promise declared. The creation is God's triumph, the establishing of being over non-being and nothingness, the framing of order against chaos, the enabling of a surging upward into light. In our own lives there is the fragmentary, anticipatory yet real victory of grace over sin, of mercy over judgment, of room over restriction, of consolation over desolation, of hope over despair. Both turn on the unique prevailing of light over darkness, of life over death, of acceptance over rejection, of affirmation over negation, when God himself once and for all both uttered and heard the cry, *Eloi, Eloi, lama sabachthani.* With the shattering of the tomb on the first Easter that cry was answered, the victory of the Creator proclaimed, and the promise written in the act of creation sealed. The unity of the Spirit was manifested as God's *own* self-consistency as Father and Son, Creator and Redeemer, and thereby also as the unbreakable bond between Creator and creation.

> Whither shall I go from thy Spirit?
>   Or whither shall I flee from thy presence?
> If I ascend to heaven, thou art there!
>   If I make my bed in Sheol, thou art there!
> If I take the wings of the morning
>   and dwell in the uttermost parts of the sea,
> Even there thy hand shall lead me,
>   and they right hand shall hold me.   (Ps. 139. 7–10)

CHAPTER TEN

FATHER, SON AND HOLY SPIRIT

The doctrine of the Trinity has not been our primary theme, but it has been impossible not to refer repeatedly to it. Nor could we very well conclude without noticing—albeit very briefly and selectively—some specifically trinitarian applications of the concepts introduced in the last chapters and relating them to the understanding of the Holy Spirit as the 'third person of the Trinity'. In addition, serious questions have been raised both about the meaning and validity of the classical trinitarian scheme and about the description of the Spirit as a divine 'person'.

1. Geoffrey Lampe and Paul Tillich

Several of these are laid before us in the rejection of trinitarianism by Geoffrey Lampe's recent *God as Spirit*.[1] Lampe's argument rests essentially on the identification of the Spirit as the immanent presence and activity of the transcendent God. He is not of course alone in wishing to cast the entire understanding of God in this kind of two-sided mould. Process Theology, for instance offers something similar, and at the same time gives fresh content to the transcendence/immanence scheme by distinguishing God's 'primordial' and 'consequent' natures. The first is the infinite wealth of the divine potentiality, the creative source of all being, luring it into activity, life and relationship with him. The second is God himself as he is conditioned and formed by his own universal relatedness, his com-present and com-passionate involvement in every minute event in the cosmic process. By and large, however, Process thought remains true to its Idealist ancestry, displaying the trade-mark of the universal threefold rhythm; it engages with science in a way that Lampe does not; and while it can be developed, as in Hartshorne's 'neo-classical theism', in the direction of a modified Unitarianism, it can also be opened out in trinitarian style, as by Norman Pittenger.[2] By contrast, while Lampe can sketch a broadly similar world-view (e.g. p. 207), and throughout treats 'spirit' as meaning 'active presence and relation', he betrays little sign of being profoundly influenced by any school of modern philosophy or theology, except in the sense that his positive views are those of a simplified Liberalism. They are spelt out especially in his closing chapter, 'God as Spirit and the Holy Spirit' (pp. 206–228).

'Theology pays too little attention, on the whole,' to the divine immanence (p. 206). The reason is the prevalence of the idea that God enters the world only 'by a kind of invasion from outside ... or, in the case of the Christ-event, a personal descent, from heaven into a "world below".' (p. 206) This is the heart of the matter, for Lampe proposes to replace the particular incarnation in Jesus Christ with the universal, immanent, creative presence of God as Spirit—a presence which was somehow decisively effective and manifest in Jesus (p. 228)—with 'God indeed becoming immanent in man in order that man may be moved to respond as a free son and so to achieve transcendence in union with God.' (p. 208) The Spirit is neither an 'impersonal influence' nor a 'divine entity or hypostasis which is a third person of the Godhead', but 'God himself, his personal presence, as active and related.' (p. 208)

This, which Lampe holds to be the authentic biblical understanding, was obscured by the patristic hypostatization of the Spirit as the third person in the Trinity, a development reflecting the preceding objectification of the man Jesus as the eternal Logos or Son (pp. 210 ff.). Lampe approves of this to the extent that it was 'entirely right to affirm that when we speak of "the Spirit of God" or "the Holy Spirit" we are referring to God himself,' (p. 219) but maintains that the doctrinal structure framed upon such concepts as 'generation', 'procession', 'person' and 'inner-trinitarian relations' was entirely artificial and wholly devoid of assignable meaning. No clear distinction could actually be drawn between the 'Son' and 'Spirit', 'generation' and 'procession', or indeed the separate divine activities ascribed to each person by the medieval theory of 'appropriations', which cut across the acknowledged principle that *opera trinitatis ad extra sunt indivisa*, 'the external workings of the Trinity are undivided', and thus revealed the incoherence and inconsistency of the whole pattern of thought.

Some of these criticisms as applying to the Augustinian and subsequent medieval Western doctrinal development resemble those of Karl Rahner,[3] who has diagnosed and rejected the separating-off of the 'immanent Trinity' from the 'economic Trinity' and from the doctrine of 'the One God' in Scholastic theology. Lampe's critique is, however, more sweeping than Rahner's because he avers that things went wrong far earlier than Rahner allows. So, while gladly echoing Rahner's warning against 'wild and empty conceptual acrobatics,' he adds, 'I do not, nevertheless, share his conviction that by going back to the elements of Christian experience we shall find . . . the Trinity itself, for I believe that the Trinitarian model is in the end less satisfactory for the articulation of our basic Christian experience than the unifying concept of God as Spirit.' (pp. 227–228)

Lampe's main contribution is perhaps to have made it crystal clear that an interpretation turning *solely* on the transcendence/immanence axis must drastically alter the substance as well as the form of Christian theology; for it dissolves away both Trinity and incarnation as utterly as either dualism or pantheism. Nor are his exegetical and historical arguments without serious flaws reflecting the questionable nature of his fundamental assumptions.[4] Yet he does force us to consider on what the doctrine of the Trinity is grounded, and how valid was its explication in the early church and subsequently.

Paul Tillich's approach is much more positive. He reaches the Trinity at the end of the fourth part of his *Systematic Theology*, so that it concludes the theological exposition of the doctrines of God, Christ and the Spiritual Presence contained in parts two to four,[5] for 'the trinitarian symbolism must be understood as an answer to the questions implied in man's predicament. It is the most inclusive answer and rightly has the dignity attributed to it in the liturgical practice of the church.' (p. 285) He identifies three motives for trinitarian thinking: 'first, the tension between the absolute and the concrete element in our ultimate concern; second, the symbolic application of the concept of life to the divine ground of being; and third, the threefold manifestation of God as creative power, as saving love, and as ecstatic transformation. It is the last of the three which suggests the symbolic names, Father, Son and Spirit; but without the two preceding reasons ... the last group would lead only into a crude mythology.' (p. 283)

Tillich lays special weight on the second factor, the symbolic identification of God as Life, which shows that the doctrine of the Trinity 'is neither irrational nor paradoxical but, rather, dialectical ... the trinitarian symbols ... reflect the dialectics of life, namely the movement of separation and reunion.' (p. 284) Hence 'the number three implied in the word "trinity,"' (p. 292) for it 'seems most probable that the three corresponds to the intrinsic dialectics of experienced life and is, therefore, most adequate to symbolize the Divine Life.' (p. 293) Yet 'all this is preparatory for the developed trinitarian doctrine in Christian theology which is motivated by the third basic reason ... the manifestation of the divine ground of being in the appearance of Jesus as the Christ.' (p. 285)

Just here, however, it can be asked how the second and third factors are connected, and, more particularly, what the place of Jesus Christ is in Tillich's system. That the system is triadic in its account of God, Christ and the Spiritual Presence as answering to the 'questions' of finitude, estrangement and ambiguity is clear; that pattern does also show a certain parallel to the triplicity of the 'symbol' of life; and 'the appearance of Jesus as the Christ' appears to be pivotal for the whole. Yet in what sense is it central? The question is sharpened by Tillich's handling of 'the Trinitarian Dogma' (pp. 286–291). There he strenuously defends the doctrine of the Logos, for 'it is impossible to develop a doctrine of the living God and of the creation without distinguishing the "ground" and the "form" in God, the principle of abyss and the principle of the self-manifestation... He who sacrifices the Logos principle sacrifices the idea of a living God, and he who rejects the application of this principle to Jesus as the Christ rejects his character as Christ.' (p. 288) Yet we cannot 'introduce into the Logos a finite individuality with a particular life history, conditioned by the categories of finitude,' or 'attribute to the eternal Logos in himself the face of Jesus of Nazareth or the face of "historical man" or of any particular manifestation of the creative ground of being ... the trinitarian manifestation of the divine ground is Christocentric for man, but it is not Jesu-centric in itself.' (p. 290)

In other words Jesus Christ is a *manifestation* of the Logos-principle *for us*, and the doctrine of the Trinity does not turn on him, nor chiefly articulate the network of relations in the Spirit between Christ and the Father, or between the Father, Christ and ourselves. It reflects the transcendent dynamics of the Divine Life, and only 'a radical revision of the trinitarian doctrine and a new understanding of the Divine Life and the Spiritual Presence' can make it possible again 'to say without theological embarrassment or mere conformity to tradition the great words, "In the name of the Father and the Son and the Holy Spirit."' (p. 292) Since the 'Spiritual Presence' is one of Tillich's primary terms for the Holy Spirit, it would seem that he is recommending a reworking of the Trinity from the angle of pneumatology, directly correlated with anthropology, and focused most centrally by the symbolic description of God as 'Spirit' and therefore as 'Life'.[6]

In broad outline, if not in every detail, this proposal reminds us of Wheeler Robinson's approach to God as Spirit. By comparison with Lampe, both preserve a great deal of the pattern of classical trinitarian teaching. Tillich's debt to Idealism and to the philosophy of Life enables him to affirm meaning hidden to Lampe in the divine triunity, and he also sets great store by the Logos christology which Lampe dismisses as illegitimate. Yet there remains a question whether the whole system is coherently integrated at the centre, whether such a pneumatological/anthropological approach supplies an adequate basis for christology, whether this doctrine of God stamped by the 'symbols' of Spirit and Life might not itself form, if not a 'crude', nevertheless a *speculative* 'mythology'. Could the doctrine of the Trinity be more radically focused on Jesus Christ himself than is apparent here?

2. Karl Barth

These questions can direct us to the distinctive and in many ways quite fresh approach to the Trinity pioneered by Karl Barth throughout his *Church Dogmatics*, and initially developed in his exposition of 'The Triune God' at the very beginning of his discussion of the nature of revelation.[7] For Barth, the doctrine of the Trinity is not a final synthesis or conclusion reached at the end of the systematic theological enquiry. Rather, the pattern of the divine triunity is constitutive throughout in every dimension. He does not mean by this that the doctrine as such is the starting-point for theology, for the only starting-point (and point of contintuing orientation) is the gracious mystery of God's revealing himself in and through Jesus Christ. Yet already there we are confronted with the trinitarian question because 'the Christian concept of revelation already includes within it the problem of the doctrine of the Trinity.' (p. 304) '*God* reveals Himself. He reveals Himself *through Himself*. He reveals *Himself* ... this subject God, the Revealer, is identical with His act in revelation and also with its effect.' (p. 296) 'Thus to the same God who in unimpaired unity is the Revealer, the revelation and the revealedness, there is also ascribed in unimpaired differentiation within Himself this threefold mode of being ... we are set before the problem of the doctrine of the Trinity.' (p. 299)

What Barth calls 'The Root of the Doctrine of the Trinity' (p. 304–333) is to be found in the statement, summing up the witness of Scripture, that 'God reveals Himself as the Lord.'

(p. 307) He expands this into the formula, 'Revelation in the Bible means the self-unveiling, imparted to men, of the God who by nature cannot be unveiled to men,' which can be analysed in three complementary ways (pp. 315–333) as meaning, *first*, that God 'becomes His own *alter ego*' (p. 316), takes 'temporal form' (p. 320), and 'differentiates Himself from Himself, being not only God the Father but also … God the Son' (p. 320); *second*, that even as the *deus revelatus*, God manifested, he remains in the mystery of his freedom the *deus absconditus*, God hidden (p. 321), 'the Father of the Son in whom He takes form … God who always, even in taking form in the Son, does not take form' (p. 324); *third*, that 'the historical event' (p. 325) of 'God's being revealed makes it a link between God and man' (p. 331) so that 'God reveals Himself as the Spirit … this self-disclosing unity, disclosing itself to men, of the Father and the Son.' (p. 332) The order, Son–Father–Spirit is important, for Barth insists that what is central and primary is the revelation in Jesus Christ: the deity of the second person of the Trinity is what opens up on the one hand the deity of the Father, on the other that of the Spirit (pp. 314–315). So he emphasises 'in the biblical witness to revelation the three elements of unveiling, veiling and impartation, or form, freedom and historicity, or Easter, Good Friday and Pentecost, or Son, Father and Spirit' as showing 'that revelation must indeed be understood as the root or ground of the doctrine of the Trinity' (p. 332). No other 'root' can be sought for, and especially not in any *vestigium trinitatis* in the created order (pp. 333–347), nor can Christian theology be properly directed to its concrete subject unless it is clear from the start that it is of *this* triune God that it has to speak (pp. 300–301).

Whatever might be said about some of the details of his argument, Barth does drive to the heart of the matter. That can admittedly be overlooked if we attend only to his handling of revelation or debate solely his particular interpretetation of the Trinity. What really matters is that these are both gathered up in a lively movement of theological reflection, guided and directed by 'Easter, Good Friday and Pentecost' by *Jesus Christ* as the manifestation of the *Father* meeting and engaging with us *in the Spirit*. That is the true matrix of the Christian doctrine of the Trinity. To it, Tillich points, but only ambiguously, while Lampe points only to one side. In Barth, by contrast, the trinitarian dogma is revitalised by the tapping of its primal spring. That releases it to become once more creatively constitutive in dogmatic theology, recentring the elements which in Tillich remain only arbitrarily associated. Here Barth made an enormous advance, and it is no accident that trinitarian theology has more recently flourished particularly where his influence has been felt. There are, however, two further aspects of his position that must be noticed as bearing directly on the Holy Spirit: (a) the general understanding of the divine triunity; and (b) his apparent leaning towards modalism.

(a) The general pattern is well outlined by the seven theses in which, towards the end of his *The Doctrine of the Trinity*,[8] Eberhard Jüngel sums up his own interpretation of Barth's teaching. These are somewhat abstractly formulated, but the material treated in our last chapters has paved the way for them and should help to make them comprehensible.

1. What may be known and said about God's being may only be known and stated from God's being-for-us.
2. The fact that what is to be known about God's being is made known to us from God's being, is based on the fact that God's being-for-us is event in Jesus Christ. This event is called revelation and as such is God's interpretation of himself.
3. God's being-for-us does not define God's being but certainly God in his being-for-us interprets his being.
4. Interpretation lives from that which is to be interpreted. As relational being God's being-for-us is the reiteration of God's self-relatedness in his being as Father, as Son and as Holy Spirit.
5. In reiteration that which is to be reiterated lets itself be known. In God's being-for-us God's being-for-himself makes itself known to us as a being which grounds and

makes possible God's being-for-us.

6. God's being corresponds to itself
   (a) in the event of God's self-relatedness: as the relation of Father, Son and Holy Spirit.
   (b) in the event of revelation: as the relation of God's being-for-us to God's being in the event of his self-relatedness.

   The correspondence-relation (b) derives its onto-logical power from the correspondence-relation (a). The correspondence-relation (a) constitutes the correspondence-relation (b).

7. This constituting is itself to be thought of as the power which is proper to the correspondence-relation (a), in which the *hidden* God is the God who *reveals* himself. God's being hidden and God's being revealed is, as relational being, a being in the power of becoming. (pp. 105–106)

This is in effect the application to God's 'being-for-himself' and 'being-for-us' of the dynamic and relational Kierkegaardian conception of the self. So Jüngel adds:

God's self-relatedness thus springs from the becoming in which God's being is ... a becoming out of the word in which God says 'Yes' to himself. But to God's affirmation of himself there corresponds the affirmation of the creature through God ... as this affirmation becomes event in the incarnation of God, God reiterates his self-relatedness in his relation to the creature, as revealer, as becoming revealed and as being revealed. This Christological relation to the creature is also a becoming in which God's being is. But in that God in Jesus Christ *became* man, he is as a creature exposed to perishing. Is God's being in becoming, here, a being unto death?

The witness of the New Testament answers this question with the message of the death and resurrection of Jesus Christ. The message witnesses that here, where God's being-in-becoming was swallowed up in perishing, the perishing was swallowed up in the becoming. Therewith it was settled that God's being *remains* a being in becoming. With his 'Yes' to man God remains in the event of the death of Jesus Christ true to himself as the triune God. In the death of Jesus Christ God's 'Yes', which constitutes all being, exposed itself to the 'No' of the nothing. In the resurrection of Jesus Christ this 'Yes' prevailed over the 'No' of the nothing. And precisely with this victory it was graciously settled why there is being at all, and not rather nothing. (pp. 107–108)

Nothing less is affirmed here than that the triune being of the God who affirms and relates to himself has gone forth into creaturely being in the incarnation, the death and resurrection of Jesus Christ, and, shining out there in the triple light of revelation, shows itself to be the ground of all being which, in Christ, God affirms and relates to himself. The triunity of God meshes with the incarnation and, beyond that, with the whole grounding of creation, bespeaking an engagement of God with what is other than himself yet more radical than that of which Process Theology seeks to speak.[9]

The range and power of this conception are quite breathtaking. Yet there are two possible dangers in drawing upon the Kierkegaardian understanding of the self to describe God as self-affirming and self-relating, and so also as other-affirming and other-relating. One would be to forget Barth's own warning against allowing any kind of *vestigium trinitatis* not merely to *interpret* but to *illustrate* (and so explain away) the mystery of God's revelation,[10] and to assume that the human self is self-evidently *the* key to the triunity of God. Another would be to allow the sheer suggestive and explanatory power of the analogy of the self-relating and self-affirming self surreptitiously to insinuate that God is adequately characterised as a kind of 'transcendent Self' or 'absolute Subject', a 'Super-self', like the human, raised to the power of infinity, and defined essentially as the lordly 'I' positing himself over against all that is not God. This would cancel the profoundest implications of the words just quoted by denying the authenticity of the divine involvement in and with the creation.

Jürgen Moltmann, who is equally concerned to affirm and interpret the engagement of the triune God with the world and its history, is particularly sensitive to this second danger. He directs attention to the eschatologically open 'trinitarian history of God' opening out from the cross and resurrection of Jesus.[11] Consequently, he stresses the *distance* opened up between the Father and the incarnate Son in Jesus' abandonment and cry of dereliction; and with this both opens up a larger inner space within the Trinity and assigns a more decisive and distinctive role to the Holy Spirit as the overcomer of that distance which at the same time drives towards God's future kingdom. Consistently with this, his most recent study[12] is sharply critical of the general tendency in modern Western theology to treat God as 'absolute Subject', and consciously follows the line of a 'social' understanding of the Trinity in which the triple identity of Father, Son and Holy Spirit will not be submerged in the single identity of God. As Barth is among those whom he here criticises, this can lead us on to the question of Barth's apparent modalism.

(b) Modalism? In line with the general Augustinian trend in the West, while Barth emphasises both the unity and the threefoldness within God, he tends to give effective priority to the former.[13] God's triple *reiteration of himself* is much more prominent than his *relation to himself*; the note of 'otherness' is more muted than that of 'self-expression'; tritheism is sensed to be a greater threat than Sabellianism. He is especially critical of the concept of divine 'persons', preferring the other ancient term 'mode of being'.[14] Further, the 'mode of being' of the Spirit as the event of the divine self-relating tends to reduce simply to the presence and action of the Father or of Christ. Consistently with this, he strenuously defends the *filioque* on quite traditional Western grounds.[15]

The direction in which Barth here seems to be pointing has been followed further by Hendrikus Berkhof in the closing section (pp. 115–121) of *The Doctrine of the Holy Spirit*.[16] He had previously argued (pp. 111–115) that the concept of 'person' was obscure when it was first introduced by Tertullian; that its questionability had been demonstrated by its Augustinian and scholastic reinterpretation as 'subsisting relation'; that it became even less suitable for trinitarian theology with Boethius' sixth century definition of *persona* as *individua substantia rationalis naturae*, 'an individual substance of a rational nature', and completely unusable with the rise in the last two centuries of the modern notion of 'personality' as an autonomous, self-conscious power. Today, he feels, 'We have even more reason to say farewell to the person-concept in pneumatology,' for, 'the word "Spirit" is basically a predicate to the nouns "God" and "Christ",' and, 'modern biblical theology has made it clear that in the New Testament the Spirit is the name for the exalted Christ acting in the world.' (p. 115)

> What we see before us in biblical revelation is a great divine movement, the movement of God as Spirit, moving toward the Son and out of the Son ... which urges us to utter three words: God–Christ–Spirit, or ... Spirit–Son–Father. These three names ... point to a movement of the one God, not to a static community of three persons. They are the description of an ongoing movement of condescendence, in which God reaches out ... in the Spirit of Christ. Then the Spirit leads man to Christ, and in Christ man finds God. So we must recognize a double movement: God stretches out his arm and his hand towards his fallen world and next draws man up toward himself...
>
> In all this God is Person, acting in a personal way, seeking a personal encounter. *The triune God does not embrace three Persons*; he himself is Person, meeting us in the Son and in his Spirit. *Jesus Christ is not a Person beside the Person of God*; in him the Person of God becomes the shape of a human person. *And the Spirit is not a Person beside the Persons of God and Christ.* In creation he is the acting Person of God, in re-creation he is the acting Person of Christ, who is no other than the acting Person of God. Therefore we must reject all

presentation of the Spirit as an impersonal force. The Spirit is Person because he is God acting as a Person. *He is a Person in relation to us, not in relation to God*; for he is the personal God himself in relation to us. (p. 116; our italics)

The first of these paragraphs is unexceptionable, but the second, especially the critical negations we have italicised, must provoke some puzzlement. What can it possibly mean to say that Jesus Christ is not a person beside the person of God? Berkhof's resounding affirmations suspiciously resemble Sabellianism, which could indeed acknowledge different forms of God's *outward* expression *in revelation*, but not a genuine *inner* differentiation *in being*, which could make place for an 'economic Trinity' but not for an 'immanent' triunity in God's own nature. Berkhof is aware of that difficulty, but the way in which he seeks to meet it, indeed to turn the tables, to trump the objection, effectively concedes it. He insists that 'the history of God's condescendence is not only a history for men but also a history within God himself. His movement is not outside of himself. He is himself involved in his own movement. He himself is the movement.' (p. 119) It is therefore adequate to speak of 'God's trinitarian extension in history' along the lines first proposed by Marcellus of Ancyra in the fourth century (pp. 119–121). It would appear that the ideas of 'double movement' and 'extension in history' can replace and express all that was validly intended by the doctrine of the Trinity; and both can also be taken to mean that God is a *single* 'subject', or 'Person'.

It would of course be wrong to accuse Barth of subscribing to Berkhof's proposal; for, as Jüngel's third thesis above makes clear, God is *in himself* what he is *towards us*, but these two ways of being are not simply identified: the second is grounded on the first, whereas in Berkhof's Marcellanism the first is collapsed into the second. Yet may that collapse itself signal an underlying danger in the preference for 'mode of being' over 'person'? That is, perhaps, what has led to Berkhof's curious remark about Jesus Christ. What preserves Moltmann's 'trinitarian history of God' from such modalism is

precisely his emphasis on the distinctness of the Son from the
Father, which in turn makes space to recognise and affirm the
distinctness of the Spirit. And in spite of Berkhof's views (here
resembling Lampe's as well as Barth's) concerning the
meaning of 'Spirit' in the Bible, closer attention to the
Scriptural material as outlined in our opening chapters
scarcely supports his conclusions. Whatever else may properly
be said about the logic of the term, it is a drastic simplification
to treat it as 'predicate' to the 'nouns' 'God' and 'Christ'.
Moltmann has grounds for his observation that if we really
start from the biblical witness we must begin with the three
'persons' involved in the history of Christ, and not with a
philosophical postulate of an absolute divine unity which
makes the threefoldness problematical from the outset[17]—and
also for his shrewd observation that the standard polemic
against tritheism (to which no Christian theologian has in fact
subscribed) commonly serves only to conceal one's own
modalism.[18] It is also no accident that Moltmann is
particularly concerned to achieve a reconciliation between
East and West on the matter of the *filioque*.[19] His distancing of
himself from the modalising tendencies of ancient and modern
Western trinitarianism is certainly one of the prerequisites for
any such rapprochement.

3. Final Reflections

Space does not permit us to take this all too summary survey
any further, but enough has perhaps been said to introduce
questions which are very much alive at the present time. We
may however try to draw some threads together by a few
observations on three central and inter-related topics: (i) the
basis and significance of the doctrine of the Trinity itself; (ii)
the understanding of the Holy Spirit as the 'third' 'person' or
'hypostasis'; (iii) the *filioque*.

(i) The Doctrine of the Trinity

As so far we have referred somewhat critically to over-hasty
rejection or dubious interpretation of the doctrine, we must
now add on the other side that this does not imply that the

classical teaching is quite unproblematic, or that there is no
basis for criticisms of the kind we have briefly touched upon.
The general difference in approach between East and West is a
salutary warning against imagining that all is already settled,
or that our choice is simply between good, orthodox
trinitarianism and sundry versions of heresy which are thereby
automatically condemned. Nor should we forget that none of
the councils of the early, undivided church undertook a formal
definition of the Trinity as such. Reflection through the
centuries has been formed and guided less by *dogmata*,
authoritative definitions, than by *theologoumena*, theological
opinions and judgments of an essentially provisional
character.

So far as the early patristic development is concerned, it
must be admitted that the teachings of, say, the fourth and
fifth centuries concerning the Father, Son and Spirit, cannot
simply be read off the pages of the Bible. Yet, as we have tried
to show in our earlier chapters, this does not mean that the
development can properly be dismissed with an air of
patronising superiority as 'unbiblical'. The trinitarian
problem is posed by the New Testament itself, and the
attempts of the fathers to rearticulate in debate with the
questions arising in their day the profoundest implications of
its witness must be measured by their adequacy to that
purpose and nor merely by the shallowness of a proof-text
comparison with biblical statements. Further, it is only to the
extent that we too enter into a similar engagement with that
witness and with the questions they were compelled to address
that we can either understand or make serious judgments
about what they found themselves having to say. In that
process, we need to be aware of the conscious or unconscious
standpoint we are ourselves adopting, and seek to draw it into
the same critical light. Awareness both of the alternative
positions that the early church found itself driven to reject, and
of the destinations at which we ourselves might land were we
to depart from its conclusions, can itself become a powerful
inducement to look more favourably upon its achievement.

On this ground, we would certainly not agree, for example,

with all of Lampe's criticisms. We would however not only accept but strongly maintain that from the fourth century onwards the doctrine of the Trinity was in grave danger of taking off into the air, of becoming a mystic formula concerning the inner life of God which could and did increasingly detach itself—especially in the West—from the history of Christ and the Spirit at work in human life. This stage was certainly reached by the high Middle Ages. It was reflected in the Eastern distinction between the *essence* and *energies* of God; and in the West, as Karl Rahner has shown, in the separating off of the 'economic' from the 'immanent' Trinity, of the Trinity of salvation from the Trinity in God's own being, and also of the treatise *De Deo Trino* from that *De Deo Uno* in the great scholastic systems—which also, by giving the latter the priority, treated the being of the One God as a (straightforward) truth of natural theology, the Trinity as an (obscure) mystery of revelation.[20] Another revealing illustration is the straits to which Anselm was reduced in explaining why, of all the three persons of the Godhead, it was the Son who became incarnate.[21] It was, he replied, appropriate that the Son of God in eternity should also be Son of God in the incarnation so that there should not be two different 'Sons' in the Trinity; and also that the one who is the image of the Father should also restore man to the likeness of God in himself. Anselm here undeniably discerns the essential connection, but it is hard not to feel that the question is being put back to front, that he and those with whom he is debating have forgotten that it is only in the recognition of Jesus as Son of God that we have any basis for speaking of an eternal Son. So the doctrine of the Trinity threatens to become a recondite speculation which must cast about for some other foundation—as in the long tradition of applications of sundry *vestigia trinitatis*, up to and including Tillich's appeal to the dynamics of life, or even Barth's reliance on the category of the self-affirming and self-relating 'I' in his initial account of the Trinity.

The heart of the matter is that the doctrine of the Trinity is not an abstract mathematical puzzle, not the articulation of the rhythm of life, nor the projection upon the ultimate of the manifold triplicities that a little inspired imagination can easily suggest to us. It arises from the fundamental recognition that Jesus Christ is Immanuel, God with us, a recognition which is itself enabled by awareness of participation in the Spirit in that same mystery. The rhythm is that of faith and of worship, and the mystery at the centre is the crucified and risen Christ, the sacrament and pledge of the reconciling and redeeming good favour of the Father extended even to us. Yet just because he is God with us, the awareness of faith opens into recognition of the triune being of God, for nothing less is required if the truth of the Gospel is not in the last resort to be set aside. Sabellianism, open or concealed, implies that the trinitarian structure of redemption has nothing really to do with the nature of God, and loses hold on God in his own reality, like a climber on a rock face who can find no crevice to give him a grip.[22] Only if there is genuine differentiation within God is there space and room for him so to reach out that he engages us with himself, going forth to become his own creature and at the same time enabling and empowering an authentic creaturely response. In this sense, the doctrine of the Trinity cannot and must not be understood as the speculative projection of the theological mind into realms too high for it, but as the doxological answer evoked in us by the divine condescension that in Christ comes down to meet us and in the Spirit bears us up from within.

(ii) The Spirit as 'Third Person'

Two connected questions arise here: the application of the term 'person' in trinitarian theology, and the identification of the Spirit as the 'third' 'person' or 'hypostasis' in the Godhead. The objections to the use of 'person' that we have already briefly mentioned are indeed formidable, especially from the general standpoint of Western theology; for on the one hand the word in normal usage has come to mean a conscious, active individual, on the other the general tendency in Augustinian approaches to the Trinity has been in a modalist direction which can lead to the conclusion that talk of 'personhood' must apply globally to God rather than to the distinct identities of the Father, Son and Holy Spirit, and encourages preference for such alternative terms as 'mode of being' or 'subsisting relation'—in other words, for *functional* analogies rather than personal ones—to express the three dimensions of God's being. Eastern Orthodoxy, on the other hand, has followed the Cappadocians in feeling able, with qualifications, to depict the Trinity on the model of three persons, as in the splendid 15th century Russian ikon of Rublev. It therefore puts especial weight on the *three* hypostases.

In any discussion of the suitability of such terms as 'person' or 'hypostasis' in this connection, it must be kept in mind that they were initially drawn into service to *refer to* rather than to *define* the distinct identities of the Father, of Jesus Christ, or the Holy Spirit. God is neither 'one person' nor 'three persons' in any ordinary sense of 'person'. Rather this technical language must be kept open to the realities to which it refers and not become a kind of substitute for them. The possibility must therefore always be reckoned with that the non-theological development of their meaning may render them too opaque for them to continue to be helpful in trinitarian formulation. To this extent, the modern criticisms of 'person' as a trinitarian concept cannot be simply dismissed. At the same time, however, we have traced some grounds for suspecting that the criticism may also rest upon more questionable modalist assumptions, and risk rejecting, not only the word 'person', but also an element of valid meaning which it serves to protect. What might that meaning be?

The key to the unfolding of the whole pattern lies in christology: it was the need to recognise and give place to the distinct identity of Jesus Christ as the Son of the Father that led to the use of *persona* and *hypostasis* as specifically theological and eventually trinitarian technical terms. It is hard to see how that need can be met unless the being of God is expressed in *supra*-personal rather than *merely* personal terms. This would seem to defuse one main objection to the use of 'person' in trinitarian theology, at least so far as the Son and the Father are concerned. But what of the extension and application of the same term to the Spirit? Is this equally legitimate or required? Or did something go wrong, as Lampe suggests, when the fathers in the fourth century came to describe the Spirit in ways paralleling the description of the Son? (Lampe of course holds that the essential error lay back at the stage of christology; but even if we do not accept his view there, the question he poses about the pneumatological development can still be recognised as needing to be answered.)

Here, everything turns on how the formulae referring to God in three 'persons' or 'hypostases' are to be understood. Are the Father, Son and Holy Spirit each *in the same way* a divine 'person', three members, as it were, of a class?[23] Or is each a 'person' quite distinctively, as Father, as Son, as Spirit? It cannot be denied that much trinitarian thought in East and West alike from the earliest period onwards would seem to drive in the first direction, whether in the envisioning of the Trinity as like three individuals, or in the more abstract accounts of three *personae* encountered, for instance, in the Athanasian Creed. Yet the legitimacy of this way of thinking must be seriously questioned. It runs counter to the profoundest motive for the framing of fully trinitarian theology in the fourth century, where the application to the Spirit of the logic of argument already developed in reference to the Son itself depended upon the recognition that the pattern of God's work of salvation is complete in triunity, not in biunity, that the movement issuing from the Father through the Son reaches us in the Spirit, that in the Spirit we are renewed in the image of the Son and drawn through him to the Father. Interlocking complementarity rather than simple threefold repetition determines and characterises the pattern. Hence the need felt by the fathers to develop pneumatological concepts that would not simply *parallel* the Spirit to the Son, but also make essential *distinctions* between them—hence such terms as 'procession'. The same motive can be traced in Augustine's attempts to devise models for the Trinity which would not present it simply as 'one plus one plus one', but as an organic three-dimensional unity.

If we are right in this view of the matter, then it remains legitimate to describe the Spirit as the 'third person' (or whatever other term may be preferred) *provided* it is recognised that each of the three is 'person' in distinctive fashion, as Father, as Son, as Holy Spirit. In particular, the difference and complementarity between the Son and the Spirit should not be effaced. The Spirit is God, but God acting within, directing us, not to himself as Holy Spirit, but to the incarnate Son, and in him, to the Father.[24] It is for this reason that we have throughout described the Spirit as 'it'—not to deny a distinct *hypostasis* or *persona*, a genuine agency and purpose, but to hint, albeit inadequately, at the Spirit's self-effacingness, at the other-directedness of its activity as the light that is seen by what it illuminates. Too highly 'personalised' language—as in the slogan of the 'personality of the Holy Spirit'—may encourage a misleading sense of the Spirit as a 'personality' external to and even competing with our own. It can indeed *reduce* the divine Spirit to too human dimensions and hide the greatness in humility of the God who searches, answers and hopes even in us as our search, answer and hope.

(iii) *The Filioque*

The long history and recent renewed discussions of the *filioque* involves a host of different issues. Here, without entering into too many technicalities, we must restrict ourselves to some brief remarks chiefly suggested by the train of thought in the preceding paragraphs.

Just as in both East and West there was a certain tendency for the doctrine of the Trinity to become detached from its concrete reference to the history of Christ and the Spirit, and with it the danger of treating the divine persons as corresponding equivalents to each other, there also was at work an inclination to set up further parallels within the Trinity, arranging the three persons into a group of two and a third standing over against the others. The East depicted the Father as the sole source and origin of the Son and Spirit, each issuing from him in the appropriate, parallel but distinct modes of generation and procession. The West, by contrast, came to posit the Father and the Son together as the single source of the Spirit, their common love and gift. This is certainly not all there is to say about either Eastern or Western trinitarian theology, but it may serve to focus the difference in approach expressed on the one hand by the medieval Western defence of the *filioque* as stated in the Councils of Lyons and Florence, and on the other by Photius' insistence in the eighth century that the Spirit proceeds *ek monou tou patros*, 'from the Father alone'.

If we have been at all on the right track in the last pages, then neither of these positions can be regarded as entirely satisfactory. The Trinity cannot be thus subdivided into 'two here' and 'one there', or 'two of this sort' and 'one of that', without doing violence to the pattern and dynamic of God's being and movement as Father, Son and Holy Spirit. The Son and Spirit are not adequately depicted as two parallel productions 'from the Father alone', nor can the Father and Son be effectively conflated in the breathing-forth of the Spirit. In the East the relation and distinction between the Son and Spirit, in the West those between the Father and the Son fall too far into the background, whereas in each case the relation and distinction between these pairs and the remaining person is placed in the centre of attention. Neither view is adequately trinitarian; both reflect a double rather than a triple pattern.

Consistently with this non-trinitarianism, neither approach is easily reconcilable with the history of Christ and the Spirit as presented in the New Testament. A Spirit proceeding *from* (rather than *to*) the Son in eternity squares ill with a Spirit coming upon, being received by, and then given from the Son in history. Similarly, however, a Spirit that proceeds in eternity from the Father alone would seem to stand in a different eternal relation to the Son from that enacted and realised in the movement from incarnation to Pentecost. Must room not somehow be found to affirm a double relationship between the Son and Spirit which is as ultimate in the life of God as in the work of salvation? Otherwise must not the doctrine of the Trinity at its heart and centre remain detached from its roots, by which alone we have access to it? In one way it may be suggested that Augustine's arguments for the *filioque* did drive in the needed direction; for as we saw, he described the procession of the Spirit as *principally* from the Father, yet as opening up in the generation of the Son in such a fashion that the Spirit proceeds from both. And, to follow up the motif of the *vinculum caritatis*, it proceeds both from the Father to the Son and from the Son to the Father. This avenue was later closed by the medieval concentration on the other Augustinian theme of the *unity of being* of the Father and the Son; but it could offer a conception of the inner-trinitarian relations which would better correspond to the pattern of the economy of salvation than either the medieval Western or the Photian roads.

That is one side of the matter. The other, of course, is that the *filioque* combined with the *vinculum caritatis* model has the tendency to project a sense of the Spirit as being somehow less 'real' or 'personal' than the Father and the Son. This is justified to the extent that it recognises the distinct nature of the Spirit's 'person', but it can be taken to the point where the Spirit effectively disappears from view as the living and present and working Spirit *of God*. As T. F. Torrance has pointedly observed, the *filioque* in the West has commonly been replaced by an *ecclesiaque* or an *homineque*, the Spirit *of Christ* displaced by the spirit of the church or of man himself.[25]

The answer here is not, however, simply to restate in Photian fashion the distinct procession of the Spirit from the Father alone. While that might serve in part to reinforce awareness of the distinct divinity of the Spirit, it is all too exposed to Lampe's charge of an over-hasty transference to the Spirit of the scheme of theology first applied to christology, a transference which is insufficiently grounded in the relation of the Spirit to Christ and Christ to the Spirit. That connection, to which the *filioque* inadequately witnesses, remains crucial if the Spirit of God is truly the Spirit of the Son, in whom we too cry, 'Abba! Father!', and may also say

Glory be to the Father,
  and to the Son,
  and to the Holy Spirit,
As it was in the beginning,
  is now,
  and ever shall be,
  world without end.

Amen.

SELECT BIBLIOGRAPHY

(More extensive suggestions for reading are given in the footnotes.)

A. *General.* Particularly useful are:

H. Berkhof, *The Doctrine of the Holy Spirit.* London: Epworth, 1965

G. S. Hendry, *The Holy Spirit in Christian Theology.* Revised and enlarged. London: S.C.M. Press, 1965

B. *Biblical.*

C. K. Barrett, *The Holy Spirit and the Gospel Tradition.* Second edition. London: S.P.C.K., 1966

F. D. Bruner, *A Theology of the Holy Spirit. The Pentecostal Experience and the N.T. Witness.* London: Hodder & Stoughton, 1971

J. D. G. Dunn, *Jesus and the Spirit.* London: S.C.M. Press, 1975

M. E. Isaacs, *The Concept of Spirit. A Study of Pneuma in Hellenistic Judaism and its Bearing on the New Testament.* Heythrop Monographs 1. London: Heythrop College, 1976

C. F. D. Moule, *The Holy Spirit.* London: Mowbrays, 1978

E. Schweizer et al., *'Pneuma, pneumatikos'. TDNT* 6. Grand Rapids: Eerdmans, 1968, pp. 332–455; also published separately as *Spirit of God.* London: A. & C. Black, 1960

E. Schweizer, *The Holy Spirit.* London: S.C.M. Press, 1981

A. W. Wainwright, *The Trinity in the New Testament.* 4th impr. London: S.P.C.K., 1977

C. *Historical.* A useful summary overview up to the turn of the century can be found in:

W. H. G. Thomas, *The Holy Spirit of God.* Lectures on the L. P. Stone Foundation, Princeton Theological Seminary, 1913. Repr. in *The Evangelical Classics Library.* London: Church Book Room Press, 1974

For greater detail:

H. B. Swete, *The Holy Spirit in the Ancient Church.* London: Epworth Press, 1912

H. Watkin-Jones, *The Holy Spirit in the Mediaeval Church.* London: Epworth Press, 1922

H. Watkin-Jones, *The Holy Spirit from Arminius to Wesley.* London: Epworth Press, 1928

On the *Filioque*:

L. Vischer (ed.), *Spirit of God, Spirit of Christ*. Ecumenical Reflections on the Filioque Controversy. Geneva: W.C.C., 1981

D. *Recent and Contemporary*:

F. W. Camfield, *Revelation and the Holy Spirit. An Essay in Barthian Theology*. London: Elliot Stock, 1933

M. Green, *I Believe in the Holy Spirit*. London: Hodder & Stoughton, 1975

W. Hollenweger, *The Pentecostals*. London: S.C.M. Press, 1972

E. Jüngel, *The Doctrine of the Trinity*. God's Being is in Becoming. Edinburgh: Scottish Academic Press, 1976

H. Küng & J. Moltmann (ed.), *Conflicts about the Holy Spirit. Concilium* 128 (1979)

G. W. H. Lampe, *God as Spirit*. Oxford: O.U.P., 1977

R. Laurentin, *Catholic Pentecostalism*. London: Darton, Longman & Todd, 1977

J. Moltmann, *The Trinity and the Kingdom of God*. London: S.C.M. Press, 1981

H. Mühlen, *A Charismatic Theology. Initiation in the Spirit*. London: Burns & Oates, 1978

K. Rahner, *The Trinity*. London: Burns & Oates, 1970

H. Wheeler Robinson, *The Christian Experience of the Holy Spirit*. London: Nisbet, 1928

T. A. Smail, *Reflected Glory*. The Spirit in Christ and Christians. London: Hodder & Stoughton, 1975

J. V. Taylor, *The Go-Between God*. The Holy Spirit and the Christian Mission. London: S.C.M. Press, 1972

P. Toon & J. Spiceland (ed.), *One God in Trinity*. An Analysis of the primary dogma of Christianity. London: Samuel Bagster, 1980

C. Welch, *The Trinity in Contemporary Theology*. London: S.C.M. Press, 1953

NOTES

Footnotes to Chapter One

1. A full survey of the various senses of 'spirit' in the Old and New Testaments and other relevant ancient literature is given in the encyclopaedic article, *'Pneuma, pneumatikos'*, by Kleinknecht, Baumgärtel, Bieder, Sjöberg and Schweizer, in Kittel/Friedrich, *Theological Dictionary of the New Testament*, translated and edited by G. W. Bromiley, vol. 6 (Grand Rapids: Eerdmans, 1968), pp. 332–455 (hereafter referred to simply as *TDNT* 6). The Old Testament section is by Baumgärtel, pp. 359–367. Another study is D. Lys, *'RUACH'. Le Souffle dans l'Ancien Testament*. Paris, 1962. Two older but still useful articles are C. A. Briggs, 'The Use of *Ruach* in the Old Testament'. *JBL* 19 (1900), pp. 132–145; and W. R. Shoemaker, 'The Use of *Ruach* in the O.T. and of *Pneuma* in the N.T.' *JBL* 23 (1904), pp. 13–67.

2. For the sake of completeness, it should perhaps be added that *ruach* can also be used in quite the opposite sense of 'hot air'! 'Behold they are all a delusion; their works are nothing; their molten images are empty *ruach*.' (Isa. 41.29; cf. also Jer. 5.13; Job 6.26; 15.2)

3. H. W. Robinson, 'Hebrew Psychology', in A. S. Peake (ed.) *The People and the Book*. Oxford: Clarendon, 1925, pp. 353–382. Along with this shift in psychology ran a similar shift in the meaning of *ruach* itself: through the Old Testament era it came to be used less and less of natural forces, or even of supernatural realities, and increasingly of human moods or the human self—cf. Lys, *op. cit.*

4. For a suggestive exploration of this theme, see G. A. F. Knight, *A Biblical Approach to the Doctrine of the Trinity*. *SJTh* Occasional Papers 1. Edinburgh: Oliver & Boyd, 1953; repr. 1957. Knight argues that the Old Testament conception of God is not of a 'monad', but of a dynamic and organic unity, and is therefore not only consistent with the later Christian articulation of the doctrine of the Trinity, but opens the way to a genuinely biblical understanding of it. See also A. W. Wainwright, *The Trinity in the New Testament*. London: SPCK, 4th impr., 1977, ch. 2.

5. For a different assessment, see C. F. D. Moule, *The Holy Spirit*. London: Mowbrays, 1978, pp. 17–21; 24–29; 43–51. It may be felt, however, that Moule makes rather heavy weather of the New Testament's silence on a creative or cosmic role of the Spirit.

6. On prophecy in the Old Testament and the ancient world generally, see D. Hill, *New Testament Prophecy*. London: Marshall, Morgan & Scott, 1979, ch. 1. The ways in which *ruach* was or was not associated with prophecy at different periods were explored in a seminal article by S. Mowinckel, '"The Spirit" and the "Word" in the Pre-Exilic Reforming Prophets'. *JBL* 53 (1934), pp. 199–227; also in his 'Postscript' in *JBL* 56 (1937), pp. 261–265; *cf.* also C. K. Barrett, *The Holy Spirit and the Gospel Tradition*. London: SPCK, 2nd edn, 1966, pp. 145–153.

7. See the illuminating discussion by A. C. Auld, 'Poetry Prophecy, Hermeneutic: Recent Studies in Isaiah'. *SJTh* 33 (1980), pp. 567–581.

8. This is very clearly brought out by P. Schäfer, *Die Vorstellung vom heiligen Geist in der rabbinischen Literatur*. Munich, 1972. It may be added that in rabbinic Judaism, as in Jewish theology throughout the Christian era, the Holy Spirit has been a far less central theme than in Christianity.

Footnotes to Chapter Two

1. For the uses of *ruach* in Palestinian Judaism, see Sjöberg's contribution in *TDNT* 6, pp. 375–389; particularly p. 386 on the weakening sense of the creative role of the Spirit by contrast with the emphasis on prophecy and the bestowal of the Spirit on the righteous. Also, on the same point, Barrett, *op. cit.*, pp. 20–21.

2. Further passages are given by Barrett, *op. cit.*, pp. 42–44.

3. These and other documents can be found in R. H. Charles (ed.), *The Apocrypha and Pseudepigrapha of the Old Testament*. Oxford: Oxford University Press, 1963 (1913).

4. Further references to the Messiah's anticipated conquest of evil spirits are quoted by Barrett, *op. cit.*, pp. 57–59.

5. The main documents are translated by G. Vermes *The Dead Sea Scrolls in English*. Harmondsworth: Penguin, 1962. The quotations we give below are from this edition, pp. 75–78.

6. For a balanced assessment, see G. R. Driver, *The Judaean Scrolls*. Oxford: Blackwell, 1965.

7. E.g. 1QH xvi (Vermes, p. 197):
And I know that man is not righteous
    except through Thee,
and therefore I implore Thee
    by the spirit which Thou hast given (me)
    to perfect Thy (favours) to Thy servant (for ever), purifying me by Thy
Holy Spirit. . . .
On the various uses of 'spirit' in the Scrolls, see Schweizer in *TDNT* 6, pp. 389–392, and A. A. Anderson, 'The Use of "Ruah" in 1QS, 1QH and 1QM'. *JSSt* 7 (1962), pp. 293–303.

8. On this whole area: A. P. Hayman, 'Rabbinic Judaism and the Problem of Evil'. *SJTh* 29 (1976), pp. 461–476.

9. A variety of papers can be found in J. H. Charlesworth (ed.) *John and*

Qumran. London: Geoffrey Chapman, 1972; cf. also Driver, op. cit., pp. 532–562. A particularly important early investigation was O. Betz, *Der Paraklet.* Leiden: Brill, 1963; a critique and modification of his position is given by G. Johnston, *The Spirit-Paraclete in the Gospel of John.* Cambridge: Cambridge University Press, 1970, ch. 7.

10. The similarities and contrasts are explored in detail by W. D. Davies. 'Paul and the Dead Sea Scrolls: Flesh and Spirit', in K. Stendahl (ed.), *The Scrolls and the New Testament.* London: S.C.M., 1958, pp. 157–182.

11. So, for example, in I Cor. 2.12, 'Now we have received not the spirit of the world, but the Spirit which is from God,' the primary antithesis is not Spirit/spirit, but God/world.

12. On gnostic thought, see Schweitzer, *TDNT* 6, pp. 392–396; also R. M. Wilson, 'The Spirit in Gnostic Literature', in B. Lindars and S. Smalley (ed.), *Christ and Spirit in the New Testament.* Studies in honour of C. F. D. Moule. Cambridge: Cambridge University Press, 1973, pp. 345–355. The flow of thought from Qumran through gnosticism into Alexandrian Christian theology is traced by W.-D. Hauschild, *Gottes Geist und der Mensch.* Munich, 1972.

13. On *pneuma* in Hellenistic Judaism, see Bieder, *TDNT* 6, pp. 372–375, and M. E. Isaacs, *The Concept of Spirit. A Study in Hellenistic Judaism and its Bearing on the New Testament.* London: Heythrop College, 1976, with a useful classification of the various occurrences on pp. 150–152.

14. Isaacs, *op. cit.*, pp. 10–17, gives a detailed analysis of the use of *pneuma* in the LXX, and the other ways in which *ruach* could be translated. See also Baumgärtel, *TDNT* 6, pp. 367–368, and E. Hatch and H. A. Redpath, *A Concordance to the Septuagint and Other Greek Versions of the Old Testament.* repr. Graz, 1954, vol. 2, pp. 1151–1153.

15. A full account of the senses of *pneuma* in the Greek world is given by Kleinknecht, *TDNT* 6, pp. 334–359.

16. Isaacs, *op. cit.*, pp. 96–112.

17. Isaacs, *op. cit.*, pp. 45–51; on the pagan notion of inspiration, see also Kleinknecht, *loc. cit.*, and G. W. H. Lampe, *God as Spirit.* Oxford: Oxford University Press, 1977, pp. 53–60.

17a. On this complex development, see R. S. Barbour, 'Creation, Wisdom and Christ', in R. W. A. McKinney (ed.), *Creation, Christ and Culture. Studies in Honour of T. F. Torrance.* Edinburgh: T. & T. Clark, 1976, pp. 22–42.

18. The reference here is not to *moral* purity, but to the 'rarified' nature of 'spirits' such as the human mind or indeed 'disembodied spirits'. The point is that, no matter how 'fine' they may be, Wisdom is 'finer' and 'subtler' still, which is why she can 'pass through' them. Stoic language is being used here, but in order (not entirely adequately) to express the idea of a transcendent 'spirit' of a qualitatively different order from anything creaturely or material.

19. *Gig.* 5.

20. This is well brought out by Isaacs, *op. cit.*, pp. 13–14; 52–58.

Footnotes to Chapter Three

1. For the New Testament material in general: Schweizer *TDNT* 6, pp. 396–451; also his *The Holy Spirit*. London: S.C.M., 1981; Isaacs, *The Concept of Spirit*, pp. 65–157; and the old but still useful surveys by E. W. Winstanley, *Spirit in the New Testament*. Cambridge: Cambridge University Press, 1908, and H. B. Swete, *The Holy Spirit in the New Testament*. London: Macmillan, 1909. Less technical coverage of the ground is in A. M. Ramsey, *Holy Spirit. A Biblical Study*, London: S.P.C.K. 1977; Moule, *The Holy Spirit*, ch. 3; Wainwright, *The Trinity in the New Testament*, chs. 11–12. Extensive further bibliographies are given by Isaacs; J. D. G. Dunn, *Jesus and the Spirit*. London: S.C.M., 1975; and F. D. Bruner, *A Theology of the Holy Spirit. The Pentecostal Experience and the N.T. Witness*. Grand Rapids: Eerdmans & London: Hodder & Stoughton, 1971. The recent studies of D. Hill, *New Testament Prophecy*. London: Marshall, Morgan & Scott 1979, and J. Wilkinson, *Health and Healing. Studies in New Testament Principles and Practice*. Edinburgh: Handsel Press, 1980, offer useful introductions to these related topics.

2. On the Gospels see C. K. Barrett, *The Holy Spirit and the Gospel Tradition*. London: S.P.C.K., 2nd edn, 1966 (1947); on Acts, Bruner, *A Theology of the Holy Spirit*, ch. 5, and J. H. E. Hull, *The Holy Spirit in the Acts of the Apostles*. London: Lutterworth, 1967; and on both, Dunn, *Jesus and the Spirit*; Schweizer, *TDNT* 6, pp. 396–415.

3. This preference of Luke's may be reflected in the fact which we mention below that Luke 11.13 speaks of the Holy Spirit where the parallel in Matt. 7.11 has 'good things'. Conversely, Matt. 12.28 refers to the Spirit of God whereas the parallel in Luke 11.20 talks of God's 'finger'. Overall, though, Luke speaks much more often of the Spirit than either Matthew or Mark.

4. See Barrett *op. cit.*, chs. 8 & 10. Dunn, *op. cit.* chs. 2–4 seeks to explore further Jesus' consciousness of the Spirit, and finds in it the essential complement to his sense of Sonship. This carries theological systematization rather further than the Synoptic writers do, but Dunn's perception is basically sound.

5. This is not to say that the Synoptics sought *wholly* to explain Jesus in terms of the Spirit, much less that a 'christology of inspiration' of the sort recently advocated by G. W. H. Lampe, *God as Spirit*. Oxford: Oxford University Press, 1977, and by some of the contributors to J. Hick, (ed.), *The Myth of God Incarnate*. London: S.C.M. Press, 1977, can replace a 'christology of incarnation'. On the general theme of 'inspiration and incarnation', see Moule, *The Holy Spirit*, ch. 5; on Lampe's proposal, C. Tuckett, 'Christology and the New Testament'. *SJTh* 33 (1980), pp. 401–416; on *The Myth*, A. Heron, 'Doing without the Incarnation?' *SJTh* 31 (1978), pp. 51–71; on both, E. L. Mascall, 'Quicunque vult. Anglican Unitarians', in his *Whatever Happened to the Human Mind?* London: S.P.C.K., 1980, pp. 97–127.

6. *cf.* Dunn, *Jesus and the Spirit*, chs. 5–7.

7. Schweizer, *TDNT* 6, pp. 415–437; Dunn, *Jesus and the Spirit*, chs. 8–11;

N. Q. Hamilton, *The Holy Spirit and Eschatology in Paul. SJTh Occasional Papers* 6. Edinburgh: Oliver and Boyd, 1957; A. M. Hunter, *Paul and his Predecessors*, rev. edn. London: S.C.M. Press, 1961, ch. 10 and pp. 145–147.

8. Colossians, like Ephesians and the Pastoral Epistles, was most probably not composed by Paul; we mention it here only as illustrating a Pauline usage.

9. See Isaacs, *op. cit.*, ch. 8; Moule, *op. cit.*, ch. 2.

10. See in particular R. Bultmann, *Theology of the New Testament*, vol. 1. London: S.C.M. Press, 1965, pp. 232–246. Bultmann distinguishes two broad conceptions of the Spirit. One is more animistic, personal, and particular, and specifically Jewish; the other more impersonal, general, dynamic, and chiefly Hellenistic; and Paul modifies the former by the latter. See also Schweizer, *loc. cit.*, and Wainwright, *The Trinity in the New Testament*, pp. 200–204.

11. Here lies the prime weakness of Lampe's thesis—see *God as Spirit*, ch. 3, and Tuckett's criticisms (*supra*, n. 5). For more accurate analyses of the way in which Christ and the Spirit are related in Paul's thought, see Dunn, *Jesus and the Spirit*, pp. 318–326; Wainwright, *The Trinity in the New Testament*, pp. 204–223, Isaacs, *The Concept of Spirit*, pp. 113–124.

12. This may be one reason for the New Testament's fondness for the designation, 'Holy Spirit'—Moule, *op. cit.*, pp. 22–23.

13. For a detailed analysis, *cf.* Bruner, *op. cit.*, ch. 7.

14. Hamilton, *The Holy Spirit and Eschatology in Paul.*

15. Schweizer, *TDNT* 6, pp. 437–444; Dunn, *Jesus and the Spirit*, pp. 350–357; G. Johnston, *The Spirit-Paraclete in the Fourth Gospel.* Cambridge: Cambridge University Press, 1970; R. E. Brown, 'The Paraclete in the Fourth Gospel'. *NTS* 13 (1966–67), pp. 113–132; and other literature listed above, ch. 2, n. 9.

16. In the light of this, the 'living water', the 'gift of God' of which Jesus speaks to the Samaritan woman in 4.10-15 may also be seen as a symbol of the Spirit, and connected with the later vv. 23–24. The same metaphor seems to be used in Rev. 21.6; 22.1ff.

17.'Docetism' (from *dokein*, 'to seem') taught that Jesus was a spiritual being who only *appeared* to be a man of flesh and blood, and did not really suffer on the cross.

18. We cannot here explore the question raised by Bultmann in his great *Commentary* on John whether the 'sacramental' strand in the Fourth Gospel is the work of the original writer or a later redactor, nor the complex matter of the authorship of the Gospel and the Johannine Epistles. For the purposes of our survey, they can be taken together, though it may well be that they are the work of more than one hand in the 'Johannine circle'.

19. To this extent, the reading known to some of the early fathers in I John 5.7, though certainly an interpolation, is not very far off the intention of the passage; 'There are three witnesses in heaven, the Father, the Word, and the Holy Spirit; and these three are one.'

20. On the motives leading to this delineation, cf. Johnston, op. cit., chs. 6–9. He argues persuasively that the combination of the 'Spirit of truth' with the 'Paraclete' was intended to combat heretical claims to possess an angelic intercessor as spiritual guide and guardian, and against them to identify the authentic Spirit-Paraclete as God's Spirit which is also the Spirit of Christ.

21. cf. J. Moltmann, The Crucified God. London: S.C.M. Press, 1974, esp. pp. 235–249 ('Trinitarian Theology of the Cross').

Footnotes to Chapter Four

1. On the field covered in this and the next chapters J. N. D. Kelly, *Early Christian Doctrines*, 5th edn. London: A. & C. Black, 1977; G. L. Prestige, *God in Patristic Thought*. London: S.P.C.K., 1952; C. Stead, *Divine Substance*. Oxford: Oxford University Press, 1977; H. B. Swete, *The Holy Spirit in the Ancient Church*. London: Epworth, 1912; J. McIntyre, 'The Holy Spirit in Greek Patristic Thought'. *SJTh* 7 (1954), pp. 353–375; J. H. S. Burleigh, 'The Doctrine of the Holy Spirit in the Latin Fathers'. *SJTh* 7 (1954), pp. 113–132. Several of the passages we quote below, together with numerous others, can be found in the extremely useful anthology of H. Bettenson, *The Early Christian Fathers*. London: Oxford University Press, 1969 (1956); also the companion volume; *The Later Christian Fathers*. London: Oxford University Press, 1972 (1970).

2. The classic studies are, respectively, H. von Campenhausen, *Ecclesiastical Authority and Spiritual Power in the Church of the First Three Centuries*. London: A. & C. Black, 1969; and J. N. D. Kelly, *Early Christian Creeds*, 3rd edn. London: Longmans, 1972.

3. The vexed question how far Tertullian really became a Montanist has been freshly explored by G. L. Bray, *Holiness and the Will of God. Perspectives on the Theology of Tertullian*. London: Marshall, Morgan & Scott, 1979, pp. 54–63.

4. Notably in the vigorous, not to say vitriolic, *De Pudicitia*. Tertullian was the first great master of polemical theological invective; his heights of sarcasm have rarely been equalled and never surpassed. At least he is never dull!

5. As, before him, did Theophilus of Antioch—*Ad Autolycum* II.xv; xviii. The identification was probably well established in Irenaeus' homeland.

6. Kelly, *Early Christian Doctrines*, ch. 5.

7. For Tertullian's place in the general development of these ideas: A. I. C. Heron, '"Logos, Image, Son": Some Models and Paradigms in Early Christology', in R. W. A. McKinney (ed.), *Creation, Christ and Culture. Studies in Honour of T. F. Torrance*. Edinburgh: T. & T. Clark, 1976, pp. 43–62.

8. D. L. Balás, 'The Idea of Participation in the Structure of Origen's Thought. Christian Transposition of a Theme of the Platonic Tradition', in H. Crouzel, G. Lomiento & H. Rius-Camps (ed.), *Origeniana. Quaderni di Vetera Christianorum* 12. Bari, 1975, pp. 257–275.

9. Origen's concern in developing the theme of the eternal generation of

the Son was not to put the Son on a level with the Father, but to preserve the unchangeable integrity of the Father himself, which would have been threatened had he *become* Father only at the point of creation. In the next century, Athanasius was to reverse the argument, and find in the eternal generation of the Son support for the *homoousios* of Nicea—*cf.* M. F. Wiles, 'Eternal Generation'. *JTS* NS 12 (1961), pp. 284–291; also Kelly, *Early Christian Doctrines*, pp. 128–132; 243–245; and Heron, '"Logos, Image, Son" ...' (*supra*, n. 7).

10. *Hypostasis,* literally 'substance', 'that which stands under', was a term with a long and complex history in Greek, traced in great detail by H. Dörrie, *Hypostasis, Wort- und Bedeutungsgeschichte. Nachrichten der Akademie der Wissenschaften in Göttingen* 1, philologisch-historische Klasse, 1955, 3. It eventually came in Christian theology to be used as equivalent to the Latin *persona,* and so to designate the individual members of the Trinity; it also had the wider sense of a 'really existing thing or person' as opposed to what was 'anhypostatic', 'insubstantial', The application to the Father, Son and Spirit is found in Origen, *Comm. John* II.10 (6), and the resemblance to the Neo-Platonist use is probably no accident. Because it was employed by Arius in his radically subordinationist theology, it was not until 362, with Athanasius' *Tomus ad Antiochenos,* that it was declared acceptable to Nicene orthodoxy.

11. Didymus of Alexandria (| 398) is a striking example of a spiritual descendant of Origen whose pneumatology was deeply influenced by Origen's, but whose orthodoxy compelled him, without ever really conceding the fact to build only on one side of the master's thought: A. I. C. Heron, 'The Holy Spirit in Origen and Didymus the Blind. A Shift in Perspective from the Third to the Fourth Century', in A. M. Ritter (ed.), *Kerygma und Logos. Festschrift für Carl Andresen.* Göttingen: Vandehoek & Ruprecht, 1979, pp. 298–310. The Cappadocians also learnt much from Origen, but similarly avoided his subordinationism. The outstanding Origenist among Arius' sympathisers was Eusebius of Caesarea; Arius himself owed little to him, and reflected his thought only in a very refracted fashion—*cf.* T. E. Pollard, 'Logos and Son in Origen, Arius and Athanasius'. *Studia Patristica* II.2 (*TU* 64) (1957), pp. 282–287. Nevertheless, Origen's work easily lent itself to an Arian interpretation, and this was one reason for the shadows clouding his reputation from the end of the fourth century, and for the eventual condemnation of his teaching at the insistence of the Emperor Justinian just before the Fifth Ecumenical Council in 553.

Footnotes to Chapter Five

1. On the problems surrounding the origins of this creed and its connection with the Council of Constantinople, see Kelly, *Early Christian Creeds.* Although it has nothing directly to do with the Council of Nicea, we shall follow the customary usage and call it the 'Nicene Creed'.

2. Apart from the writings we shall mention, another major Greek

contribution was the *De Spiritu Sancto* of Didymus of Alexandria, probably dating from about 370, but only preserved in the Latin translation by Jerome. On Didymus' approach, *cf. supra*, ch. 4, n. 11.

3. On the origins of the Tropici and the nature of their position, see C. R. B. Shapland, *The Letters of St Athanasius Concerning the Holy Spirit.* Translated with Introduction and Notes. London: Epworth Press, 1951, pp. 18–34; T. Campbell, 'The Doctrine of the Holy Spirit in the Theology of Athanasius'. *SJTh* 27 (1974), pp. 408–440; and, for a somewhat different interpretation, A. I. C. Heron, 'Zur Theologie der "Tropici" in den Serapionbriefen des hl. Athanasios: Amos 4.13 als pneumatologische Belegstelle'. *Kyrios* 14. 1–2 (1974), pp. 3–24. For Athanasius' theology of the Spirit: Shapland, Campbell, and T. F. Torrance, '*Spiritus Creator.* A Consideration of the Teaching of St Athanasius and St Basil', in his *Theology in Reconstruction.* London: S.C.M., 1965; repr. Grand Rapids: Eerdmans, 1975, ch. 12.

4. In the subsequent MS tradition, the second letter was incorrectly divided into two, so that what is now referred to as *Ad Serap.* III is in fact the second part of the second letter, while *Ad Serap.* IV is really the third. Further, *Ad Serap.* IV.8ff are not part of the letters, which end at IV.7 (Shapland, pp. 11ff).

5. *cf. Ad Serap.* I. 10–11 and Shapland's notes *ad loc.*

6. *Trias*: the Greek counterpart to the Latin *trinitas.* 'Triad' and 'triadology' are standard terms in Eastern Orthodoxy.

7. The Alexandrian theologians following Athanasius took a position on the relation between the Son and Spirit which was much closer to what developed in the West: *cf.* Didymus, *De Spir. S.* 34 and Cyril of Alexandria, *Ep.* 17; also Theodoret of Cyrrhus, *Repr. Anath. Cyrilli* 9. This approach was not followed in later Eastern Orthodox thinking—no doubt partly because the Alexandrian tradition ran on into monophysitism, and so became separated from the main stream.

8. See the remarks of C. C. Richardson in E. R. Hardy & C. C. Richardson (ed.), *The Christology of the Later Fathers.* London: S.C.M., 1954, pp. 241–244; also R. W. Jenson, 'Three Identities of One Action'. *SJTh* 28 (1975), pp. 1–15. A full study of Gregory's pneumatology is M. Parmentier, *St Gregory of Nyssa's Doctrine of the Holy Spirit.* Oxford D. Phil diss., repr. as a series of articles in *Ekklesiastikos Pharos* 58 (1976), pp. 41–100; 387–444; 59 (1977), pp. 323–429; 60 (1978), pp. 697–730.

9. Quoted by K. Ware, 'The Holy Spirit in the Personal Life of the Christian', in *Unity in the Spirit—Diversity in the Churches.* Report of the 8th (1979) Assembly of the Conference of European Churches. Geneva: Conference of European Churches pp. 139–169. Fr. Ware's paper offers an excellent introduction to this dimension of Eastern theology; *cf.* also E. Timiadis, 'The Centrality of the Holy Spirit in Orthodox Worship'. *Ekklesiastikos Pharos* 60 (1978), pp. 317–357. The finest summary exposition of Orthodox pneumatology for Western readers is probably the 8th chapter of V. Lossky, *The Mystical Theology of the Eastern Church.* London: James

Clarke, 1957; repr. 1973; *cf.* also S. Bulgakov, *Le Paraclet.* Paris: Aubier, 1946.

10. Lossky, *op. cit.*, ch. 2, 'The Divine Darkness', and ch. 4, 'Uncreated Energies'; also the recent study by D. Wendebourg, *Geist oder Energie.* Munich: Kaiser, 1980. The theologian whose work definitively established this pattern of Eastern mystical theology was Gregory Palamas (1296–1357/8).

Footnotes to Chapter Six

1. H. Watkin-Jones, *The Holy Spirit in the Mediaeval Church,* London: Epworth Press, 1922; Swete, *The Holy Spirit in the Ancient Church*; and other works mentioned above, ch. 4, n. 1.

2. Best known in the 17th century translation by John Cosin, 'Come, Holy Ghost, our hearts inspire, And lighten with celestial fire...' Another well-known rendering is John Dryden's, 'Creator Spirit, by whose aid The world's foundations first were laid...'

3. Translated by John Mason Neale as, 'Come, thou Holy Paraclete, And from thy celestial seat Send thy light and brilliancy...'

4. *De Trinitate* VI.7.

5. J. N. D. Kelly, *The Athanasian Creed.* London: A. & C. Black, 1964, pp. 35ff.

6. *cf.* Watkin-Jones, *op. cit.*, pp. 181–191.

7. Karl Rahner, *The Trinity.* London: Burns & Oates, 1970, pp. 115–120, gives a brief but penetrating analysis; *cf.* also Bernard Lonergan, *De Deo Trino.* Rome, 1964. A summary of Lonergan's application of the 'psychological analogy' is given by Hugo Heynell in *One God in Trinity (infra,* n. 10), pp. 95–110.

8. *cf.* Watkin-Jones, *op. cit.*, pp. 199–213.

9. G. R. Evans, 'St Anselm's Images of Trinity'. *JTS* NS 27 (1976), pp. 46–57, brings this out with a wealth of illustration.

10 On the history of the *filioque* and on recent discussion, see especially the papers presented to a W.C.C. working party in 1978 and 1979 and edited by L. Vischer: *Spirit of God, Spirit of Christ.* Ecumenical Reflections on the Filioque Controversy. Geneva: W.C.C., 1980; also A. Heron, 'The *Filioque*', in P. Toon and J. Spiceland (ed.), *One God in Trinity.* London: Samuel Bagster, 1980, pp. 62–77; and H. Küng and J. Moltmann (ed.), *Conflicts about the Holy Spirit. Concilium* 128, (1979).

11. V. Lossky, 'The Procession of the Holy Spirit in the Orthodox Triadology', *Eastern Churches Quarterly Review,* suppl. vol. 2 (1948), pp. 31–53, repr. with alterations as chapter four of his *In the Image and Likeness of God.* London: Mowbrays, 1975; see also the W.C.C. volume mentioned above (n. 10). It should however be added that not all Eastern theologians agree wholly with Lossky, as is clear in that volume: *cf.* also Heron, *op. cit.*

12. A. Flannery (ed.), *Vatican Council II. The Conciliar and Post Conciliar Documents.* Dublin: Dominican Publications, 1975, p. 356. Where Popes Leo

and Pius had affirmed directly that 'as Christ is the Head of the Church, the Spirit is its Soul,' Vatican II spoke here of the Spirit as giving life to the whole body, and commented, 'Consequently, his work could be compared by the Fathers to the function that the principle of life, the soul, fulfils in the human body.' The analogy is thus applied in that slightly more open and flexible style which marks much of the ecclesiology of the Council—*cf.* A. *Dulles, Models of the Church*. Dublin: Gill & Macmillan, 1976.

13. See the summary exposition of medieval sacramental teaching in the *Decretum pro Armeniis* of the Council of Florence (*DS* 1310–1327), especially the opening paragraph; also T. F. Torrance, 'The Roman Doctrine of Grace from the Point of View of Reformed Theology', in his *Theology in Reconstruction*. London: S.C.M., 1965, repr. Grand Rapids: Eerdmans, 1975, pp.169–191.

13a. This point is made with particular emphasis by Rahner, *op. cit.*, pp. 9–48.

14. Karl Adam, *The Spirit of Catholicism*. London, 1934, p. 53.

15. The flavour of these diverse yet interconnected streams can be tasted in two useful anthologies: *Late Medieval Mysticism*, ed. R. C. Petry. London: S.C.M., 1957; and *Apocalyptic Spirituality*, translated and introduced by B. McGinn, in the series, *Classics of Western Spirituality*. London, 1980.

Footnotes to Chapter Seven

1. See in general Watkin-Jones, *The Holy Spirit in the Mediaeval Church*, Part IV; and his *The Holy Spirit from Arminius to Wesley*. London: Epworth Press, 1928; also W. H. G. Thomas, *The Holy Spirit of God*. Lectures on the L. P. Stone Foundation, Princeton Theological Seminary, 1913, repr. in *The Evangelical Classics Library*. London: Church Book Room Press, 1974; H. Berkhof, *The Doctrine of the Holy Spirit*. London: Epworth Press, 1965; G. S. Hendry, *The Holy Spirit in Christian Theology*. London: S.C.M. Press, 1965.

2. In his introduction to Abraham Kuyper's *The Work of the Holy Spirit*, p. xxxiii, quoted by Thomas, *op. cit.*, p. 102.

2a. *cf.* T. F. Torrance, *Theology in Reconstruction*. London: S.C.M., 1965, repr. Grand Rapids: Eerdmans, 1975, ch. 13: 'The Relevance of the Doctrine of the Spirit for Ecumenical Theology'.

3. On this, and on Luther's doctrine of the Spirit in general, *cf.* Regin Prenter's vigorous study, *Spiritus Creator. Luther's Concept of the Holy Spirit*. Philadelphia: Muhlenberg Press, 1953; also J. Pelikan, *Spirit versus Structure. Luther and the Institutions of the Church*. London: Collins, 1968.—On *caritas* in the Augustinian and medieval tradition see, e.g., A. Nygren, *Agape and Eros*. Part One. London: S.P.C.K., 1932, pp. 34–40.

4. A comprehensive study is W. Krusche, *Das Wirken des heiligen Geistes nach Calvin*. Göttingen: Vandenhoek & Ruprecht, 1957.

5. *cf.* Thomas, *op. cit.*,chs. 21–22; Berkhof, *op. cit.*, pp. 45–50; 66–93; Moule, *The Holy Spirit*, ch. 6.

5a. See H. Cunliffe-Jones, *Christian Theology since 1600*. London:

Duckworth, 1970; also A. Heron, *A Century of Protestant Theology*. London: Lutterworth, 1980.

6. For the general shift in perspective from Calvin to the *Westminster Confession*: R. T. Kendall, *Calvin and English Calvinism to 1649*. London: Oxford University Press, 1979. On Puritan teaching: G. F. Nuttall, *The Holy Spirit in Puritan Faith and Experience*. Oxford: Basil Blackwell, 1946.

7. Many of the Puritan classifications of the stages in this process were considerably more complex. A splendidly fearsome example can be found in the diagram attached to William Perkin's *The Golden Chaine* (1592), reproduced in I. Breward (ed.), *The Work of William Perkins*. Abingdon: Sutton Courtenay Press, 1970. Here the whole plan of salvation and damnation, from the primordial divine decrees to the ultimate destiny of the individual soul in heaven or hell, is laid out with the precision of an engineering blue-print.

8. The doctrine of evidences is spelt out at length in the mid-seventeenth century *Sum of Saving Knowledge*, which was commonly bound up together with the Westminster documents as edifying reading. For the problems that it generated, see J. B. Torrance, 'Covenant or Contract?' *SJTh* 23 (1970), pp. 51 76, and 'The Contribution of John McLeod Campbell to Scottish Theology'. *SJTh* 26 (1973), pp. 295–311; and on the 'practical syllogism', Dirkhof, *op. cit.*, pp. 79–85.

9. E. A. Dowey, *The Knowledge of God in Calvin's Theology*. New York: Columbia University Press, 1965 (1952); see also Hendry, *op. cit.*, chs, 4 and 7.

10. C. G. Strachan, *The Pentecostal Theology of Edward Irving*. London: Darton, Longman & Todd, 1973, is particularly to be recommended.

11. On the theologians mentioned here and in the remainder of this chapter: C. Welch, *Protestant Thought in the Nineteenth Century, vol. 1: 1799–1870*. New Haven: Yale University Press, 1972; K. Barth, *Protestant Theology in the Nineteenth Century*. London: S.C.M., 1972; A. Heron, *A Century of Protestant Theology*, ch. 2.

12. Forsyth († 1921), one of the outstanding British theologians of his day, was describing in this remark (made in his *Positive Preaching and the Modern Mind*. London: Hodder and Stoughton, 1907, and quoted here from A. M. Hunter, *P. T. Forsyth. Per Crucem ad Lucem*. London: S.C.M., 1974, p. 17) his own pilgrimage from a broadly Liberal position to one which led to his being posthumously described, not unjustly, as 'a Barthian before Barth'.

13. Hendry, *op. cit.*, ch. 5.

14. S. Kierkegaard, *The Sickness Unto Death*. Translated with an Introduction by Walter Lowrie. London: Oxford University Press, 1941, pp. 17; 19—*cf.* also Lowrie's note on the translation (pp. 219–220).

Footnotes to Chapter Eight

1. H. Wheeler Robinson, *The Christian Experience of the Holy Spirit*. London: Nisbet, 1928.

2. E.g. W. Herrmann, *The Communion of the Christian with God*. London: Williams & Norgate, 1906 (ET of the 4th German edition of 1903); H. R. Mackintosh, *The Christian Experience of Forgiveness*. London: Nisbet, 1929; John Oman, *Grace and Personality*. Cambridge: Cambridge University Press, 1917.

3. F. W. Camfield, *Revelation and the Holy Spirit: An Essay in Barthian Theology*. London: Elliot Stock, 1933.

4. See especially the short paper on 'The Humanity of God' in his collection of essays under that title (London: Collins, 1961), pp. 33–64.

5. *cf.* the diagnosis of H. Berkhof, *The Doctrine of the Holy Spirit*. London: Epworth, 1965, pp. 13-29.

6. Berkhof, *op. cit.*, p. 29. He refers especially to Barth's treatment in *Church Dogmatics* IV/2. Edinburgh: T. & T. Clark, 1958, §64.4 (pp. 264–377).

7. Berkhof, *op. cit.*, pp. 109–121; *cf. infra*, ch. 10.

8. *cf.* T. F. Torrance, 'The Mind of Christ in Worship: The Problem of Apollinarianism in the Liturgy', in his *Theology in Reconciliation*. London: Geoffrey Chapman, 1975, pp. 139–214.

9. *cf.* J. D. G. Dunn's opening comments in *Jesus and the Spirit*. London: S.C.M., 1975.

10. See Nils Bloch-Hoell, *The Pentecostal Movement. Its Origins, Development, and Distinctive Character*. London: Allen & Unwin, 1964; Walter Hollenweger, *The Pentecostals*. London: S.C.M., 1972; F. D. Bruner, *A Theology of the Holy Spirit*. London: Hodder & Stoughton, 1971; and, for a popular account, Michael Harper, *As At The Beginning. The Twentieth Century Pentecostal* Revival. London: Hodder & Stoughton, 1965.

11. L. Newbigin, *The Household of God*. London: S.C.M., 1953; 2nd edn, 1964.

12. *E.g.* Berkhof, *The Doctrine of the Holy Spirit*; also A. B. Come, *Human Spirit and Holy Spirit*. Philadelphia: Westminster Press, 1959; J. G. Davies, *The Spirit, the Church and the Sacraments*. London: Faith Press, 1954; H. P. van Dusen, *Spirit, Son and Father*. New York: Charles Scribner's Sons, 1958; G. S. Hendry, *The Holy Spirit in Christian Theology*. London: S.C.M., 1965; P. Tillich, *Systematic Theology*, vol. 3. Chicago: University of Chicago Press, 1963.

13. These movements have generated a vast amount of writing, much of it somewhat anecdotal or concerned more to testify than to inform. The Roman Catholic wing has produced the most considerable quantity of serious theological discussion, represented, for example, by R. Laurentin, *Catholic Pentecostalism*. London: Darton, Longman and Todd, 1977; K. McDonnell (ed.), *The Holy Spirit and Power: The Catholic Charismatic Renewal*. Garden City: Doubleday, 1975; H. Mühlen, *A Charismatic Theology. Initiation in the Spirit*. London: Burns & Oates, 1978; E. D. O'Connor, *The Pentecostal Movement in the Catholic Church*. Notre Dame, Indiana: Ave Maria Press, 1971; K. & D. Ranaghan, *Catholic Pentecostals*. New York: Paulist Press, 1969;

Cardinal Suenens, *A New Pentecost?* London: Darton, Longman and Todd, 1975; S. Tugwell, *Did You Receive the Spirit?* London: Darton Longman and Todd, 1972. For developments on the Protestant side, see M. Harper (ed.), *Bishops' Move.* London: Hodder & Stoughton, 1978; W. Hollenweger, *New Wine in Old Wineskins. Protestant and Catholic Neo-Pentecostalism.* Gloucester, 1973; T. A. Smail, *Reflected Glory. The Spirit in Christ and Christians.* London: Hodder & Stoughton, 1975; J. Rodman Williams, *The Era of the Spirit.* Plainfield, N. J.: Logos International, 1971.

14. J. Massyngberde Ford, *Which Way for Pentecostals?* New York: Harper and Row, 1976, traces two emerging wings in American Roman Catholic Neo-Pentecostalism, one wholly integrated, the other threatening to separate off from the Roman tradition; *cf.* also R. H. Culpepper, 'A Survey of Some Tensions Emerging in the Charismatic Movement'. *SJTh* 30.5 (1977), pp. 439–452.

15. This is brought out clearly in the writings of Suenens, Tugwell and Laurentin (*supra*, n. 14).

16. Smail, *Reflected Glory*; also his *The Forgotten Father.* London: Hodder & Stoughton, 1980.

17. This is constantly reiterated, for instance, by Tugwell, *Did You Receive the Spirit?*; *cf.* also the closing chapter of Smail, *Reflected Glory.*

18. Tugwell, *Did You Receive the Spirit?*, pp. 59–74; Suenens, *A New Pentecost?*, pp. 99–104; Smail, *Reflected Glory*, pp. 134–152; Laurentin, *Catholic Pentecostalism*, pp. 58–99. Laurentin's splendid discussion is in a class of its own—see also his excellent bibliography on glossolalia (pp. 213–221). The Classical Pentecostal position is presented in detail by Bruner, *A Theology of the Holy Spirit*, pp. 56–129, and equally painstakingly demolished, pp. 225–284 (but see also Smail's replies in *Reflected Glory*, pp. 32; 39–40; 81; 84; 95–96; 140–147).

19. See especially Laurentin, *loc. cit.*

20. Laurentin is again helpful on this—*op. cit.*, pp. 100–121; also J. Wilkinson, *Health and Healing.* Edinburgh: Handsel Press, 1980, and the valuable bibliography offered there (pp. 181–185).

21. *E.g.* Bruner, *A Theology of the Holy Spirit*, pp. 56–129; 225–284; G. W. H. Lampe, *God as Spirit.* Oxford: Oxford University Press, 1977, pp. 198–205; also J. D. G. Dunn, *Baptism in the Holy Spirit.* London: S.C.M., 1970, *passim.*

22. *E.g.* Tugwell, *Did You Receive the Spirit?*, pp. 40–49; Suenens, *A New Pentecost?*, pp. 79–88.

23. Smail, *Reflected Glory*, pp. 134–152; Laurentin, *Catholic Pentecostalism*, pp. 26–47. Laurentin draws on traditional Roman distinctions in sacramental theology to suggest that water baptism is the *sacramentum tantum*, the 'sign', Christ the *sacramentum et res*, the 'sign and reality', and the reception of the Spirit the *res*, the 'spiritual reality within us', and in this way believes one might integrate Classical Pentecostal ideas of 'baptism in the Spirit' with established teaching. From his somewhat different Reformed

standpoint, Berkhof, *The Doctrine of the Holy Spirit*, pp. 85–93, discusses whether there might be a 'third element in regeneration' to which the Classical Pentecostal emphasis witnesses. The sensitive point in these (or any comparable) efforts to accommodate the concerns of Pentecostalism is of course the uncomfortable question whether the identification of a specific 'gift' (*i.e.* glossolalia) as the new and decisive outpouring of the Spirit and so as the *res sacramenti* or the 'third element' in regeneration is accepted. If it is not, the treaty is not being negotiated on terms acceptable to Classical Pentecostalism.

24. Smail, *Reflected Glory*, p. 150.

25. A prayer from the missal for English-speaking Canada, cited by Suenens, *A New Pentecost?*, p. 47.

Footnotes to Chapter Nine

1. *Supra*, ch. 7. For a range of approaches to the analogy and relation between divine Spirit and human spirit which extends somewhat more widely than those mentioned here, one might take together: A. B. Come, *Human Spirit and Holy Spirit*. Philadelphia: Westminster Press, 1959, concentrating on the ideas of communion, person, and love to relate the work of the Spirit to human potential for personal growth; L. Dewar, *The Holy Spirit and Modern Thought*. London: Mowbrays, 1959, enthusiastically and thoroughly questionably dissolving the Spirit into the occult deeps of the psyche; and G. S. Hendry, *The Holy Spirit in Christian Theology*. London: S.C.M., 1965, ch. 5, focusing on the theme of man's freedom and the drive for transcendence. This diversity leaves H. Berkhof, *The Doctrine of the Holy Spirit*. London: Epworth, 1965, pp. 96–99, doubtful whether any analogy at all should be sought: 'The search for similarity cannot produce more than formal results, discovering analogies in terms of structure, like: responsibility, communication, relation, personality, etc. As soon as it goes beyond that, it becomes arbitrariness or is in danger of blurring the distinction between God and man.' (p. 98) The warning needs to be heard, but the *meaning* of 'spirit' still needs to be considered. For issues raised by some earlier modern approaches, see W. H. G. Thomas, *The Holy Spirit of God*. Repr. London: Church Book Room Press, 1974, chs. 24ff.—In this section I am particularly indebted to some references and suggestions first drawn to my attention by Paul W. Newman's article, 'Humanity with Spirit', *SJTh* 34 (1981), pp. 415–426.

2. Hence such famous affirmations as, 'Thou hast made us for thyself, and our hearts are restless till they find their rest in thee,' and 'Thou couldst not seek me hadst thou not already found me.' The second is for Augustine God's word to man—though in Barth (see below) it might well (and rightly) become man's word to God.

3. M. Buber, *I and Thou*. A new translation with a prologue and notes by Walter Kaufmann. Edinburgh: T. & T. Clark, 1970, p. 89.

4. See especially Hendry, *op. cit.*, pp. 100–108. Among the more modern

exponents one might especially mention M. Scheler, *On the Eternal in Man*. London: S.C.M., 1960, and N. Berdyaev, *Spirit and Reality*. London: Geoffrey Bles, 1939.

5. G. F. Thomas, *Spirit and Its Freedom*. University of North Carolina Press, 1939, p. 49 (quoted from Hendry, *op. cit.*, p. 103).

5a. The classic account of this difference, tracking back to the underlying conceptions of human and divine love, is A. Nygren's *Agape and Eros*. London: S.P.C.K., 1932; *cf.* esp. ch. 7.

6. E. Brunner, *Man in Revolt. A Christian Anthropology*. London: Lutterworth, 1939, pp. 237–239.

7. Brunner, *The Christian Doctrine of Creation and Redemption* (*Dogmatics*, vol. II). London: Lutterworth, 1952, pp. 62–63. A summary outline of the general understanding of the Spirit in Barth, Brunner, Tillich and Bultmann is offered in the second half of J. Rodman Williams, *The Era of the Spirit*. Plainfield, N.J.: Logos International, 1971.

8. The English translation in this passage uses 'spirit', but this does not seem either to catch Barth's sense, or to be consistent with the usage elsewhere in the same section of the translation.—On Barth's pneumatology in general: P. Rosato, *The Spirit as Lord. The Pneumatology of Karl Barth*. Edinburgh: T. & T. Clark, 1981. Barth's own attitude to the Hegelian glorification of the 'self' is developed on the chapter on Hegel in his *Protestant Theology in the Nineteenth Century*. London: S.C.M., 1972.

9. K. Rahner, *Spirit in the World*. ET London: Sheed & Ward, 1968. It was first published in German in 1939. A brief notice of other Roman Catholic 'philosophies of Spirit' in this and the last century, chiefly in France, Italy and Spain, is given by A. J. McNicholl, in the *New Catholic Encyclopedia*, vol. 13 (1967), pp. 572–573.

10. J. B. Metz, 'Foreword' to *Spirit in the World*, p. xvi. 'Pre-apprehend' is a somewhat helpless translation of the German *vorgreifen*, expressing an initial, anticipatory seizing of that which one is yet grasping after. 'Prehend' as employed in Process philosophy might perhaps be more adequate; it would at any rate correspond more closely to the etymology of the German.

11. Newman, 'Humanity with Spirit'.

12. Hendry, *op. cit.*, pp. 108 117, is sharply critical of Barth on this score. 'In his treatment of the doctrine of creation, Barth resolves the Berkleian doubt as to the existence of the world by merging it in its salvation: *esse est salvari*. The sovereignty of grace has become totalitarianism.' (p. 109) Similar criticisms are made, much more intemperately, by R. H. Roberts 'Karl Barth's Doctrine of Time', in S. W. Sykes (ed.), *Karl Barth—Studies of his Theological Methods*. Oxford: Clarendon Press, 1979, pp. 88–146. It does however demand something of a suspension of disbelief to accept that Roberts' polemic does simple justice to the full implications of Barth's position, which become increasingly apparent in the later volumes of the *Church Dogmatics*—that God himself freely defines himself as God *for* man, God *for* the world. Here R. D. Williams' paper, 'Barth on the Triune God',

in the same collection (pp. 147–193) shows a surer touch. Torrance's recent comments respecting the related controversy about natural theology are apposite here too: 'The failure to understand Barth at this point is highly revealing, for it indicates that his critics themselves still think within the dualist modes of thought that Barth had himself long left behind, in his restoration of an interactionist understanding of the relation between God and the world ... which God himself has already established ... Barth's objections ... are on grounds precisely the opposite of those attributed to him.' (T. F. Torrance, *The Ground and Grammar of Theology*. Belfast: Christian Journals, 1980, p. 87.)

13. P. Tillich, *Systematic Theology,* vol. 3 London: S.C.M., 1978, pp. 11–294. This volume was first published in 1963 (University of Chicago Press).

14. *Systematic Theology,* vol. 1 London: S.C.M., 1978, pp. 59–66. First published in 1951 (University of Chicago Press).

15. Karl Popper, *The Open Society and its Enemies.* 2nd edn. London: Routledge and Kegan Paul, 1952.

16. cf. Thomas, *The Holy Spirit of God,* chs. 23–24. Thomas, like many others, therefore largely restricts the Spirit's role to redemptive activity in believers and through the Word of the Gospel. C. F. D. Moule, *The Holy Spirit.* London: Mowbrays, 1978, shows similar hesitation, and wonders whether the lack of New Testament reference to a creative or cosmic work of the Spirit 'may be a theological pointer to something distinctive in the Christian understanding of incarnation.' (p. 21) In view of the tack taken by such a contemporary eminence as G. W. H. Lampe, *God as Spirit.* Oxford: Oxford University Press, 1977, Moule's reservations are comprehensible. Yet to limit the scope of the Spirit in Moule's fashion in order to safeguard the uniqueness of the incarnation runs perilously close to a binitarianism likely in the long run to prove as dangerous a short-circuit as Lampe's substitution of the immanent Spirit for the incarnate Son.

17. Early Dialectical Theology, the mature existentialist theology of Rudolf Bultmann, and the 'theocentric' rather than 'christocentric' approach of John Hick respectively illustrate these variations on the dualistic theme. Of all contemporary theologians, Thomas Torrance has been most acute and incisive in diagnosing and challenging it: see, most recently, *The Ground and Grammar of Theology* (*supra,* n. 12).

18. J. V. Taylor, *The Go-Between God. The Holy Spirit and the Christian Mission.* London: S.C.M., 1972. See especially the first three chapters.

19. Gerard Manley Hopkins, *God's Grandeur.*

20. J. Moltmann, 'Theology of Mystical Experience'. *SJTh* 32 (1979), pp. 501–520; *cf.* also the fourth chapter of his *The Trinity and the Kingdom of God.* London: S.C.M., 1981

21. cf. T. F. Torrance, *Space, Time and Incarnation.* London: Oxford University Press, 1969; *Space, Time and Resurrection.* Edinburgh: Handsel Press, 1976.

22. For a brief survey, see my *A Century of Protestant Theology.* London:

Lutterworth, 1980, pp. 196–214. Taylor in *The Go-Between God* quotes from a number of writers and relates their arguments specifically to pneumatology. A range of selections from a variety of writers is given by I. G. Barbour (ed.), *Issues in Science and Religion*. London: S.C.M., 1965; *Science and Religion. New Perspectives on the Dialogue*. London: S.C.M., 1968.

23. *e.g. The Phenomenon of Man*. London: Collins, 1959; *Science and Christ*. London: Collins, 1968.

24. *Christian Theology and Natural Science*. London: Longmans, 1956; repr. Archon Books, 1965.

25. *Christian Faith and Natural Science* and *The Transformation of the Scientific World-View*. Both London: S.C.M., 1953.

26. *Science and the Christian Experiment*. London: Oxford University Press, 1971; *Creation and the World of Science*. London: Oxford University Press, 1979.

27. *Nature and God*. London: S.C.M., 1965.

28. *Theological Science*. London: Oxford University Press, 1969; *The Ground and Grammar of Theology* and *Christian Theology and Scientific Culture*. Both Belfast: Christian Journals, 1980.

29. *e.g.* J. Monod, *Chance and Necessity. An Essay on the Natural Philosophy of Modern Biology*. London: Collins, 1972.

30. My italics; *cf.* Barth, *Church Dogmatics* III/1, pp. 57–59; Berkhof, *op. cit.*, pp. 94–96.

Footnotes to Chapter Ten

1. G. W. H. Lampe, *God as Spirit*. Oxford: Oxford University Press, 1977.—For studies of a wider range of modern approaches to the doctrine of the Trinity than we can cover here, see *e.g.* C. Welch, *The Trinity in Contemporary Theology*. London: S.C.M. Press, 1953; E. J. Fortman, *The Triune God*. London: Hutchinson, 1972; P. Toon and J. Spiceland (ed.), *One God in Trinity*. London: Samuel Bagster, 1980; R. W. Jenson, *The Triune Identity*. Philadelphia: Fortress, 1982.

2. N. Pittenger, *The Holy Spirit*. Philadelphia, 1974; *cf.* Spiceland's article, 'Process Theology', in *One God in Trinity*, pp. 133–157.

3. K. Rahner, *The Trinity*. London: Burns & Oates, 1970. For discussions of Rahner, see T. F. Torrance, 'Toward an Ecumenical Consensus on the Trinity'. *Theologische Zeitschrift* 31 (1976), pp. 337–350; J. Moltmann, *The Trinity and the Kingdom of God*. London: S.C.M., 1981, pp. 144–148.

4. *cf. supra*, ch. 3, nn. 5; 11. It may be added that in his discussion of the patristic development Lampe is strangely shallow: he does identify certain dangers and internal problems, but does not seem to have engaged deeply with what was really controlling the thought of the fathers. Contrast, for instance, the incomparably profounder treatment by T. F. Torrance, 'Spiritus Creator', in his *Theology in Reconstruction*. London: S.C.M., 1965; repr. Grand Rapids: Eerdmans, 1975, pp. 209–228, and 'Athanasius: A Study in the Foundations of Classical Theology', in his *Theology in Reconciliation*. London: Geoffrey Chapman, 1975, pp. 215–266.

5. *Systematic Theology*, vol. III. repr. London: S.C.M., 1978, pp. 283–294. In placing the Trinity at the end, Tillich follows, approvingly, the example of Schleiermacher and is sharply critical of Barth for not doing likewise (p. 285).

6. There is a certain similarity here to the approach that Barth observed Schleiermacher might have followed (but did not) towards 'a theology which, beginning with man, is intended as a theology of the Holy Spirit.' (*Church Dogmatics* III/3. Edinburgh: T. & T. Clark, 1960, p. 324).

7. *Church Dogmatics* I/1. 2nd edn. Edinburgh: T. & T. Clark, 1975, pp. 295–489.

8. E. Jüngel, *The Doctrine of the Trinity. God's Being is in Becoming.* Edinburgh: Scottish Academic Press, 1976.

9. *cf.* C. Gunton, *Becoming and Being: The Doctrine of God in Charles Hartshorne and Karl Barth.* Oxford: Oxford University Press, 1978.

10. *Church Dogmatics* I/1, p. 345.

11. See especially *The Crucified God*. London: S.C.M., 1974; also R. Bauckham, 'Jürgen Moltmann', in *One God in Trinity*, pp. 111–132.

12. J. Moltmann, *The Trinity and the Kingdom of God.*

13. Moltmann, *The Trinity and the Kingdom of God.* pp. 139–144; also R. D. Williams, 'Barth on the Triune God', in S. Sykes (ed), *Karl Barth—Studies of his Theological Methods.* Oxford: Clarendon, 1979, pp. 147–193; and, a trifle dyspeptically, R. Roberts, 'Karl Barth', in *One God in Trinity*, pp. 78–94.

14. Barth, *op. cit.*, pp. 348–368.

15. *op. cit.*, pp. 473–487; *cf.* A. Heron, ' "Who Proceedeth from the Father and the Son." The Problem of the *Filioque*'. *SJTh* 24 (1971), pp. 149–166, and the critique of Barth offered by Hendry, *The Holy Spirit in Christian Theology.* London: S.C.M., 1965, pp. 42–52.

16. H. Berkhof, *The Doctrine of the Holy Spirit.* London: Epworth, 1965. In his more recent *Christian Faith.* Grand Rapids: Eerdmans, 1979, esp. pp. 330–337, 'The Covenant as Tri(u)nity', he presents a rather different position, speaking of the Father as the divine partner in the covenant, the Son as the human representative, the Spirit as the bond between them, so that the Trinity is the covenantal event between God and man. This comes somewhat closer to Moltmann's position, but if less Marcellan, is still wholly 'economic'.

17. *The Trinity and the Kingdom of God*, p. 167.

18. *op. cit.*, p. 243, n. 43. The remark is directed against Barth, but could easily be more widely applied.

19. *op. cit.*, pp. 178–190; also his contribution to L. Vischer (ed.), *Spirit of God, Spirit of Christ.* Ecumenical Reflections on the Filioque Controversy. Geneva: W.C.C. 1980.

20. Rahner, *The Trinity.*

21. *De Incarnatione Verbi Dei*, ch. 10.

22. T. F. Torrance, *The Ground and Grammar of Theology.* Belfast: Christian Journals, 1980, ch. 6.

23. *cf.* Moltmann's acute remarks on this—*op. cit.*, p. 188.

24. *cf.* T. F. Torrance, 'The Epistemological Relevance of the Holy Spirit', in his *God and Rationality*. London: Oxford University Press, 1971, pp. 164–192.

25. 'The Relevance of the Doctrine of the Spirit for Ecumenical Theology'. *Theology in Reconstruction*, pp. 229–239.

INDEX OF BIBLICAL PASSAGES

INDEX OF EARLY JEWISH WRITINGS

INDEX OF EARLY CHRISTIAN WRITINGS

INDEX OF NAMES AND TOPICS